ORDINARY MEN

EXTRAORDINARY SERVICE

The World War I Experiences of the 9th Battalion (Queensland) AIF & Reflections on the Gallipoli Campaign.

Chris Lowndes

First published 2011

National Library of Australia Cataloguing-in-Publication entry

Author:	Lowndes, Chris.
Title:	Ordinary men, extraordinary service : the World War I experience of the 9th battalion (Queensland) AIF & reflections on the Gallipoli campaign / Chris Lowndes.
ISBN:	9781921555862 (pbk.)
Subjects:	Australia. Army. A.I.F. (1914-1921). Battalion, 9th.
	World War, 1914-1918--Participation, Australian.
	World War, 1914-1918--Campaigns--Turkey--Gallipoli Peninsula.
Dewey Number:	940.412994

Typeset in Arno Pro 12 pt.

Published by Boolarong Press, Salisbury, Brisbane, Australia.

Printed and bound by Watson Ferguson & Company, Salisbury, Brisbane, Australia.

Photo front cover – Men from D Company 9th Battalion commanded by Captain JA Milne, aboard the British Destroyer HMS Beagle on their way to Gallipoli Peninsula for the landing on 25th April 1915 (AWM WDJ0157)

Contents

Foreword

Brigadier R.A. Hamilton, CSM, RFD
CO 9 RQR 1988–1991
Regimental Colonel RQR 2003–2009
Patron, 9th Battalions' Association 2008–present

I am delighted to make a few observations by way of foreword to this fine work.

When I first joined the 9th Battalion, The Royal Queensland Regiment, as a junior captain in 1973, it was my great privilege to be able to assist in hosting the Annual Reunions of the members of the 9th AIF. Meeting those outstanding men, who served their country so magnificently, I was moved by many emotions. "First Ashore" was continually in my mind as I spoke with these elderly, dignified gentlemen.

And yet there was humour among the gathering, as old stories were retold. One veteran of the landing insisted that he would have been ashore ahead of Duncan Chapman, save that he dropped an ammunition box on his groin, thus dealing himself an incapacitating blow! Two of the old chaps had their backs to each other, neither having spoken to the other since one declined to share a mug of tea with the other on the third day after the landing. There was a quietly spoken, reserved gentleman who had won not one, but two Military Medals, and there was the officer who, despite having won a Military Cross at Pozieres, was still regarded as a "reo" for not having joined the Battalion until the Western Front. When one of these men played a shaky rendition of the "Last Post" on a battered bugle that had been carried ashore at the landing, there were straight backs but few dry eyes in the room. Such was this group of men. In later years, when I had the great honour of commanding the

Battalion, it was my sad yet ennobling duty to attend, with my RSM, many of their funerals.

I wish to heartily congratulate Chris Lowndes on his comprehensive account of the 9th AIF during the Great War. He writes in an attractive, conversational style that is eminently readable and enjoyable. He reaches out to the reader as someone with whom Chris genuinely wishes to share the fruits of his research. While there is substantial detail in his work, it does not subsume the human element of the 9th story.

This piece of scholarship demonstrates a commendable rigour of research, suitably referenced. The maps and contemporary photographs are of great assistance, as are the helpful colour photographs taken more recently. I was interested to read the asides as to the later stories of those who survived, and how the Great War impacted on the home front both during and after the conflict. Chris emphasises quite frequently the commitment and self–effacement of these men, such as one badly wounded soldier in a letter home who "didn't want to make a fuss about himself". The final chapter contains interesting reflections about the process and outcomes of his research.

I strongly commend Chris Lowndes' account and assessment of our history to both those in the military and to the general reading public. Well done!

Rod Hamilton
March 2011

Acknowledgements

In the absence of the old AIF diggers, the work of earlier 9th Battalion writers and historians were critical sources of information. In particular, Clarrie Wrench (also a distinguished officer of the 9th Battalion, AIF) in his book titled "Campaigning with the Fighting 9th – In and out of the line with the Ninth Battalion AIF" and Norman Harvey's book titled "From Anzac to the Hindenburg Line – The History of the 9th Battalion AIF", were of great assistance. Their dedication to ensuring the detailed accounts of the Battalion's activities and interviews with serving members of the AIF during World War I were a critical platform for my research and understanding of the men. I owe both authors my appreciation for taking the time to capture the history for another generation.

No writer who has written about the AIF during World War I could afford not to become familiar with the work of Charles Bean. The ease of access that we have to his work, especially through the Australian War Memorial website, ensures that his significant contribution to the history of Australians at war is available as a reference point for all interested in understanding more about the men that fought in the war. Clearly his work, in conjunction with other references with which to corroborate, was critical for my book.

Over the last two years, I have had the honour of becoming a member of the 9th Battalions' Association. This has provided an opportunity to spend time with others within the Association, most having served in a 9th Battalion unit, who have a similar interest in ensuring the history of the 9th Battalion is preserved and passed onto new generations of Australians. The work and dedication that members of the Museum Trust have, and continue to expend on the 9th Battalion museum and the maintenance, preservation and presentation of 9th Battalion items is very special. The support they provided, their input into this book and the encouragement that Brigadier Rod Hamilton (Patron of the 9th Battalions' Association), Colonel Mark Plath (President of the Association), Major Alan Reed (Treasurer) and others such as Major (Retd) Peter Newland, Mal Black and Dan Penman within the Association is much appreciated and helped to keep me driven to finish what I had started.

I have also to thank the Sherwood/Indooroopilly RSL sub branch for their support and assistance with making this book a reality. In particular, Ron McElwaine (President of the sub branch) and members such as Ron Aumann and Miles Farmer who spent time reading, advising and supporting this work.

To my good friend Tony Nicholls and his family and friends such as Roger Lamb, I owe a great deal of gratitude. Your friendship, input and encouragement for my work inspired me and kept me focused and energized. The thoughts and many discussions we have shared regarding your father's service within the 9th Battalion AIF was a constant inspiration, and I have enjoyed the journey of discovery with you.

I am appreciative of the editing work that was undertaken by Alison Slykerman on an early draft of the manuscript, your time and dedication ensured the quality of writing from an early stage.

Thanks to Dan Kelly and Amanda Quick at Boolarong Press, your support and guidance for a first time writer, and taking the time to ensure that a quality final product eventuated is appreciated.

Thanks also to the staff of the Australian War Memorial that have fielded my questions and requests across many departments and provided consent to use materials quoted. In addition, thanks to the following institutions for allowing me to quote their resources and provision of helpful staff; the John Oxley Library – State Library of Queensland, the Mitchell Library at the State Library of New South Wales, the Imperial War Museum in London, the Alexander Turnbull Library – National Library of New Zealand and the National Army Museum – Waiouru, New Zealand.

Special thanks to my patient guide and teacher while touring the Gallipoli Peninsula, Kenan Celik AO and the staff at the Hotel Kum that helped me with plans and directions during my stay on the Peninsula.

Finally a special thanks to my wife, Monique and my children, Brianna and Joshua for their understanding and support while Dad worked on his special "hobby".

Introduction

Right from my early years as a boy growing up in Brisbane, I have always had an interest in Australians at war, in particular, the Gallipoli campaign of World War I. The amazing story of what Australian soldiers did so long ago, the trials and sacrifices made by these men, compelled me to better understand what these men were like, why they went to war and what they endured during the course of the war. Rather than glorifying war, it was for me personally all about the men and their character, the ordinary men that had performed extraordinary services for their country and each other. Australian men at the time just prior to the war possessed a strength of character that stood tall in the face of adversity and hardship, a character that required that you stand by your mate in tough times and see the job through. The Gallipoli campaign was made for such men. As author Les Carlyon puts it, the Anzac tradition is about both the perceived and the real elements of the character of the men involved, not the generals or officers (many Australians today could not name the key commanders during the campaign), but the ordinary Australian soldier, the lowest ranking private.[1]

Even though Australia is a relatively young country, it has forged a long and distinguished war service history. Like most Australians born and bred here, and part of a family that has lived in this country for several generations, I have had relatives who served in the two World Wars and have only ever been told brief accounts of their deeds. Possibly because as I have uncovered, those involved in the wars were often very reluctant to recount their experiences and stir the nightmares.

From an early age the story of the Gallipoli campaign attracted my interest, so much so that in my grade 11 year at school, I selected to write a diary of an Australian soldier who landed at Gallipoli, entirely made up, but based on what I had learnt about the campaign for my English assessment piece. Many Australians are compelled to research and set out on family pilgrimages to the battlefields of Gallipoli and the Western Front in a quest to bond with a long lost great-grand father who served in World War I and fill in some of the gaps that family stories had left out. For me, however, the compulsion was not so much a personal journey of discovery, but for most of my time of research, it was just about them, the beaming faces of young men that volunteered to fight for their country. These Australian soldiers from another time managed to get under my skin. Their remarkable feats at arms and the very personal and touching accounts that they share in their diaries, notes and letters about what they were going through, and more often than not, the way they dealt with extreme hardship and death, are compelling. I desired to know more about the men who fought, the world they lived in at that time and then what happened following the war. A book was always destined to become the end result. With each Anzac Day service that comes around, the emotion has served to solidify my resolve to tell their story.

It was only later, when nearing the completion of my first draft of this book that I uncovered a great-great-uncle of mine, 22 year old Fred (Freddie) Williams from Brisbane, who had fought and died with the 25th Battalion AIF on the Western Front. With a strong sense of anticipation, my research had suddenly turned personal. I had a bond now and someone to research, which also explained a part of the Lowndes family history. My interest in the World War I was now more driven than ever. Slowly I uncovered the war story of a young man who lived a relatively short life, and while never having had the opportunity to meet him, as a young boy I was cared for by his brother for whom I have seen in photos and was told stories about his mother from my grandmother. By the end of reading his personal war service record, which fortunately were quite extensive, his hospitalisation records, his Battalion's history and letters written to his mother from abroad, I began to feel myself getting close to him. Like many other men that served in World War I, his story came to an abrupt end. Freddie was killed in action on the battlefields of the Western Front in 1918, the last year of the war.

Australian soldiers during World War I, more so than other wars since, wrote diaries and expressed their feelings and emotions on paper, a lasting communiqué for future generations to get to know them and understand them. They did not have phones or computers, but communicated with loved ones via letters and diary entries, in which they bare their soul and let us know what they are thinking. This is probably part of the reason why of all the battlefields that Australians fought in across many wars, the most highly remembered, reflected on and written about, and the one to bring out so much emotion and enduring patriotism among Australians young and old, is the Gallipoli campaign of 1915. The number of visitors at each Anzac Day ceremony on the Gallipoli Peninsula seems to increase in size year on year, and the interest at home in Anzac services, even though there are no more of the old Diggers around, does not wane.

Another trigger that drove me to write about this campaign in particular, was the famous picture of a group of over 800 Australian soldiers of the 11th Battalion AIF, who were recruited from Western Australia, on the Great Pyramid of Khufu (Cheops) near their Mena training camp in Egypt in 1915. This Battalion, along with the 9th, 10th and 12th Battalions, formed the 3rd Brigade of the First Division of the Australian Imperial Force (AIF) and it was this brigade that was selected to land first at Gallipoli on 25th April, 1915. It was also among the first of the infantry brigades formed during World War I. Looking at the faces and the relaxed carefree poses of the men, I often reflected on the fact that they seemed so proud, confident, happy and full of anticipation. They were looking for action and adventure, they were with their mates and together they would use this as a way to prove themselves worthy of the British Empire. Who could defeat the might of the empire! However, there was a dark side to this picture snapped in a moment in time, for little did these young Australian's realise what would happen to them soon. A large portion of these happy-go-lucky Aussies would be dead or horribly wounded within a few weeks following this gathering, and if they were lucky to survive Gallipoli, then they went on to the European Western Front to a fate worse still. Most would describe the Western Front as a living hell. A man was lucky to survive both campaigns and most of the originals in this Brigade that did survive were wounded in action, often numerous times. In the first five days following the landing at Anzac Cove, the men of the 11th Battalion, suffered 378 casualties, over a third of its strength dead or wounded.

For these proud men on the pyramid and their comrades making up the 3rd Brigade, reality over the next four years was going to be a hard pill to swallow. They would never be the same again physically, mentally or emotionally. Their grandiose ideas of what the war would be about were shattered following the landing at Gallipoli, and certainly if they were not disillusioned at this time, then it would sink in before the end of the eight months of the campaign. The survivors would be forever changed upon returning home following the four years of a long, drawn out war.

The war was not in reality a romantic adventure, nor was it an event to look forward to or to develop fond memories as they had initially thought. Young Australian men died in their thousands, and many friends, fathers and brothers were lost in this cruel war. War was in its reality a chilling horror story that seemed to never be capable of ending for those involved. It was full of sadness, cruelty, horror, death and disease. The glory of war certainly never eventuated for these men and when there were moments of happiness they were brief and soon faded. Their mates were killed and maimed before their eyes. They saw things that men their age should never have to see, and they were let down by their officers and forced to fight in battles that were ill-conceived and poorly planned by their superiors. Our British comrades were very different to ourselves, but even more so, those senior military officers proved time and again that they could not be trusted with making decisions that would make a difference to the course of the war or minimise the loss of life. The Australian soldiers summed the British officers up very early in the War, viewing them as pompous, out of touch with reality and ready to sacrifice men's lives in an instant as if playing a game of chance, for fame or vainglory and in most cases for little gain. They were cruel and their actions contributed greatly to the brutality of, arguably, the cruelest war there has been.

But amazingly, through all this the Australian soldiers stuck it out, courageous under fire and brave to the point of reckless. They maintained a courage and bravery that few men in today's world would display, the Australian larrikin way and our sense of humour could not be stymied even in the worst of scenarios. They had a willingness throughout to put their life on the line for their mates, country and King. In fact, many became fatalistic and had accepted the fact that they would not last long at all.

The Australian soldier acquired a reputation that continues today as one of the finest fighters on the battlefield, dependable, ingenious, resourceful men who got the job done under tremendous duress. During the World War I, the Australian soldiers would be given the most difficult of tasks and would have the greatest casualty rate of any of the Allied armies assembled. They would go on to achieve some of the highest battlefield honours and successes during the war and prove to the British generals, who considered them ill disciplined and unreliable, very wrong. They would do their country proud.

The questions regarding what these men were like, how they felt on joining up, what drove them to enlist, how did they feel over the days just before and during the landing at Gallipoli and then tracking these young men through the period from raw recruitment to battle- weary veterans of the Gallipoli and Belgium/France battlefields needed answers. This book reveals my quest to understand and to document the answers I found. I wanted to put faces to names and bring individuals to light and show that, most importantly, they were ordinary men who did extraordinary service.

While some pages in the appendices are devoted to following up men of the 11th Battalion who feature in the photo on the Great Pyramid of Khufu (Cheops), my focus has been on the first of the Queensland Battalions raised for the AIF in World War I. While selecting a Queensland unit was a necessity for a proud Queenslander, the main reasons to select one unit of men was for very much a practical reason, in that by narrowing the field to a specific Battalion one could get closer to them, present more detail and provide a focus for research. A broader base would lose this effect and there are already many fine books that cover in depth all the proceedings and most of the Australian units. The 9th Battalion, 3rd Brigade, 1st Division AIF therefore became the basis. While references are made to many other battalions throughout this book, the 9th takes pride of place. These Queenslanders were also the first Australian soldiers to land at Anzac Cove on the morning of 25th April, 1915.

During my research, two books in particular, have been invaluable in providing an insight into the war and specifically the men of the 9th Battalion. Both are battalion histories that are written by men who had either firsthand experience through fighting with the 9th Battalion, like Lieutenant Clarrie Wrench, or a historical inclination such as Norman Harvey. Both devoted many years to researching, talking to returned servicemen about their experiences and piecing together a very detailed history of the 9th Battalion throughout the World War I. It is from their books that most of my understanding and written facts about the 9th Battalion have been taken. At a broader level, the work of Charles Bean forms the foundation reading for my research and provides factual accounts for many of the pages in this book. Bean's 12 volumes, which cover predominately Australians fighting in the World War I, are an essential reference tool for anyone contemplating any research into this topic.

Why was Gallipoli such an important event for Australia and why is it still remembered more than any other battle or event in Australia's wartime history? The battle itself was not successful for the Allies, who were not able to achieve their key objectives and suffered a significant loss of life. In fact, there were more Australian lives lost in a single day on the Somme battlefields of the Western Front than during the whole Gallipoli campaign. Most Australians today would be aware of what happened, even broadly, over the course of the Gallipoli campaign and the sacrifices made by many Australians on foreign soil. But how many really know what the common soldier went through, why they were there, the courageous deeds of bravery that the men performed against great adversity and the different opinion that Australians would have towards the British homeland following the war. Gallipoli was the place where the nation's eyes were opened to the horrors of war and it would forever taint our view of "giving our all for King and Country" and would, I believe, set us on the track of being independent, having a nationalistic view and discovering our unique identity. We were not like our English brothers any more, we were Australians.

The Gallipoli campaign was also important given that this was the very first time our men had been called upon for any significant war service. While Australians prior to the World War I had served in the Boer War and some other smaller hostilities, they were in these campaigns much smaller units of Australian soldiers fighting as part of the British Army. Gallipoli, however, was the first time they went into battle under the Australian flag. The Australian nation and her soldiers were given a chance finally to prove their metal in the face of overwhelming adversity and they performed and endured.

While the Gallipoli campaign is the main theatre for this book, there are also chapters covering the Belgium and French battles of the Western Front that Australians fought in following the Gallipoli campaign. Again the main focus is on those battles where the 9th Battalion was involved and their part in the fighting. These campaigns lasted significantly longer and actually cost far more Australian lives, presented many more victories and successes for the Australian Army than did the whole Gallipoli campaign. But to truly outline the 9th Battalion soldier's war experience and post-war years, some writing needed to be dedicated to this theatre also.

All wars create terrible suffering to both combatants and innocents, however, World War I was particularly heinous compared to other wars given its scale, callousness and disregard of human life. It was fundamentally a war of attrition. The 60,000 Australian soldiers' lives lost were too many for a young country of just under 5 million to bear. The best of the young Australian men of that time were part of the 1st Division AIF who volunteered for service.

Britain let these men down so many times. Their military leaders were often too old or incompetent, many having gained their knowledge through earlier wars that used military strategy that was woefully unsuitable for this war and were ineffective commanders of men. Most were not held to account for the horrendous orders that were demanded of the men on the battlefield, the waste of lives that followed and the sheer bloody-mindedness of their decision making. An example of this was the battle at Passchendale in 1917, which like Gallipoli was marked by great courage from the men involved, but a battle that ultimately achieved very little. The four month battle cost 570,000 lives, 300,000 on the Allies' side, including more than 36,000 Australians. Including the number wounded, the casualties would reach to an estimated three quarters of a million. Incredibly, after a few months following the battle, the Germans were able to win back every inch of the ground taken in just three days.[2]

It is inconceivable in today's age that battles could be fought this way and that the casualty rates and daily loss of life could be tolerated for any longer than a week or two, let alone spanning a four year period. The primitive channels used to communicate information from the front-line back to the public, the stringent levels of censorship imposed and heavy restrictions placed on journalists at the time all helped to cover up mistakes and minimise the impact of heavy casualties. There is stark comparison against today's standards of communication, technology and in particular, the involvement and scrutiny of the media in the modern battlefields. The best contrast is provided by the death of an Australian SAS Trooper, Private Jason Marks, during operations in Afghanistan in April of 2008. His platoon was attacked by an overwhelming force of Taliban fighters and he was killed in the ensuing battle. Just a few hours after his death, the Defence Chief of the Australian Army was woken early in the morning at about 1am Australian time and was briefed. By 7.00am that same morning the Australian public was being told about his death and already the media were starting to ask probing questions aimed at trying to determine whether there had been any mismanagement or negligence. As you will see further on in this book, during the war on the Gallipoli Peninsula it would take some weeks before the Australian public were even aware of the scale of death of its soldiers abroad. It would take a week just to know where they were fighting. Even then, many telegrams would be so filtered, inaccurate and overly positive about a desperate situation to ensure that the recruitment drive would continue. Rather than a source of accurate news, many of the early reports seemed more like propaganda pieces being used to stir the nation to support the war effort. Limited scrutiny of the campaign was undertaken by journalists and media here in Australia during the first few months. Orders given and the conduct of specific battles were left to the British generals. It was certainly not the "done thing" in those days to question their wisdom. Even if our politicians or military leaders were in a position to raise the harder questions, everything reported seemed to indicate all was well and in hand. How things have changed. Certainly truth in the early stages of the World War I was, as the US Senator Hiram Johnson stated in 1917, the first casualty when war arrives.

Incredibly, within 15 years, another German Army would rise up under a ruthless dictator and start making trouble again and the world would be plunged into another World War. The conditions of the surrender of the German Army at the end of the World War I were severe. Some argue overly so for the German nation, people and economy to properly recover and the people too proud to remain destitute for any extended time period. The victorious Allies had, inadvertently, laid the foundations for aggression to take place again in 1939.[3]

It is difficult to write about the full Gallipoli campaign, let alone the frantic first day of hostilities after the Australians landed at Anzac Cove and provide the justice it deserves without writing a 400 page book, for which I did not have the time to commit to, nor was this the purpose of my writing. There are already many books that provide very detailed and meticulous accounts, especially of the landing and the first week . What you will find in this account though is a focus on the 3rd Brigade and specifically the actions of the 9th Battalion during the campaign, while providing some references to the key events that were happening in the Anzac sector throughout their stay on the peninsula.

Rather than cover some detailed military actions here, I have outlined a number of the key battles such as the charge at the Nek and Lone Pine in the appendices to this book. I also recognise that the Anzacs were not the only Allied soldiers fighting in this campaign. The British (including Gurkha and Sikh units) and French had far more men committed to the war and indeed lost far more lives. Hence, it would not be complete without devoting some time to the British and their landings, especially at the beaches at Cape Helles and for that fact, the New Zealanders' heroic effort at Chunuk Bair. I have therefore covered these as separate appendices at the back of this book.

The final chapter outlines a trip to the Gallipoli Peninsula and what it meant to me. It gave me some closure on this book and allowed me to understand the context of the Gallipoli campaign and provided a better idea of what the men endured. It gave me time to reflect on the locations described in this book, view the beautiful panoramas that they would have gazed upon and walk in their footsteps across the battlefield. It was critical for me to see firsthand the battlefield and what is left of the trenches and fortifications, understand the terrain, visit the final resting places of Australians from the 9th Battalion in particular that have been referred to in this book and last but by no means least, understand the perspective of the Turkish soldier and what this battle meant to them.

I have pleasure in presenting this small account of the Australian soldiers who landed at Anzac Cove and went on to the Western Front and hope that it provides further background to answer the questions of why and how ordinary men provided extraordinary service to their mates, families and country.

Chris Lowndes
2011

Brisbane's Bert White, who enlisted in the 25th Battalion, could not see any reason to remove his cigarette for this official pre-war portrait with his mate. He is typical of the irreverent larrikin from Queensland that volunteered to fight for his country in World War I. (King)

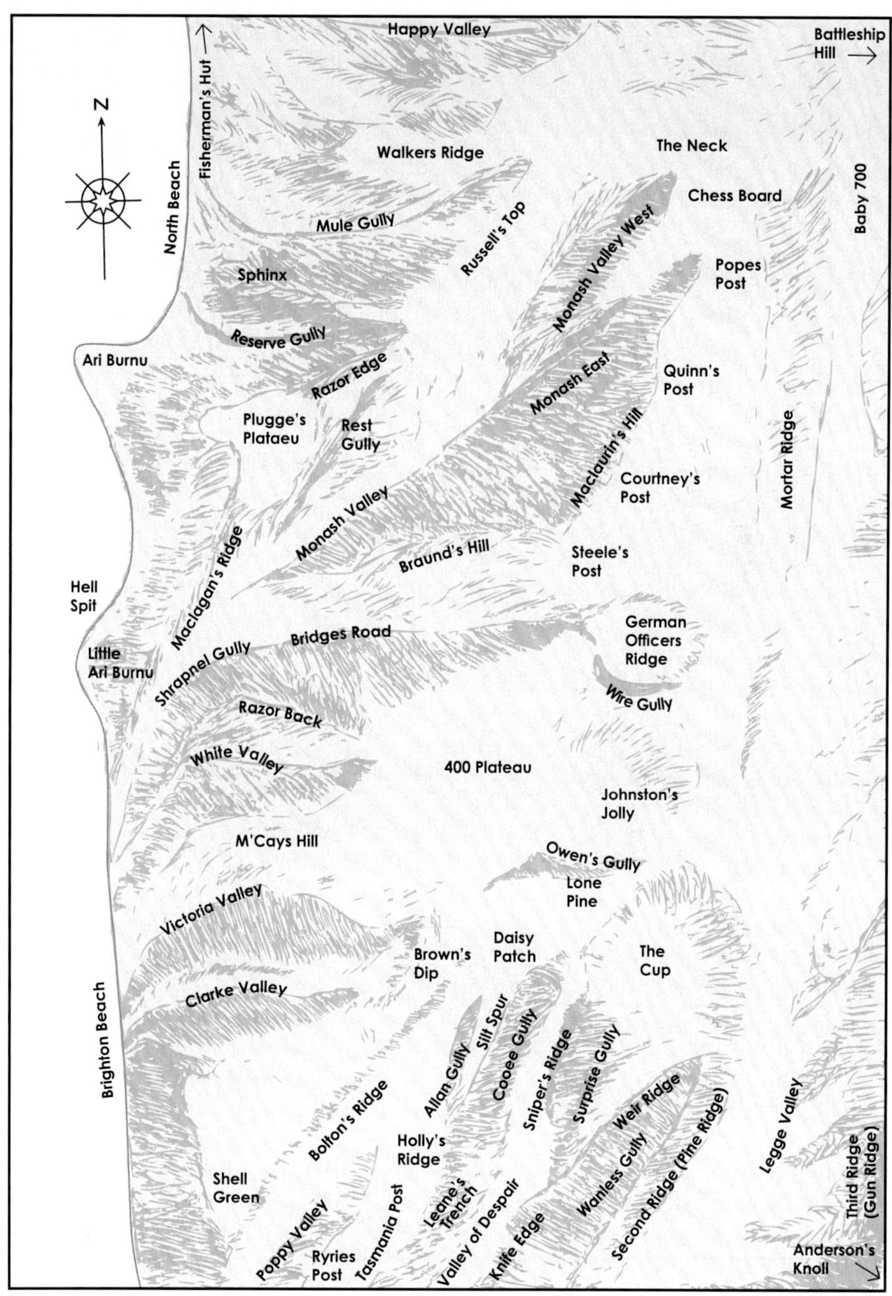

The Anzac Battlefield - Gallipoli

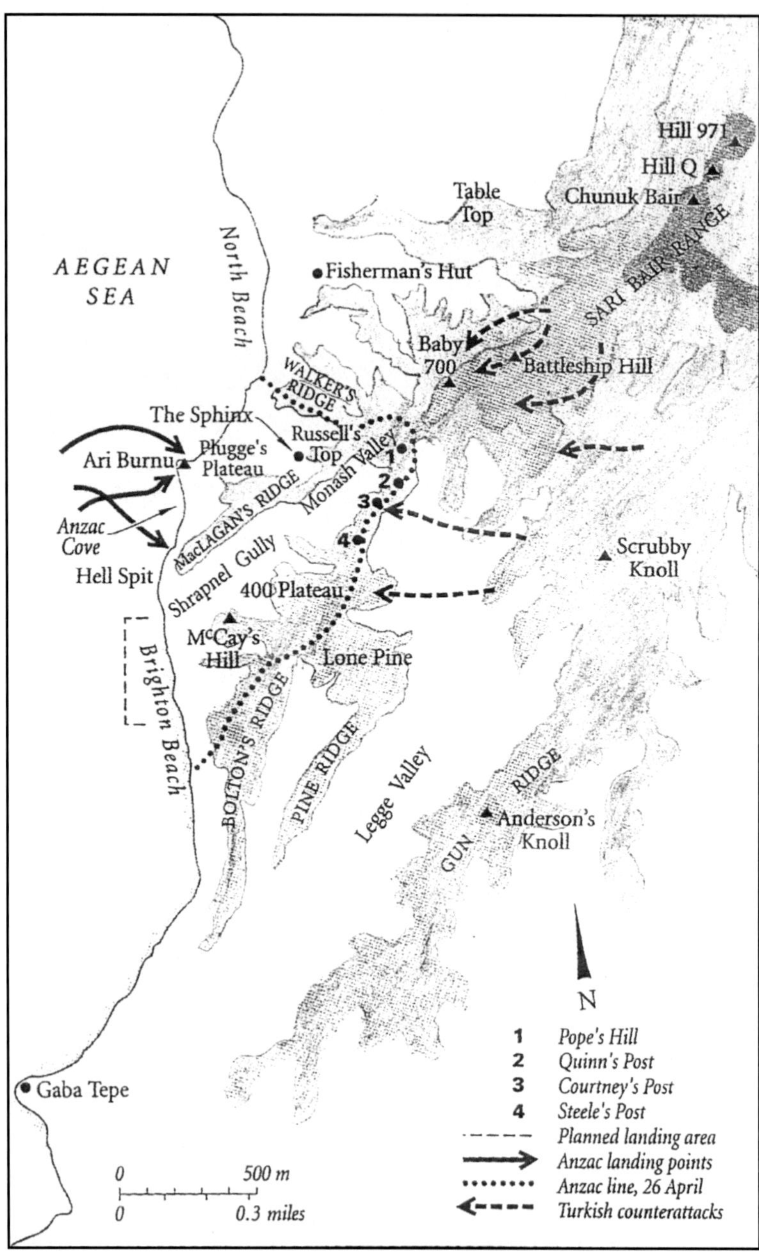

The Anzac Sector – Gallipoli Peninsula. (Pedersen)

Australian and New Zealand Military Units – Fighting in the Anzac Sector Gallipoli Campaign

Australian and New Zealand Army Corps

Commanded by Lieutenant General Sir W.R. Birdwood

Made up of two Divisions:

1st Australian Division

Commanded by Major General W.T. Bridges

1st Brigade (NSW) – (Landing from 5.30am onwards, all ashore by 9am, 25th April)

Commanded by Colonel H.N. MacLaurin

- ***1st Battalion***
- ***2nd Battalion***
- ***3rd Battalion***
- ***4th Battalion***

2nd Brigade (Victoria) – (Started to land around 5am, all ashore by 9am, 25th April)

Commanded by Colonel J.W. M'Cay

- ***5th Battalion***
- ***6th Battalion***
- ***7th Battalion***
- ***8th Battalion***

3rd Brigade (Mixed – Covering Force) – (First to land 4.30am, 25th April)

Commanded by Colonel E. Sinclair–MacLagan

- ***9th Battalion (Qld)***
- ***10th Battalion (SA)***
- ***11th Battalion (WA)***
- ***12th Battalion (SA, WA & Tasmania)***

Australian and New Zealand Division

Commanded by Major General Sir A. Godley

4th Brigade (Mixed) – (Landed after 5.30pm on 25th April)

Commanded by Colonel J. Monash

- ***13th Battalion (NSW)***
- ***14th Battalion (Victoria)***
- ***15th Battalion (Qld & Tasmania)***
- ***16th Battalion (SA &WA)***

NZ Infantry Brigade

Commanded by Brigadier General H.B. Walker

- ***Auckland Battalion*** (Landed 10.45am on the 25th April)
- ***Canterbury Battalion*** (Landed 10.45am on the 25th April)
- ***Otago Battalion*** (Landed late at night on the 25th April)
- ***Wellington Battalion*** (Landed late at night on the 25th April)

NZ Mounted Rifle Brigade – (Landed mid to late May 1915)
Commanded by Major General Sir Andrew Hamilton Russell

- ***Auckland Mounted Rifles***
- ***Canterbury Mounted Rifles***
- ***Wellington Mounted Rifles***
- ***Otago Mounted Rifles***

Note: The Australian 2nd Division, which included 5th, 6th and 7th Brigades, landed later in the campaign to take part in the offensive in August 1915.

The **Australian Light Horse Brigades** were also involved in the Gallipoli campaign. Their work was as infantry and their horses were left behind in Egypt:

- ***1st Light Horse Brigade*** (landed 12th May 1915)
- ***2nd Light Horse Brigade*** (landed late May 1915)
- ***3rd Light Horse Brigade*** (landed late May 1915)
- ***4th Light Horse Brigade*** (landed partly May {4th LHR} and the other regiments landed in August 1915)
- ***5th Light Horse Brigade*** (only 13th LHR saw action and landed in September 1915)

Chapter 1

Prelude to War

The World War I started at a time when tensions in Europe were at breaking point. Countries were primed for war and were seeking any reason to bring their burgeoning armaments to bear and show the rest of Europe their military might. In fact some historians still argue whether the Great War was necessary at all. Beyond the doubtful virtues of imperial breast-beating, there seems to have been no sound moral, religious, territorial or economic reason for it to have taken place.[4] Big egos among politicians and national patriotism within countries was very high in the decade leading up to the World War I, each country regarding the other with increasing suspicion.[5] In addition, there was a complex web of agreements and coalitions between countries, many negotiated around access to raw materials or out of necessity because they needed the support of larger, more influential countries. It seems, however, that some of the early treaties secured could not be relied upon as much as their predecessor signatories would have envisaged and most arrangements were very fickle and could be subject to change without notice.

One such agreement was the Triple Entente agreement between Britain, France and Russia signed in 1907, which required that these countries work together in foreign affairs. Unfortunately, this agreement did little to enhance a sense of security in Europe, but instead created an arms race, with each power feeling it had to be ready for war to fulfil its obligations.[6] Germany was also pursuing a policy of expanding its powerful standing in Europe by building up a vast arsenal of military hardware, in particular a focus on battleship construction that would rival the current British naval supremacy.

Crowd in Trafalgar Square in London cheer Britain's declaration of war. Singing "God Save the King". (Cross)

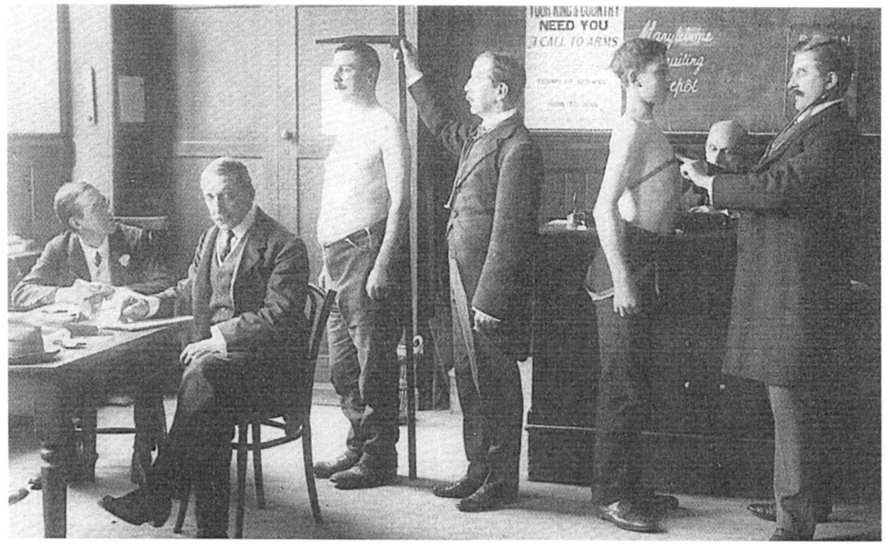

British volunteers undergo their enlistment medical examination. Similar to the Australian experience, for the first wave of hopefuls there were many rejects.

Indeed, Germany which had dominated Europe for many years (since defeating the French in the Franco–Prussian war of 1870–1871 in which it claimed the territory of Alsace to Lorraine from the French), seemed determined to go to war. It had a longstanding strategy for war known as the Schlieffen Plan, which was conceived in 1905 and involved invading and defeating France quickly before the large Russian Army had a chance to mobilise and come to the aid of its treaty partner.[7]

During the early exchanges of the European powers following the assassination of Archduke Ferdinand, Britain saw herself as the greatest imperial power in the world, but was about to lose her influence in Europe. The actions of Germany served to bring Britain and France closer together and they were actively working on a plan that would enable the dispatch of a British expeditionary force to France in the event of war with Germany. When German troops marched into Belgium on the 4th August 1914, Britain was already in possession of an old treaty made in 1839, 75 years previously, in which Britain agreed to guarantee Belgium's neutrality. It was the excuse needed to get involved and so the "war to end all wars" was given the go ahead to move forward by all participants.[8]

This powder keg was therefore fused during the year 1914.

The following points outline the road to World War I.[9]

- The assassination of Archduke Franz Ferdinand, heir to the Austro–Hungarian Empire and his consort at Sarajevo on 29th June, 1914. Austria had replaced the Ottoman Empire in 1908 as Bosnia's new rulers.
- Austria presented to Serbia, whom it thought responsible for the assassination, an ultimatum with very difficult demands, which all had to be accepted within 48 hours. Serbia, acting on Russian advice, accepted all demands except two which she asked to be reserved for the Hague tribunal.
- Austria declared war on 28th July against Serbia. Russia, an ally of Serbia, replied by partly mobilising its forces against Austria.
- On 31st July, 1914, Germany, because of its alliance with Austria, sent an ultimatum to Russia to demobilise. This did not occur and Germany then declared war on Russia, and in turn France, which was an ally of Russia by treaty.

- The King of the Belgians appealed to King George V for the British Government to safeguard the integrity of Belgium. The British Foreign Secretary, Sir Edward Grey, spoke to the French and German Governments on 31st July regarding whether they would respect the neutrality of Belgium so long as no other power violated it. France gave a pledge, Germany gave no reply.
- On 4th August, 1914, England demanded assurances from Germany, but by this time German troops were already in Belgium and had been there for some days. The British Government sent a final instruction on 4th August, which reached Berlin at 7pm. They indicated that they were bound to uphold the neutrality of Belgium and take all steps in their power. Immediately after these instructions reached Berlin, the German Government, without waiting for the ultimatum to expire, announced England had declared war. (Never probably in the history The world has there taken place such a display of warlike passion as manifested itself in the most civilised countries of Europe at the beginning of August 1914 – *The Times History of War.*)
- War was declared between Britain and Germany on 4th August, 1914.

The British public went wild with excitement. They had not the slightest doubt that Britain was the greatest and most powerful nation on earth, the many dominions that the country had all over the world, which included Australia, the great empire on which the sun never set, holding significant resources and wealth, would ensure that they would be victorious. The British Navy was considered the mightiest in the world and at the time comprised 80 destroyers, 10 battle cruisers, 12 light cruisers and more than 20 battleships. With such an armada and many more merchant men guarding their shores and blockading Germany's access to resources, they believed the war would be quick and over before Christmas.[10] With patriotic fervour, hundreds of thousands of young men throughout Britain enlisted and marched off for the great adventure.

Not everyone was so positive about the outcome though and the statesman Sir Edward Grey uttered the sad words on hearing the news of war, *"The lamps are going out all over Europe – we shall not see them lit again in our lifetime."* Sir Grey knew that Germany would certainly not be a pushover. Germany had a burning ambition for a great united Teutonic State encompassing the whole of Europe and it was greedy to acquire the rich natural resources of Russia and France. He also knew that the Prussian generals commanded an army of very well trained and disciplined troops and had enough resources to mount a long and aggressively fought war.[11]

The array of alliance relationships that existed between European countries and their dominions in the early 1900s had been well covered by Australian newspapers over the years. Hearing of the events outlined above, Australians understood that the peace of the world was under threat. However, they also knew that other Balkan crises had come and gone without a major incident.

But this was going to be different, the pressure cooker that was Europe and the egos that drove foreign policies could no longer be controlled.

The Australian formal response to a Britain now at war was clear:[12]

- Senator Millen, Minister for Defence – 31st July, 1914 stated,

  If necessity arises, Australia will recognise that she is not merely a fair- weather partner of the Empire, but a component member in all circumstances.

  This was at the time when it was becoming increasingly evident that Britain would be involved in the war.

- On the same night, Andrew Fisher (Leader of the Opposition Party – Labor) declared,

  Should the worst happen, after everything has been done that honour will permit, Australians will stand behind the mother country to help defend her to our last man and our last shilling.

- The night after, Joseph Cook – Prime Minister of Australia (Liberal Party) said,

  If there is to be a war, you and I shall be in it. We must be in it. If the old country is at war, so are we.

- Sir John Forest – Treasurer of the Commonwealth (a man who was greatly respected by all Australians irrespective of political persuasions) on Monday, 3rd August said,

  In the past, Australians were proud to think of the glories of England. We shared her victories and triumphs. Justice and reason now demand that we must be prepared to share her difficulties, and, if need be, her disasters. If Britain goes to her Armageddon we will go with her. Our fate and hers, for good or ill, are as woven threads.

War was declared at 9am on the 5th August, 1914 by Australia. The mood of euphoria then swept Australia as the news quickly spread through extra editions of the newspapers, which were published at lunchtime that day. In Melbourne, police struggled to keep an impatient crowd under control as hundreds gathered outside the offices of the Argus newspaper, awaiting the news.

While the Australian Army in the years leading up to war used similar equipment to their English peers, senior Australian soldiers were sent to London to work with Imperial Staff and enlist their help in the development of plans that could be implemented for the defence of Australia. There was a feeling of insecurity within Australia at the turn of the century and increasing concern about the threat of a possible invasion. Russian invasions scares had been raised along with a perceived threat from China. The Japanese Navy was also developing a name for itself following its defeat of the Russian Navy in 1905, and of course the Germans were establishing themselves throughout the Pacific Rim. Plans were subsequently drawn up on the advice of the Imperial Staff, although it should be noted there was no authority by the British over any of the Dominion Armies. No force could be brought to bear by Britain, or any other country for that matter, to compel Australians to go to war.

Australians had first gone on active service with British forces over a half a century earlier. In 1860, they ferried British garrisoned troops across to New Zealand and supported operations against the Maori camps. In 1885, New South Wales sent a contingent of 770 men to help subdue the Dervish rebels in Sudan, but were not involved in any actions. Small contingents of Australian soldiers also supported the British in the China Boxer rebellion in 1900. However, the first real action came in 1899 when Australians fought with the British against the Boer soldiers during the war in South Africa. Queenslanders, it seemed, even at that stage could hardly wait for war. As early as July 1899, when it first appeared that hostilities would break out between the Boers and the British in South Africa, the Government of Queensland, acting on a recommendation from the commandant of the Queensland Defence Forces, offered a contingent of 250 mounted infantry with a machine-gun section. The governments of New South Wales and Victoria quickly matched the offer. In the end, six contingents of Queenslanders would be sent to the Boer War. Victor Jones' sad claim to fame is that he is believed to be the first Australian, and the first Queenslander, to be killed in battle. He died and was buried at a place called "Sunnyside" in South Africa on 1st January, 1900, a little over two months after he and 22 mates from the Mount Morgan mine region had caught a train from Rockhampton to Brisbane to join the first contingent of the Queensland Mounted Infantry bound for South Africa.[13]

The men enlisting for service in the Boer War were drawn mainly from prior established militia units and were used as mounted infantry and were referred to as "Bushmen Units". The British praised them for their initiative, courage and hardiness. When the war ended in 1902, 16,175 Australians had served in it, 606 of whom were killed.[14] In fact, it was the many heroic stories and tales of daring that came back with the returning veterans from the Boer War that assisted with fuelling some of the patriotic fervour that developed as men rushed to volunteer, eager to enlist in the armed services.

On 1st January, 1901, the six colonies had federated, becoming the Commonwealth of Australia, a self-governing dominion of the British Empire. It remained dependent on Britain, lacking in particular the ability to make war or peace with another country, and a limited capacity to stay neutral if Britain went to war. In the later scenario, however, Australia had the ability to determine the extent of her neutral involvement.

Following the 1908 Imperial Conference, which was attended by the then leaders of the British Dominion armies, General William Bridges was appointed Chief of Staff and responsible for the Australian Army's defence plan. Bridges was joined by a Major Charles White, who had recently returned from the British Staff College.

Compulsory military service (home training) was adopted in Australia in 1909. Both political parties of the time agreed on the need to provide for defence and expected at some time that Australians would need to fight for their existence. Lord Kitchener visited Australia in 1910 and provided advice on the organisation of the force that had been raised under the compulsory military training order and all of the strategies he outlined were adopted.

Working hard behind the scenes, Major White had formulated a plan that he believed would provide a practical means by which Australia would be able to contribute men at arms to the British war effort. White's plan would guarantee that a volunteer force of 12,000 men of all arms could be raised and organised for service abroad and to have the men ready to sail within six weeks. In the belief that Canada had offered 30,000 men, the Prime Minister (Andrew Fisher) was determined that Australia's contribution should be comparable and with White, revised their plans and agreed that 20,000 Australian soldiers could be raised and ready to sail within six weeks.[15]

On 3rd August, 1914, when it was becoming clear that Britain would soon make a declaration of war, a Cabinet meeting was held and it was decided to offer the mother country the assistance of the Australian Navy and a force of 20,000 men. A cable was subsequently sent to the British Government that indicated that in the event of war, the Australian Government was prepared to place its naval vessels under the control of the British Admiralty and dispatch an expeditionary force of 20,000 men to be at the complete disposal of the British Government. This force would, in effect, form the 1st Australian Division of the Australian Imperial Force (AIF).

In regard to the navy available, Australia had a number of ships at the outbreak of war that were transferred to the control of the British Admiralty for the duration of the war. The naval squadron comprised:[16]

Battle–cruiser	*Australia*
Light– cruisers	*Melbourne*
	Sydney
	Brisbane (which was still being built)
Destroyers	*Parramatta*
	Yarra
	Warrego
Submarines	*AE1*
	AE2

The scheme for the AIF was completed by General Bridges and Major White on August 8th, 1914. The force was to be drawn, as far as possible, from men who had undergone some training. Half of them were to be men then serving in the citizens army of Australia, mainly young men in their 20s and upwards. The other half were to be men not then in the forces, but who had once been in the Militia, or had served in the South African or other wars.[17]

Recruiting began in earnest soon after the scheme was completed. Bridges chose Brigadiers before recruiting started and had them attached to commandants in their respective States to assist in organising and training their brigades. The Brigadiers in turn selected regimental commanders and they in turn chose officers for their own units.[18]

Throughout Australia in 1911, volunteer territorial regiments, mostly infantry, had been established in all States, bearing titles indicative of the district in which they were located. These were the source of many early enlistments.

As was noted earlier from the tone of the key Australian politicians of the day, the mood of the nation was very much that they were still a colony of Britain. The population followed in the footsteps of Britain and had much the same customs, viewed the world through British eyes and were extremely patriotic to their homeland. They looked up to Britain as their guiding light, protector and for comfort. They quoted news from British papers as if it were their own, at least a quarter of the songs taught in Australian schools were patriotic of Britain (including "God Save Our King", Australians very much loved the king of the time) and students from a young age were taught both the history of Britain and Australia, although our own history was of little consequence. Every schoolchild in Australia was taught that the red parts on the map of the world "belong to us" and that to be British was a privileged state of being.[19]

Even the most supported of Australian politicians spoke fervently of Britain and the ties between the countries. The elected leaders of the country, however, were merely reflecting the opinion of the average Australian at that time. Indeed both sides of politics were blatant in their support of the Monarchy and Britain. This made a great deal of sense given that there were less than 140 years since Englishmen (white man) had first landed and settled the nation. Many Australians at that time could trace their parents or grandparents back to the homeland or had newly arrived in Australia. There was limited cultural diversity at the time, most were immigrants from Britain. The great flood of multiculturalism of the 20th century had not yet happened.

However, in reality Australians had changed a lot and it was mainly due to the fact that most did not spend time with Englishmen. While a large proportion had relatives or close family members living in England, most Australians did not travel and certainly did not mix with your average Englishman. In the 140 years or so since settlement in Australia, Australians of 1914 had adapted to a much harsher country and lost many of the "airs and graces" that their forefathers had brought with them when immigrating out from England.

As Bean notes, the generation of Australians at the time that war broke out had been left to develop themselves freely in their own way, independent of any direct involvement from the mother country, England. Australians had come to exhibit a peculiar independence of character. Their fathers, usually men of an assertive and forcible disposition, had cut loose from tradition and authority when they left the British Isles; they refused to take for granted the prescribed opinions, but faced each question for themselves and gave to it an answer of their own. If there was in them something of aggressiveness, there was also a vigorous and unfettered initiative. In them the characteristic resourcefulness of the British was developed further. They had lived so much in lonely places, where it was necessary to solve each difficulty without help and in the process they learnt to hold no practical problem insoluble.[20]

Australia was a young country and the population was very proud of its history to date, especially the history of their roots and what they had been able achieve under their "own steam". Australia had a strong rural base with a laid-back country lifestyle and "the man on the land" view of the world was evident even in the larger capital cities. Relationships were valued and most of the population had a strong work ethic, carrying themselves with dignity, manners and applying decency to those around them. When times were tough, they would get stuck in and pull each other through. They would get the job done, see it through and not give up. More importantly, they would not let their mates down and when there was tough work to do then they could be counted on.

Bean notes that so far as a prevailing creed, it was a romantic one inherited from the gold–miner and the bushman, of which the chief article was that a man at all times and at any cost would stand by his mate. This was and is the one law that the good Australian must never break. It is bred in the child and stays with him throughout his life. This was clearly demonstrated during the last few moments before the bloody attack on Lone Pine in Gallipoli, when the 3rd Australian Infantry Battalion was crowded on the fire steps of each bay of its old front–line trench, awaiting the final signal to scramble over the sandbags above, a man with a rifle in hand, bayonet fixed, came peering along the trench below. "Jim here?" he asked. A voice on the fire step answered "Right, Bill; here". "Do you chaps mind shifting up a piece?" said the man in the trench. "Him and me are mates an' we're goin' over together." The same thing must have happened many thousands of times within the Australian Divisions among men about to go into battle. The strongest bond in the Australian Imperial Force was that between a man and his mate.[21]

The influence of the rural lifestyle and living on the land were a lot stronger around the turn of the century than they are in more current times. The image and character of the "man on the land" was the guide for many young boys growing up. Even those from the city were never far from family and friends who made their living and their homes in the country. In many ways, living in the bush and outdoor work on the land were ideal foundations for the Australian soldiers of the World War I. Charles Bean noted that the bush still sets the standard of personal efficiency:

> *The bushman is the hero of the Australian boy; the arts of the bush are his ambition; his most cherished holidays are those spent with country relatives or camping out.*
>
> *He learns something of half the arts of a soldier by the time he is 10 years old – to sleep comfortably in any shelter, to cook meat or bake flour, to catch a horse, to find his way across country by day or night, to ride, or at worst, to "stick on".*
>
> *The Australian was half a soldier before the war; indeed throughout the war, in the hottest fights on Gallipoli and in the bitterest trials of France or Palestine, the Australian soldier differed very little from the Australian who at home rides the station boundaries every weekday and sits of a Sunday round the stockyard fence.*[22]

Hamilton in his book about the Australian Gallipoli sniper – Billy Sing, indicates that many young boys growing up in Australia in the pre–war years were used to handling guns and were very good marksmen even by the time they had reached their teens. Guns were readily available throughout the country following the turn of the century, gun shops were a common sight and guns could even be obtained via mail order.[23] For the buyer, it was not so much a status symbol or purchased for security purposes if needed, but it formed part of life in the bush, and to be proficient at handling a gun and the ability to shoot well were socially acceptable at the time. Moreover, the country at that time was intent on building up its own defence forces, having been stimulated to do so by the British and the increasing concern at home about an invasion by possibly either Russia or China, or even a new force from Asia that wanted to expand south. So real was the public's anxiety that in Queensland at that time, the construction of Fort Lytton was commenced and a steamer was purchased (the Otter) specifically to patrol the waters of Moreton Bay to provide a deterrent and an early warning of potential invasion. Hence, it was considered critical to bring through appropriately trained young men who could defend the country in a time of war and became an important part of the social infrastructure.

There were numerous occasions and events staged for young men to show off marksmanship skills. Sporting and competitive shooting were encouraged from an early age. So much so that a musketry instructor toured Melbourne's metropolitan schools, teaching school cadets how to shoot and maintain rifles. By the time they left school at 14, many boys could shoot using the main army weapon of the day, the Lee–Metford magazine rifle – the national weapon of Australia.[24]

In 1911, Donald MacDonald, a Melbourne journalist with the Argus, who had been the first Australian war correspondent to go to South Africa, published a best seller titled The Bush Boy's Book, which was priced at one shilling and sixpence. No fewer than three chapters were devoted to shooting and advice to boys on selecting the right weapon, safety precautions, how to shoot properly, how to hunt animals and birds, including rabbits, hares, ducks and quail and how to succeed in competitive shooting on the range.[25]

The demanding environment and harsh drought conditions in Australia at the time toughened men and they developed a practical common-sense approach which set them apart from their British ancestry. This contributed to the "can do" attitude, giving them a confidence in their own abilities and meant that they strove to make the most from what little they had available and to be frugal with what they earnt. They appreciated a good laugh, especially at someone else's expense, and everyone knew of a "Larrikin" or two in their group of friends. They did not take everything as seriously as their British counterparts, and made fun of order and standards that tended to bind them and limit the freedom the expansive country they lived in encouraged.

The Australian colonial had been brought up to believe that "Jack" was as good as his master. Hence unlike the British soldier, these young men were not accustomed to unquestioning obedience or to following orders, particularly when they thought them an insult to their intelligence. By offering themselves voluntarily for war service they believed they were entitled a say in how they were to be treated. The Australian soldier did not understand why he had to put up with poor rations and how confinement to barracks, mindless drills and long marches in new boots would help him kill Germans more effectively.[26]

The Australian soldier preferred field exercises and were skilled horsemen, therefore shooting and general skirmishing were the order of the day. This was a tradition adopted by Australians from the Boer War, where personal initiative was prized in a soldier rather than "square bashing". The result was that the officers initially engaged in the AIF possessed poor routine military skills and were not overly concerned with appearance. Highly polished boots did not make you a better horseman or help you shoot straight.[27]

Australians certainly possessed some independence from the old country, due mainly to their isolation. While there were numerous areas that Australian society still needed to place reliance on for England's support, they wanted to show themselves worthy of great deeds, stand on their own two feet and to demonstrate what had already been achieved so far from the British Isles. Australia at the turn of the century had its own political system, economy, sports teams, legal system and corporate world, all however, were still very much linked or developed based on the British model. Australia was still a very young nation and had much to show the world. Its people wanted a chance to prove their worth and how great they were, as their forefathers had a long history of achievements and conquests.

When the war came, it seemed as if they suddenly had been provided with their chance to prove themselves and showcase Australia to the world.

War was something, however, that Australians were not used to. While Britain on the other hand seemed to be always at war, it was only from afar that Australians understood it. While a small number of Australians fought in the Boer War, it was a relatively small commitment of men and was not closely followed or even understood by the average Australian. In a world where news travelled slowly, particularly in reaching Australians, when it did arrive it was often provided with a highly censored view and few would really know the true reality of war.

The Australian knowledge of war was based on the British model, and during the early 1900s the country had a minimal defence force and was very dependent on Britain to support and defend the country's sovereignty. When the country decided on active development of a national defence force, even though Britain had no say in the way Australia planned, strategised and recruited soldiers, Britain's guidance and direction was always sought. When war started, the Australian naval fleet was given over to Britain, the country's soldiers were fighting for Britain's defence and military objectives. They fought for what Britain believed in, her battles were their battles. The most senior Australian military officials were either British, educated in the British way or were Australian officers reporting to English generals.

War at that time was almost romanticized. It was where men were men and the adventurous spirit was set loose. The hero always won out against the bad guys and valor and gallantry was the true mark of a man. Courage and bravery were available to all men in war and could be proven by men. It was a time for men to be together, to be with their mates and embark on a great adventure. For them to get away from the everyday monotony of life and hardship to seek fame and fortune. Likewise, for a new country this was where they could stand and be counted for the first time. More importantly, the Australians that went to war believed they were invincible and the war would be over swiftly, for when they came on to the battlefield the enemy would shrink away. Lasting no more than a few months, nothing could stand in the way of the British Empire. In fact, this was a significant part of the rhetoric that drove the recruitment campaigns at the outbreak of war.

The Australian papers took up the stories printed in the English press regarding the Germans' barbaric behavior, which included bayoneting babies, raping and killing women. This inflamed the Australian public, which instantly turned against anything remotely German in origin. People with German names were harassed and German owned businesses and retailers were shunned by many members of the public. In fact the St Kilda Football Club felt so embarrassed at accidentally having the same team colours as the German flag that they placed Union Jacks on their jerseys and changed the team colours from red, black and yellow to red, black and white as they remain today.[28]

Volunteers following Australia's entry into the war flooded into recruiting centres across the nation, a fervor of men eager to serve and participate in the adventure. In fact, so great was the rush to enlist, the infrastructure was just not ready to process and quarter them. Makeshift shelters were erected and sporting stadiums were used to house the men upon enlistment.

Carlyon[29] indicates that innocence explains some of the headiness. Unlike France or Bulgaria, Australia had never been to a big war. It did not know what it was like to lose the best spirits of a generation, to read casualty lists that took up whole columns in the newspapers, to see young men return home old and broken and wanting nothing much to do with anyone for the rest of their lives. Australia had too much faith in the British Empire, it looked so much smarter and stronger from here.

In the book "An Anzac's Story" which was based on the diaries of Roy Kyle[30], a soldier in the AIF, it suggests that the Australia that Roy grew up in was a great contradiction. The nation was founded on misery and despair, the unwanted children of Mother England, who declared us thieves, whores and misfits and threw us out of her house, sending us to the far ends of the earth where it was hoped that we might be forgotten. In the years that many of the men who joined up were born, they were only the fourth generation of white settlement. The first two generations took up the convict era and it would be expected that memories and stories of oppression and servitude were still very much in the conscious thinking of a significant part of the men and women at that time. They should have had little reason to love England or to nurture in their offspring a loyalty to the king. Yet this appears not to have been the case, possibly due to the schooling of the younger generations of Kyle's time by newly arrived migrants extolling the values of Mother England. Paradoxically, this affection wasn't reciprocated.

This was the Australia and the men that went to war in 1914.

Chapter 2

The Queenslanders Depart for Adventure

The basis of the Australian Imperial Force (AIF) that formed in 1914 was territorial. New South Wales supplied the 1st Brigade (1st – 4th Battalions) and Victoria the 2nd Brigade (5th – 8th Battalions), with the four less populous States fielding the 3rd Brigade.

The 3rd Brigade was made up of four Battalions: 9th Battalion which was a Queensland and northern New South Wales based Battalion, the 10th Battalion, which was South Australian based, the 11th Battalion, which was Western Australian based and the 12th Battalion, which was a combination of Tasmanian, South Australian and Western Australian men. The 3rd Brigade was therefore referred to as the "all Australian Brigade".

Each Brigade had approximately 4000 men and each Battalion roughly 1000 men. The Battalions were further broken down into companies and there were four companies within a Battalion, companies A through to D, each with 250 men.

As mentioned earlier in Chapter 1, the plan was to recruit men with prior military training and /or prior active service. At the time General Bridges started to consider the men available, it was noted that the Australian Military Forces (AMF) at the time were almost entirely made up of 19–21 year old youths. Aware that they could not send away an army of boys, and wanting men who had done some military training, Bridges and Major White decided that at least half the force would be made up of volunteers aged 20 years or over from the citizen forces (cadets after the age of 18 passed into the citizen forces). The rest were to come from men who had served in the old militia or in South Africa or other conflicts. It is interesting to note that of the 32 officers to sail with the 9th Battalion to war, 26 were drawn from the Queensland Militia units. The remaining six had either served in the British Army or had seen active service in South Africa and one had graduated from Duntroon. In the wider field, only 24 out of the 631 officers in the original 1st AIF Division had never served before, and of the 609 who had served, only 99 were professional soldiers, leaving 510 officers drawn from the Militia units.[31]

Enlistees had to be at least 19 and could be no older than 38, with the exception of some senior officers, but boys as young as 14 and men as old as 59 were able to fool recruiters. The average age, however, of the Australian soldier at Gallipoli was 28; 40 per cent were over 25 years old, 40 per cent aged between 21 and 25 and 20 per cent under 21 years. Men wanting to enlist had to be at least 5 foot 5 inches tall with a minimum chest measurement of 34 inches (86 cms). Bootmakers did a roaring trade at this time, adding half an inch to the soles of young men's boots when they fell short of the height required by the recruiting sergeant. There was also an extremely high medical and dental standard in place and men that had filled teeth, false teeth, corns, varicose veins and toes that were not level could have been rejected. Almost 90 per cent of the men enlisting were unmarried.[32]

Privates would receive six shillings per day for overseas service, which was very good, in fact it was two shillings a day higher than the basic wage, and given that there was reasonably high unemployment at the time, this made enlisting a very attractive alternative. The Australian soldier would be the best-paid soldier in the war. For many the war was a godsend. Many men had never dressed so well nor earnt so much money in their life. *The Sydney Morning Herald* estimated that half of Sydney's 550 unemployed signed on.

The response when recruiting began on 11th August, 1914 was massive. Initially the only recruiting centres were in the capital cities. In Sydney, 3600 men had been selected at the end of the first day they were open and over 10000 had applied by 20th August. In Brisbane, 1400 men had volunteered on the first day at the Brisbane Town Hall. A Queensland drover was said to have walked 350 miles to Brisbane when his horse gave up. Bill Harney, a 21-year-old stockman from Townsville, upon the outbreak of war had been in the Gulf Country and travelled many miles to enlist with the 9th Battalion in Brisbane. Years later after the war he was quoted as saying, "I was dead scared when I went to join up – scared it would be all over before I got there!" Bill survived the war and returned to Australia in 1919.[33]

The great fear that the men had was rejection at the recruitment office. Captain James Bean a medical officer of the 3rd Battalion, recorded in his observations:

Funny fellows, these men, dare–devils many of them, but for the most part now quivering all over with nervousness in my extremely mild presence. They are all secretly terrified that they will be rejected, and they look at you with a pathetic, feeble smile and twitching lips, and they heave a huge sigh of relief when it is over and they are safely in… sometimes I have to refuse and they plead with me and almost break down.[34]

As almost 30,000 men had enlisted by the end of September 1914, more men were offered and accepted by Britain. By the end of 1914, 52,561 men had joined for what they believed would be the adventure of a lifetime. Many men took it also as an opportunity to get out of the humdrum or rut lifestyle they were in. They thought the war would not last long and would be over in a few months, so they therefore needed to enlist as soon as possible before the opportunity was lost. The recruitment posters urged the young men to "Join the Grand Picnic in Europe" and in *The Sydney Morning Herald*, they proclaimed that this was an opportunity for young colonials to see the mother country and be home shortly after Christmas. Such was the expectation of an early and easy defeat of Germany that the recruits became known as the "six shilling tourists".[35]

Australian war correspondent Alan Moorehead stated after the war that,

I don't think the prospect of fighting scared these young soldiers very much, or, if it did, their fear was coated over with the military trappings, the excitement, and a complete ignorance of war.[36]

Unemployment was high and the country was in the midst of a drought that was wearing down the economy. The opportunity to travel overseas was also a real incentive, given that the chance of overseas travel for the average person was unlikely and far too expensive. Men would often try other recruitment centres one after another until they were accepted. For a nation of 4.5 million people, the number of men who had signed up (almost 1 out of every 2 men by the end of the war), was a large commitment and as others have rightly pointed out, the war effort took the best of the best young men in their generation at that time into the 1st Division, AIF.

A group of recruits for the 9th Battalion at the Enoggera Camp, Brisbane. (AWM P00889.008)

General Bridges chose Brigadier Sinclair-MacLagan, aged 46 at the time, to command the 3rd Brigade. A British officer decorated in South Africa, Sinclair-MacLagan was a very capable man but tended towards pessimism.[37] He in turn chose Lieutenant Colonel H.W. Lee to command the 9th Battalion.

In the foreward to Harvey's book[38], then Major General Sinclair-MacLagan writes that most of the men who sailed (with the 9th Battalion) in the troopship "*Omrah*" from Queensland in late 1914 were typical Queenslanders of the tall, lean, wiry type – though in this Battalion there was quite a "sprinkling" of ex–soldiers of the British Regular Army.

For the 9th Battalion, its newly named C.O. Lieutenant Colonel H.W. Lee, had previously been in charge of the 47th Wide Bay Militia Regiment. One interesting fact about Lt. Col. Lee was that he and his eldest son, Captain H.W. Lee Jnr, along with another father and son combination Major W.C. Harvey and 2nd Lieutenant H.C. Harvey, were all from Maryborough and all were commissioned officers in the 47th Wide Bay Regiment. All were on their way to Brisbane to join up with the 9th Battalion within 24 hours of the war breaking out. Wrench[39] indicates that he believes this to be an unparalleled occurrence within the AIF. Both fathers were approaching fifty years of age, were highly trained militia men and dedicated to the regiment in which each had served from before the Boer War.

See appendix 1 for more detail about what happened to these four men.

There were many Australian families that had all their eligible sons enlisting in the new army drawn to support Australia's call to arms. However, two Queensland families in particular that supported the war effort and joined the ranks of the 9th Battalion were the Scrivener family from Ipswich and the Keid family from Graceville, Brisbane.

The two brothers, Frederic and Nelson Scrivener, enlisted on the 19th August 1914 with the 9th Battalion. Both men were born in Ipswich, Suffolk, England and migrated to Australia just before the war started and settled (interestingly enough) in Ipswich, Queensland. The older brother, Frederic, was a shoemaker by trade and was aged 30 when he enlisted. Nelson was 20 but noted his age as 23 when he enlisted, mainly to avoid the need for his parents to provide permission to join, which would have taken sometime. Nelson also stated that his occupation was a labourer, but according to his children, he had worked as a railway clerk before the war. One of the reasons why Nelson was so keen to enlist was that he hoped to be able to return to England to see his parents and the girlfriend he had left behind when he came to Australia. It was far too expensive to consider doing this on his pre–war wage.[40]

Charles and Mary Elizabeth Keid were born in Australia in the late 1850s. Charles was part of the first generation of the Keid family tree to be born outside of England. They settled in Pimpama, Queensland, a farming community on the outskirts of Brisbane city, and Mary Elizabeth gave birth to two daughters and seven sons (one daughter and one son died in infancy). Soon after all their children were born they moved into the Brisbane suburb of Graceville whereby they built the family home, a large Queenslander house on Molonga Terrace, which they named "Chewton". The six boys represented a good cross-section of Queensland men and their respective ages and occupations around the outbeak of war were as follows:

- Henry (Harry), age 30, selector
- Edward (Ted), age 25, farmer
- William (Bill), age 28, carpenter
- Leonard, age 28, accountant
- Walter, age 22, clerk at the Post Office
- Guy, age 19, student studying a science degree

Like most Australian families at the time of the World War I, they would have been following world events closely, joining in discussions with friends and neighbours about escalating tensions in Europe. When war did break out, the Keid boys, like many other young men in the area, were keen to join up and start the adventure before it concluded. Bill was the first of the boys to enlist on the 21st August, 1914 with the Australian 2nd Light Horse Regiment and Guy, the youngest of the boys, enlisted with the 3rd Field Ambulance, which supported the 9th Battalion soon after on the 2nd September, 1914.

Clearly, the remaining Keid boys would have been considering their own options now that their brothers had made decisions to enlist. It really would only be a matter of time before the others would follow. To be left behind and continue with the day-to-day monotony of life and work, missing the grand adventure with your brothers by your side and reading about their exploits from afar would have been unbearable.

About two weeks after war had been declared, the first members of the 9th Battalion started to assemble at a makeshift camp in the suburb of Enoggera, in Brisbane. Three days later 300 recruits from the Tweed, Richmond and Clarence River districts of New South Wales marched into camp and a large number of them were drafted into the Battalion. On August 22nd, 30 volunteers arrived from the Oxley Regiment, which had initially been called up for home service at the outbreak of war and was on duty at Fort Lytton.[41] The Fort, at that time, defended the entrance to the Brisbane River.

On August 22nd, a contingent of 123 men from North Queensland left Townsville on the SS *Bombala* and 10 more joined the ship in Mackay. They reached Brisbane on the 25th August and 77 of their number were included in the 9th Battalion and the remainder joined the Light Horse regiments and other units.[42]

During the third week in August 1914, a few military officers in uniform and a number of men in ordinary civilian clothes were noted pitching tents in Bell's Paddock, Enoggera, Brisbane. This was the formal beginning of the 9th Battalion AIF. On the 21st August the Commanding Officer of the proposed Battalion and several other officers arrived at camp. By 28th August, 52 officers and 1237 other ranks were in camp at Enoggera. This number had increased to 65 officers and 1784 other ranks by 3rd September, 1914.[43] On September 12th, it was announced that the Queensland quota of the expeditionary force was complete. Further recruits coming in began to train as the nucleus of the

15th Battalion, part of the second contingent, which trained at a temporary camp at the Exhibition grounds in mid-September following the completion of the annual exhibition in August. This new camp had to be established to cope with the overflowing numbers of recruits that were by this time "swamping" the Enoggera camp. Others became the first reinforcements for the 9th Battalion.

New recruits into the 9th Battalion AIF, donning packs near their tent lines at the Enoggera camp in preparation for a route march. The men are dressed in a mixture of civilian and military uniforms. (AWM P01875.002)

As the camp settled down, squad and company drill began, and then Battalion drill. Uniforms and then equipment was slowly acquired and issued to the men as they became available. Leave was given very sparingly, however, every Sunday afternoon the camp was opened up for visitors, relatives and friends of the troops to visit, and with the enlisted men they formed happy little picnic parties, some lasting through until 10pm.

On Saturday, September 19th, the troops who were to leave for overseas marched from the Enoggera camp into Brisbane city in full marching order, and, after traversing the main streets with fixed bayonets, to the accompaniment of a large crowd they returned to camp. A total distance of about twelve and a half miles was covered by the men that day.

The men of the 9th Battalion on board the SS *Omrah*, 24th September, 1914, at Pinkenba Wharf. (AWM H02228)

On the 23rd September, 1914, the *Western Star* reported for its outback readers, with the help of *The Courier*, the stirring scenes as the first contingent of the AIF (9th Battalion) marched through the streets and off to war past many thousands of cheering people who lined the streets waving small Union Jack flags:

> *Queensland has reason to be proud of its sons who have heard the call of the motherland in her hour of danger. From the north, west and from the south they have gathered and are still gathering, grim and resolute, their blood aflame at the challenge hurled forth by the Despot of Europe. Many of them wear on their breasts honours already won on the field of battle in South Africa and elsewhere, when they showed – as they will show again – that he who treads on the tail of the lion must also beware of the lion's cubs.*[44]

Barely six weeks after enlistment began, the 9th Battalion left camp at 4.15 on the morning of the 24th September, 1914, arriving at the Pinkenba wharf to go aboard the *SS Omrah* (8130 tonne Orient liner) for their great adventure at 8am. There was a lot of energy on board, as the ship was to sail at noon out from the Brisbane River. As the time of embarkation had not been announced to the public, there were only a few family and friends at the wharf at first, but later in the morning a couple of hundred well-wishers had gathered and were there to see the ship leave at midday. A number of the men were sick following vaccinations they had received prior to embarkation for overseas active duty.

The *Omrah* was, therefore, the first troopship to leave Queensland for the war effort. It was the ship's first voyage as a transport, but by no means its last. The *Omrah* remained on active service for nearly four years, until the ship was sunk by a torpedo off Sardinia, in the Mediterranean, on May 12th, 1918. It is worth noting that the HMT *Star of England* (A15) was also moored at Pinkenba Wharf, and on the same day troopers and their horses forming the 2nd Light Horse Regiment were embarking for Egypt. It was yet another vessel that made up the first convoy carrying the men and equipment of the first contingent AIF to Egypt.

The diary of Lance Corporal Fred Neal of the 9th Battalion has entries written between 23rd September, 1914 and 15th August, 1915. Fred was a clerk before enlisting and lived in Maryborough, Queensland. He boarded with the 9th on the SS *Omrah* and would eventually land at Anzac Cove on the morning of 25th April, 1915. He states in his earliest entries:

> *Got notice on Wednesday, September 23rd to get ready to leave on Thursday morning. Reveille sounded at 3am Thursday, 24th September and all men fell in at 4am and marched to Enoggera and sent by two special trains to Pinkenba. Met at the wharf by mother Maud and May. Boat left wharf at 12 noon, trip up the river was very smooth.*[45]

The *SS Omrah* was bound first for Port Melbourne, which it reached on 28th September and there the men remained for three weeks. During this time they continued training, with a lot of route marches and practice in attacking at Albert Park, Fisherman's Bend and Heidelberg. The reason for the extended stay in Melbourne was due to the presence in the Pacific of the German warships *Scharnhorst* and *Gneisenau,* which had also delayed the New Zealand troop ships from setting sail. Until an adequate naval escort was provided, the New Zealand Government refused to let its transports leave for Australia to join the first convoy.

On the 17th October, 1914, the men of the 9th Battalion aboard the *SS Omrah,* left Port Melbourne having been preceded by *Hororata* and the ship *Benalla* the previous day. They then arrived in Albany, Western Australia on 21st October and at 6.45am on 1st November, set sail again with the rest of the fleet bound for what they thought would be the war in Europe. Many men threw last messages over the side of their ships in bottles that implored the finders to pass them on to their loved ones.

Men of the 9th Battalion returning to the SS *Omrah* after undertaking route marches in Albany, Western Australia (Wrench)

Men of the 9th Battalion resting on the decks of the SS *Omrah* after departure from Australia. The first figure seated on the right, leaning against the deckhouse, is Corporal James Hunter, who was subsequently killed leading a charge at Tasmania Post, Gallipoli on 23rd June, 1915. (AWM C02484)

The fleet was the largest to leave Australia and had 36 transports including 10 from New Zealand, three abreast and covering an area two miles wide and over seven miles long. The convoy was lead out by the cruisers *Minotour* and the *Sydney.* The light cruiser *Melbourne* was far astern and the Japanese ship *Ibuki* was on the starboard beam. The convoy was joined two days later by the troopships *Ascanius* and *Medic* with troops from WA. On the 8th November, the *Minotour* was withdrawn and the *Melbourne* took over her lead role.

It is worth noting that on the day the convoy left Albany, WA, Britain, following the action of Russia on the previous day, declared war on Turkey. This was not known to the AIF men on board the ships, who had no thought that they would ever meet the Turks in battle. They were going to fight the Germans in Europe.[46]

All of the troops aboard the *Omrah* would have known that the Australian cruiser the *Sydney* would be one of the escort ships, so on the morning of the 9th November, 1914, they were surprised to see the *Sydney* change course and head in a westerly direction at top speed with smoke coming from all four of its funnels. Later in the morning at around 11.30, a notice was posted on deck advising that the *Sydney* had destroyed the German cruiser *Emden* in a battle off the Cocos Islands. There was great rejoicing on board the *Omrah* and the victory was celebrated by the issue of an extra ration of beer and the granting of a half-day holiday for each of the men, which meant exemption from parade and fatigues for the afternoon.

Lance Corporal Neal indicates on the 18th November, 1914:

> *Travelling 14 knots from 6pm Tuesday until midday Wednesday, travelled 285 miles. Boats left port (Port of Colombo) in three groups. Ours last to leave composed of fast boats. SS Omrah second last in line. Miltidies at rear and directly in front of us the SS Hororata. Four officers and 40 German prisoners brought aboard SS Omrah at 5pm on Tuesday, 17th November, body under escort of armed guard. Officers not on parole.*[47]

An interesting side point is made by Bean in his *Official History of Australia in the War of 1914–1918* in which he indicates that the transport fleet had a certain amount of good fortune. According to Captain Von Muller of the *Emden*, they had only been 52 miles from the convoy the evening before the *Sydney* caught up with them. Although the escort was strong, when the *Minotour* left the convoy and a reshuffling of positions occurred, the stern of the convoy was left undefended.

There were quite a few German sailors picked up while in Colombo; 44 of the survivors were taken on board the *Omrah* as prisoners of war and the 9th Battalion was required to provide a guard of 60 men. Lieutenant Colonel Lee indicates in one of his letters that the prisoners were all well treated and looked after by medical staff.[48] The German sailors were transferred off the *Omrah* and on to another ship two weeks after first coming on board, when the troopship dropped anchor at Suez Canal. One of the *Emden's* officers stated that they should have got in among the transports from astern and they would have been able to do all sorts of damage with their guns and torpedoes.

We would certainly have sunk half- a- dozen ships, possibly 12, before the escort could have come up and stopped us.[49]

In another interview after the action with Captain Von Muller (who was picked up and taken prisoner), he indicated that if he had caught up with the fleet:

I would have run alongside of the Sydney and torpedoed her. Then in the state of confusion I would have got among the transports and sunk half of them before your escort came up. I should have been sunk in the end, I expect. I always expected that.[50]

The *Emden's* objective was clear. Fortunately for the Anzacs it was never successful. Given that each of the troopships were fully laden with men, the effect would have been devastating for the nation (and potentially New Zealand) and for the future of Australia's war effort.

While Bill and Guy Keid were in Melbourne en route to Egypt with the first contingent of the AIF, two more Keid brothers, Harry and Ted, decided it was time to join. Both enlisted with the 9th Battalion as one of the first reinforcements for the Battalion on the 5th October, 1914 in the city of Townsville, where they had been living. This left Leonard Keid, the qualified accountant who was married with three young children, and Walter Keid, the clerk with the Post Office, both no doubt debating the difficult decision on whether to give up full-time careers and family to enlist with their other brothers. For Leonard, it would have been particularly difficult given his family commitments, and there was an expectation from family and friends that he would be the one to stay at home.

German prisoners from the German raider "Emden" playing leapfrog on the port saloon deck of the SS Omrah. (AWM A03346)

The Officers of the original 9th Battalion on the "Omara"

From left to right. Back row: Lieuts. H.C. Harvey, Hinton, Capt. Melbourne, Lieuts. Costin, Boase, Capts. Ryder, Jackson, Lieut. Adsett, Capt. Salisbury, Lieut. Ross, Capt. Milne, Lieuts. Chambers, Ker, Williams, Fisher, Thomas, W. McK, G. Young, Capts. S.B. Robertson, H.W. Lee, Lieut. Rigby. Middle row: Lieut. Chapman, Majors W.C. Harvey, J.C. Robertson, Lieut. Col. H.W. Lee, Capts. Brown, Butler, Lieut. Dougall. Front row: Lieuts. Haymen, Jones, Fortescue, Roberts. (Wrench)

Chapter 3

Welcome to Egypt

The arrival of the 1st AIF Division at Alexandria on the 4th December, 1914 was a great relief for the troops, who had been cooped up for many weeks on board their respective ships without any shore leave. It was not until the 6th December that the *SS Omrah* moved into the wharf, and the troops received news that they would be going to Mena Camp near Cairo. The first men of the 9th Battalion starting disembarking at 9am i.e. F, G and H companies with B, C, D and E following. All troops with the exception of A company, who remained on board for guard and other duties, left the ship by 4pm that day.

The original intention was for the troops of the 1st AIF Division to continue on to England and to be put into camp on the bleak and cold Salisbury Plains. The Australian High Commissioner in London at the time, Sir George Reid, had become aware of the inadequate preparations that had been made for their reception. He was also aware of the terrible conditions that the Canadians had earlier been subjected to and the inevitable shortening of the training program that would have occurred due to the poor local conditions. He therefore decided to take action as soon as possible given the ships were approaching the Suez Canal and have them disembark in Egypt instead for their training. Lord Kitchener agreed to the proposal.

The London Times stated that due to the changed situation in Egypt, being the declaration of Turkey to side with the German forces in waging war on the Allies, the Australians were to remain in Egypt to complete their training, strengthen the local British Garrison and help defend the Suez Canal against any land attacks that may be made by the Turkish. Wrench writes that this decision was to change the destiny of the colonial troops as well as drastically affect events in the Middle East.[51]

The first group of 9th Battalion men travelling by train reached Mena late that night, the other companies arriving the following day on the 7th December. The men of A company reached Mena on 8th December at 2am. Once reaching Mena Camp[52] they were formed up in lines of companies in the dark and were issued with two blankets each and slept in the open sand within full view of the pyramids. This must have been quite exciting for the men as most would not have travelled overseas before, in fact, many would not have travelled outside their home districts before and now they were camping right in front of one of the largest pyramids in the area. Spirits would have been very high among the troops. Harvey notes that all these new sights and tastes were enjoyed to the utmost by the Australians. Everything was so different from what they had been used to. Some of the 9th, in fact, had never been in a town in their lives until the day they passed through Cairns, Townsville or Charleville on their way to Brisbane when they enlisted, so it must have been an amazing experience for them, not only the sight and sounds, but also the companionship of so many men.[53]

The second day a number of tents were issued, but more importantly, it rained on the second night and continued for the next two days. It was a significant event in hindsight, as it did not rain again during the whole period that the Battalion was at Mena.[54]

Lance Corporal Neal writes on Sunday, December 6th,1914;

Disembarked at 4pm, joined train at wharf. Arrived Cairo midnight. Cup of coffee, bread and cheese supplied outside railway. Joined train again and moved to next station. Joined trams and moved to foot of first pyramid.[55]

Training commenced for each of the 9th Battalion companies on 10th December, and on the 14th a series of whole-day parades began in the desert. At first these consisted of one–half of the Battalion entrenching itself and being attacked by the other half. The desert around Mena had been divided into three large training areas, one area allocated specifically for each of the brigades making up the first Division i.e. 1st – 3rd Brigades.

The training of the Australian troops was carried out almost entirely by their own officers. Lieutenant Colonel Lee was an experienced militia man and as with many other members of the militia, had been a school teacher and disciplinarian. He had gained a good understanding of his unit in the early days of their enlistment and had selected a good team of young officers to support him. Many of these officers had come from militia units before the war and would have also been competent instructors. Bean noted that the training was more than just a passing mention, inasmuch as it was one of the finest achievements in the history of the AIF. The intensity was exceptional.[56]

One interesting picture which is provided on the following page, was taken at Mena Camp by Chaplain Ernest Merrington, of an Australian soldier in the foreground playing with a kangaroo, the regimental mascot. The soldiers either side of the photo are troops of the 9th and 10th Battalions on parade, so we assume it was a 3rd Brigade mascot. The question for some time has been, who is the soldier in the photo feeding the kangaroo? Peter Stanley from the Australian War Memorial indicated as part of the caption to the picture, which is held in the memorial's records, that they had no information about the soldier and would be interested to learn more. Then in the Brisbane *Sunday Mail* newspaper on 22nd April, 2007, Meg Row came forward and indicated that the photo was of her father, Walter MacTaggart, who was 26 at the time and part of the Australian Light Horse. The photo was stored in an old family album. She indicated that he had enlisted into a Light Horse Regiment and took the wallaby with him and his horse from Australia. However, on researching Walter MacTaggart, it was noted that he was not part of the Light Horse, but part of the 9th Battalion infantry at that time (which makes sense and fits with the Battalions noted by the Australian War Memorial in the photo) and was living in Ascot, Brisbane at the time of his enlistment. He boarded the *Omrah* with the other members of the first contingent of the 9th Battalion. It was noted that many other young Australian soldiers had in fact smuggled koalas and possums into the camp, feeding them on rations for the donkeys and horses. Some were subsequently given to the Cairo Zoological Gardens when the units eventually left for Gallipoli.

Very limited leave was allowed in Cairo after hours and almost from the morning of their arrival training was carried out for at least eight hours a day, every day, with the exception of Sundays. All day long, in every valley of the Sahara, for miles around the pyramids, there were groups of men advancing, retiring, drilling or squatting near their piled arms listening to their officers. Egyptian hawkers followed the marching columns with an array of foods and drinks. The 5th Battalion's historian wrote that only the soldiers were visible "until the signal was given for smoke–o, when the Gyppos (Egyptian travelling food salesmen) would spring up as if by magic from the sand".[57]

Lines of the 9th and 10th Battalions at Mena Camp. The soldier with the kangaroo is Walter MacTaggart of the 9th Battalion. (AWM C02588)

Officers standing outside tents being erected by men of the 9th Battalion at Mena Camp, Egypt. One of the officers in front of the tent on the right (first man without hat, left to right) is Lt. Joseph Costin. (AWM C02590)

Sydney Loch, who enlisted as a gunner in the Field Artillery Brigade and was made a "galloper" (running messages) for Colonel Johnson during the fighting on Gallipoli, noted in his diary entries when in Mena Camp that the vendors would shout out at the troops:

This way Australia! Australia very good, very nice!

Oranges, five for one piastre!

Nestle chocolate, only two piastres!

Donkey, sir! Or a camel, very good, very nice!

And the reply was usually, go to blazes, the lot of you! from the ANZAC soldiers.[58]

In regard to how well the men of the 3rd Brigade were held by High Command, a British officer on General Birdwood's staff is quoted as saying "a better division than the 1st Australian had never gone to war". Wrench indicates that the men of the 3rd Brigade in particular could have laid claim to this statement, for when General Bridges needed to decide which brigade should be thrown into action first, he had chosen the 3rd Brigade, despite the high average age (51) of the Battalion's commanding officers.[59]

Wrench goes on to indicate that perhaps they were influenced by an incident described by Bean that occurred during some desert training. Two Battalions were still far out in the desert sand so that they could not be seen. All that appeared was a few vague dots swimming on the line of mirage on the horizon. Presently the dots thickened and enlarged. Then out of the mirage came a line of men, all unnaturally tall, all running. They were the 9th Battalion, Queenslanders. They came at the double across a mile of sand and stone. Instead of 15 minutes that their commander had expected them to take, they took eight minutes. What struck the British and French officers who saw them was the manner in which these men threw themselves into it, as though their training was real war.

The Australians were fascinated by their ancient surroundings, especially the pyramids, which many men climbed during their free time. Often the men scratched their names in the stones of the pyramids, trying to get higher up the monument than soldiers from previous wars.

One of the most intriguing pictures is the group photo of the officers and men of the 11th Battalion, 3rd Brigade, recruited from Western Australia. The group of over 800 soldiers are spread over the side of the Great Pyramid of Khufu (Cheops) near Mena Camp. There are many stories around this photo. One of the more well known stories is that a soldier had died not long prior to this photo being taken. Rather than leaving him out of the photo, his mates brought him along and he is propped up somewhere in the crowd.

On spending some time with one of the researchers at the Australian War Memorial in Canberra, she informed me that this story was not true and merely a rumor. Even though, I have spent some time looking through the faces trying to confirm whether there was any truth to the rumor!

One other interesting feature of the photo at the bottom left-hand corner, is four men with arms linked. They are said to be a father and his three sons, all having enlisted in the 11th Battalion.

This photo conveys to me all the character and spirit of the Australian soldiers prior to the landing at Gallipoli. The larrikin smiles, the mateship, the confidence and happy-go-lucky attitude of a group of men who will very soon realise that their vision of the adventure and thrill of war will be sorely tested. A large part of the men in this photo will be dead, injured or mentally scarred by the Gallipoli legacy that awaited them in no more than a matter of weeks. For the 11th Battalion in particular, in the five days following the landing it suffered 378 casualties, over one third of its strength.

Appendix 14 provides some research into what became of the officers positioned in the front row of this photo. Captain Barnes of the 11th Battalion, who is shown sitting in the front row, four in from the left, recorded in his diary that after church (Sunday morning) the whole Battalion was marched up to the Pyramid and we had a photo taken, or at least several of them at the pyramid. Researching Captain Barnes, I noted that he was killed on the 28th April, 1915, three days following the landing at Anzac Cove.

It is also interesting to note that there were a number of injuries and indeed deaths of soldiers during their stay in Mena Camp, well before seeing enemy action. The 9th Battalion had its fair share of these as well. Lieutenant Ross of the 9th Battalion noted in his diary[60] the following incidents:

- Sergeant Joseph Moore, injured while onboard the *SS Omrah* when a primus stove he was handling exploded. The Sergeant was taken to hospital in Egypt on arrival, but died on 3rd January, 1915. Funeral service held on 4th January.

Group portrait of all the original officers and men (over 800 soldiers) of the 11th Battalion, spread over the side of the Great Pyramid of Cheops near Mena Camp. (AWM P05717.001)

- Sergeant Millward of D Company badly injured by a car.
- Private Forster of D Company was hurt when he fell off one of the pyramids on the 30th December. He later died from these injuries.
- Private F.J. Gilvarry died of unstated causes.
- Soldier (unnamed) is injured falling off pyramid.
- Private N. Matthews, in regimental transport, dropped dead.

These are the details of just one of the Battalions at Mena Camp. We could imagine the total numbers of injuries and deaths across the Australian contingent and the number of men returning home without firing a shot or setting foot on the battlefield. Often we forget that there were deaths outside the theatre of battle. It is only logical with such a large number of men that death by natural causes and injuries will inevitably occur.

The Australian soldiers were noted for their "larrikinism" during the many weeks in Egypt. There were only a limited number of places for the troops to amuse themselves outside Mena Camp. For most soldiers, the time to let down their hair was when they visited Cairo. Mena Camp lay 10 miles to the south of the city of Cairo, with which it was connected by a tree-lined road and tramway. Once in the city, many of the younger men were easily led astray by the sights, sounds, people and places that they would not have had any exposure to back home. This was another part of the great adventure and the men had money to spend, having built up big credits in their paybooks during their long period on board ship. As Bean mentions,[61] owners of hotels pressed upon the newcomers drinks amounting to poison, and the natives along the road sold them stuff of unheard vileness. "Touts" lead them to amusements descending to any degree of filth. Many a youngster was plunged into excitement that seemed only too sordid when the blood cooled. Much of this behavior was little more than high spirits. The trams to Cairo were continually crowded with soldiers taking up both the floorboards and roofs. In most cases there were more men heading into Cairo than those actually entitled to the leave.

Bean indicates that over time matters were swiftly coming to a point when discipline in the AIF must either be upheld or abandoned. Heavy drinking, desertion, attacks upon the locals and stealing were on the increase. Much of the trouble seems to come from one class of man, the old soldier leading the younger ones astray. Bean, the official Australian historian for the Gallipoli campaign, always supportive of his fellow countrymen both during their time in Egypt and throughout his time with them on the Gallipoli Peninsula, indicated that many of these older soldiers were not Australian, although there were a few Australian criminals added to them.

The AIF's discipline hung in the balance at the end of 1914. Serious misconduct among the Australian soldiers was rife. Drunkenness, venereal disease and absence without leave all soared at this time. British military police were routinely bashed and Egyptians were being assaulted and robbed. Cairo residents were fed up and began to ask when the Australians would be tied up! Pederson outlines a "farcical" case of discipline when a Captain berated an Australian sentry for eating a pie and ordered him to present arms. The sentry proceeded to ask the accompanying Colonel to hold his pie while he did so.[62]

As an indication of the level of misconduct, it was noted that early in January 1915, about 300 soldiers from the 1st Division AIF were absent without leave in Egypt. Although they were technically classed as deserters under military law, they could not under the Australian regulations, nor indeed in fairness, be shot. General Bridges understood that while some of the reason for the unruly behavior was likely contributed to by the monotony of training and the boredom of the men during their extended time at Mena Camp, he understood that the behavior of many of the men needed to change quickly. This was needed in order to ensure the AIF retained some level of respect from their peers, would be considered for active service when it came, and most importantly, would be ready to go into combat as an effective fighting force. He had rightly come to the conclusion that the normal military punishments were not working as a deterrent for the Australian soldiers. He needed some other extreme penalty to restore some form of discipline, so he resorted to sending men back to Australia to be discharged from the army. For the average Australian soldier, this punishment was considered extremely severe among the men and hence became a relatively successful way of curbing the ill-discipline. This was their greatest adventure, they were there with their mates, life was boring back home, they had not yet fired a shot after having trained so hard, and to be separated from comrades and sent home in shame was, for most, a fate worse than dying on a faraway battlefield. Bean states that for most AIF units, this was a very practical way for them to discard their most troublesome characters and restore the levels of discipline and respect that would be required before the men entered action.

On the 1st January, 1915, an important event in the structure of the AIF infantry units occurred. The Australian battalions, which up until that time had consisted of eight companies, were reorganised on a four company basis; A through to D. Hence, the original companies, E, F, G and H which the men had enlisted under and embarkation records refer to, became obsolete. In addition, each company was then subdivided into four smaller units of platoons.

For the men in camp, while the training that they had endured over several weeks was both tiresome and monotonous, it had fast developed the 3rd Brigade into a physically fit and tough unit, well trained to the extent of the limited weapons and resources available. Especially in regard to open warfare, skirmishing practice and they developed into very capable riflemen. Moreover, the men developed strong friendships and strong bonds during this period that would hold then in good stead in time of hardship. The men gleaned whatever information they could about the course of the war, especially the movements of troops in their area. Every activity that affected the trend of the war effort only stimulated their desire to get into the action for which they had enlisted, and their continued training was doing nothing but aggravating this desire. General Bridges was wise to have focused on curbing the pent–up spirits of the men by his intense training methods.[63]

The Australian and New Zealand troops by now had been organised into the Australian and New Zealand Army Corps, under General Birdwood. The well-known code name adopted to refer to this group of men, which has forever imbedded itself in our history, was the word ANZAC, which was first used, as the story goes, by a junior officer at Corps Headquarters who had been used to seeing A &N.Z.A.C. on cases stacked outside his office.

On February 9th, the 1st reinforcements for the 9th Battalion arrived at Camp Mena, approximately 100 men under Lieutenant Koch. They were absorbed into the Battalion to replace men who had become sick, been sent home or had become casualties due to accidents.

When war started between Turkey and the Allies late in October 1914 and then the news of Turkey's invasion of Egypt early in the New Year had been passed around each of the Battalions, it had the effect of enlivening their impatience. However, the Brigade was bitterly disappointed when only one of their units, the 3rd Field Company of Engineers, had been called upon to build defence trenches and floating barges. The 3rd Brigade remained on in Camp

Mena for almost three months through until 28th February, 1915, when they marched out of Cairo, then entrained for Alexandria.

For the Scrivener brothers, Corporal Fred Scrivener and his younger brother, Private Nelson Scrivener, both were keen to move on from Camp Mena along with the rest of the 9th Battalion. They had enough of the sand, heat, training and most of all the waiting. Now they were on their way to take some active part in the fighting that they had been training for over so many months. Fred was part of D Company and would be part of the team of stretcher bearers during the first action at Gallipoli. Nelson was part of B Company.

Soldiers leaving Mena Camp, bound for action at Gallipoli. (AWM P01436.007)

Lance Corporal Neal writes that on Sunday, 28th February, 1915;

Struck camp at Mena. Received orders to march into Cairo. Left camp 5pm, arrived at Barracks opposite train station 9pm. Bivouacked for night.[64]

The Battalion War Diary entry on the 28th February, 1915 by the Battalion Commanding Officer, Lieutenant Colonel Lee, indicates that the strength of the Battalion was 1081 officers and men. This number is further adjusted down due to 34 men being in hospital, one man in detention and eight men absent without leave, leaving an effective number of 1038 men.

Lance Corporal Neal[65] indicates that over the following days:

Monday, March 1st, 1915, "Entrained at railway station central at 4.30am for Alexandria arriving there about 11am. Purchased 20 ostrich feathers for 10/–."

Tuesday, March 2nd, 1915, "Left Alexandria per SS Ionian 11.30am. Travelling without escorts at rate of about 10 knots per hour. Reached the bay off Lemnos Island about 7.30pm Thursday."

It was also on the 2nd March, 1915 that Harry and Ted Keid, who had been training in Egypt since January 1915, eventually linked up with the 9th Battalion just as it was about to board the SS *Ionian* bound for Lemnos Island.

Chapter 4

The 3rd Brigade AIF is Going to War

Why did the Australians go to Gallipoli? The Australians that had enlisted in the AIF had joined up to fight the Germans, "the Hun" on the Western Front in France and Belgium. Most of the recruitment advertisements and the talk in the pubs, hotels and sportsgrounds was about joining the mother country to fight the Germans, who were summarily depicted as evil men who raped, pillaged and killed babies, more like monsters than men. Instead the German soldier was probably very similar to themselves in terms of their love for family, king and their country. They too had expected that their country would reign supreme and their enemies would be defeated quickly. The common privates in both armies, in some respects, had been deceived by the politicians, the media, the military leaders and the hysteria that surrounded the declaration of war.

Instead of the Western Front, the Australian soldiers ended up lost in a place of antiquity, in a place that many of them had not heard of until a few weeks before they landed on the Gallipoli Peninsula. The Turkish Army, in particular the Turkish soldier, was initially considered inferior and vastly underestimated by the senior British officers charged with planning the Gallipoli campaign, much to the Allies' dismay when they finally met the Turks on the battlefield where they were staunchly defending their homeland.

Carlyon[66] writes that Gallipoli, and in fact the World War I, is the tale about how little wars, much like tumors, sometimes turn into big wars, not because those in charge intend this to happen, but because the thing they have created takes on a life of its own. It grows on them, muddling their senses and slipping into places it shouldn't, until finally it gets away from them, so big and so painful that all they wish is for it to go away.

By Christmas 1914, the war in Europe was only five months old and already the war against Austria and Germany on the Western Front had reached a stalemate. The battlefield could be described as a myriad of trench systems stretching for thousands of miles packed with soldiers. So much had changed in the manner in which wars would be fought from the last great wars that Britain had been involved. Carlyon writes that barbed wire, machine-guns and trenches sat badly with the imperial opera that had played for generations: cavalry wheeling in open country, bits clanking, the Union Jack humming in the breeze, delinquent natives trembling at the sight of so much pageantry. It was not like this on the Western Front. As one German prisoner remarked it is effectively best described as the suicide of nations. A single man with a machine-gun firing 500 rounds a minute had the power of 40 infantry men. Artillery pieces such as the destructive howitzer, were much more important than 100 bayonets. For every man impaled on a bayonet, 70 would die from shrapnel, high explosive or gas. This was effectively a battle of attrition, with each of the combatants driving endless ranks of their young country men to their deaths. The machine-guns and howitzers had tipped the balance in favour of the army that was defending. Any offensives carried out by either army were therefore normally unsuccessful, and were met with overwhelming force and massive loss of life. There were effectively two sophisticated, evenly matched and determined armies facing each other in two lines of trenches stretching from the North Sea to Switzerland, which left no opportunities for flanking movements. Any flanking movement had to be outside Western Europe.

Kitchener was the War Minister at the time and as Carlyon outlines, was trying to run the Great War as though it is another of the colonial skirmishes of which he knew so well. Kitchener would often make up the rules as he went along. Given the stalemate that had bogged down the British Army in the Somme, a bold plan devised by Winston Churchill, which outlined a flanking manoeuvre via the Dardanelles, was supported by Kitchener and he was able to garner support for the idea from the War Cabinet. Even though, it must be said, that there had been clear analysis provided to members of the cabinet that any fighting on the Gallipoli peninsula would be at the very least, be hard fought. Something needed to be done quickly and the 40 year old Churchill seemed to have some ideas that the War Cabinet were quick to support. History would show that they did not assess the strategy of the campaign nearly as much as they should have, especially given the commitment of men and hardware that was being planned.

Carlyon provides a picture of the background and mindset of both Kitchener and Churchill as military strategists and soldiers of a bygone era. During the war in Sudan in 1897 against the followers of the Mahdi, the British fought a key battle at Omdurman. Lieutenant Winston Churchill rode in the charge of the 21st Lancers. In this battle ancient war tactics met modern; the Dervishes threw themselves at the British with spears, some even rode horses clanking with chain mail. The British, however, had at their disposal the latest in military sophistication such as artillery, machine-guns and gunboats. It was no match for the Dervishes and the war was over by lunchtime. For the British public, their warriors had avenged the death of General Gordon (killed at Khartoum) and slain the nonbelievers. For General Kitchener from that time on, the British public had an almost religious faith in him. Similarly, many Australians at the time would also have held him in very high regard.

Churchill wrote later in 1930 that the battle,

Was the last of a long chain of those spectacular conflicts whose vivid and majestic splendour has done so much to invest war with glamour. It was not like the Great War, however, nobody expected to be killed. Here and there in every regiment, half- a-dozen or at worst 30 or 40 would die. But to the great mass of those who took part in the little wars of Britain in those vanished light- hearted days, this was only a sporting element in a light-hearted game. We may perhaps be pardoned if we thought we were at grips with real war.[67]

The Dardanelles campaign was first conceived by Churchill as a naval operation which would allow him in his role as the First Lord of the Admiralty, to make use of the great armada of British ships of war that he had at his disposal. The naval operation would limit the need to redirect much needed Allied troops away from the Western Front, which most in the War Cabinet agreed was showing clear signs of becoming an "unwinnable" and costly disaster. The campaign, which if successful, would not only remove

Turkey from the war and divert large parts of the German Army away from the Western Front, but encourage the Balkan nations to join the Allied cause. In due course, the success of the campaign would also return to the Russians, their supply route through the Black Sea. The plan rested on the assumption that the long suffering Turkish people, who had been mistreated by their leaders for so long, would not present much resistance when the British and French battleships appeared off the coast of the capital, Constantinople, and fired into the city. It was expected that when this happened the Turkish people would revolt under the duress against the Government, which included the influential German military advisors, and it would be driven to surrender its military forces to the Allies. The city would then be eventually handed over to the Russians.

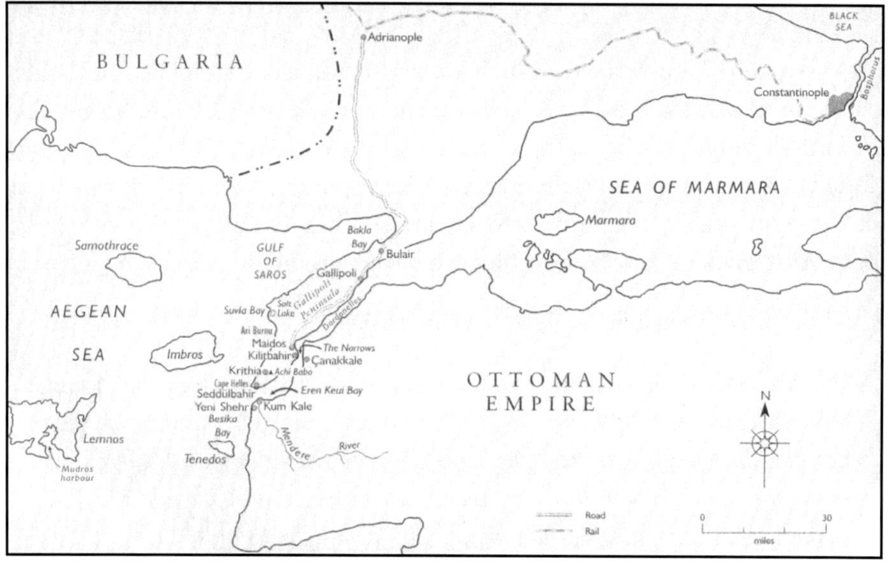

The theatre for the Dardanelles Campaign (Carlyon)

When Turkey entered the war in November 1914, siding with the Germans, the British Navy sent a squadron to attack the shore defences of the Dardanelles. While the ensuing naval bombardment of one of the Turkish forts guarding the entrance to the Dardanelles was successful in destroying the fort, it was mainly due to a fortunate direct hit on an ammunition store. While there was no infantry involvement and no British ships entered the Straits, this action did give some much needed credence to Churchill's theory that naval power alone might succeed in forcing the Dardanelles. There was even some talk early during the initial planning for the campaign that the Greeks might be prepared to provide three infantry divisions to assist the naval attack by landing and occupying the Gallipoli Peninsula. However, as so often was the case when historical differences surface between old sparring partners, this proposition soon faded when allegiances and plans with other Allied countries, namely the Balkans, were not to the Greeks' liking and they left the planning table. It is interesting to consider that it was unfortunate that the Greek invasion did not progress, as the three Greek divisions initially planned to land would have been easily able to occupy the peninsula at that time. The Turkish army's history later stated it would have been possible to have successfully conducted a landing at any point on the peninsula, and the capture of the Straits by land forces would have been comparatively easy prior to the buildup of men and defences in the months leading up to the Allied landings.[68] Australia's link with the Gallipoli campaign and its place in Australian history may never have occurred.

The whole campaign was planned with much optimism and with significant underestimation of the Turkish Armies will to fight. The battle was expected to be over reasonably quickly and the Allies rapid advance to the planned objectives. The Turks would most likely crumble and flee soon after the initial landings took place. General Sir Ian Hamilton was selected to command the military force that would primarily support the fleet. Carlyon provides a good portrayal of Hamilton and suggests that he was from the same vintage as Kitchener, and was fiercely loyal to him, even in awe of him. He had many years of experience directing men on the battlefield with which to toughen his character, but he also had a mellow, kindly character of the Edwardian gentleman below the surface. He also loved poetry and conducted himself with impeccable manners. Importantly he was considered a yes man to his superiors at all costs and even a yes man to many of his subordinates, who on numerous occasions should have been harshly refuted and brought to account for their actions and in many cases, their inaction in carrying out his orders. Hamilton was also a man very sensitive to the world of politics and understood its operation well. He knew clearly who on the War Cabinet was a supporter of the operation and who he would need to carefully communicate with over the course of the campaign.

As would eventually occur given that military force would take on the primary role in the Turkish invasion plans, Hamilton had been given an enormous task with a very basic outline of what the objectives were, although the overall milestones for success were clear. He was provided with scant information and plans of the Gallipoli area (mainly due to the fact that there was precious little), and minimal practical intelligence on the enemy positions and fighting capability. How to actually achieve this grand plan would be in reality his responsibility, although he would be significantly restricted in the men at arms he could get access to, the military hardware and infrastructure available, and most importantly, the very limited amount of time available for him to develop a detailed plan and brief his subordinates. Hamilton was a man under great pressure with a set of fundamental issues that would hinder him from the start and in effect throughout the campaign.

So these were the top three leaders, Kitchener, Churchill and Hamilton. It is important to outline this background as it not only provides the setting for the way the battle on the Gallipoli Peninsula is carried out, but also, the view the top brass had leading into the campaign. The personalities of these three men, in particular Hamilton, and those of his many incompetent senior commanders, contributed significantly to the disasters that lay ahead for the Anzacs.

The naval attack into the Dardanelles Straits began on 19th February, 1915. The fleet was comprised of mostly outdated battleships drawn predominately from the Canopus class of pre–dreadnoughts that had been destined for scrapping, and the Majestic class which had been commissioned for action around the same era. The vast minefield in the Straits and the very effective fire from Turkish gun emplacements meant that the job of the navy was perilous and slow going. After several weeks of manoeuvring and sporadic attacks, on the 11th March the British naval offensive had stalled. While a renewed attack took place on 18th March, the 21 minesweepers (which were really just North Sea fishing trawlers manned by Greek civilians) that were vital for the success of the fleet to proceed quickly up the Straits, did not, as could have been expected, complete this task when put under heavy concentrated Turkish fire and withdrew. Subsequently, with the British/French fleet moving through heavily mined waters, four battleships struck the minefield in the Narrows and three sank i.e. the French ship *Bouvet* and two British ships – the *Irresistable* and the *Ocean*. The fourth ship, the *Inflexible,* with a more modern design i.e. a compartmentalised hull, was able to limp back out to sea. Unknown to the Royal Navy, approximately one week earlier a small Turkish minelayer, the *Nousret,* had laid a single line of 26 mines parallel to the Asiatic shore in the sheltered waters of Eren Keui Bay, and it was these mines that did most of the damage. This effectively ended the naval attempt at forcing the Dardanelles and the plan to capture Constantinople from the sea.

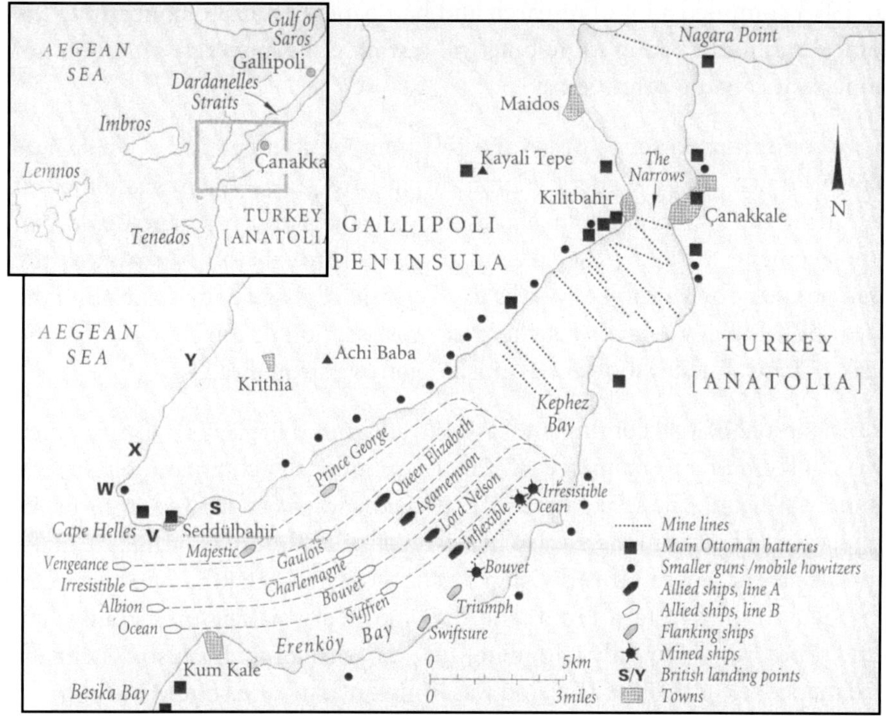

The Dardanelles: Map outlining the naval attack of the 18th March and the Cape Helles landing sites of 25th April, 1915. (Broadbent)

While it was the original objective for the troops to merely support the naval operation by helping to silence the Turkish guns that could not be destroyed by the heavy guns of the fleet and by occupying the peninsula and policing Constantinople after its fall, this plan changed significantly when the navy failed. Now the 75,000 strong Mediterranean Expeditionary Force (MEF), which included not only Anzac troops, but British, French and Indian troops, had to do much more than be an occupation force. They now had to seize the peninsula so that the fleet could get through. It now became primarily an infantry battle, rather than a naval battle.

Clearly the focus of the planning and strategy work up until that time had been centred on a naval operation, which now left precious little time available to adequately plan for an army operation. This placed significant pressure on Hamilton and his staff. It is interesting to note, however, that in Hamilton, the Allies had possibly the leading expert on amphibious landings. He had by 1913 compiled a lot of research and had papers prepared concerning the topic, even undertaking some practical testing of his research, although not under actual battle conditions.

A co–ordinated series of landings of men, equipment and supplies was hastily drawn up by General Hamilton and his staff, which was aimed at capturing the Gallipoli Peninsula, destroying the Turkish defences and gun emplacements to allow the fleet to proceed through the Narrows of the Dardanelles. The key objective was the Turkish forts and batteries around the town of Kilitbahir, which is at the narrowest section of the Dardanelles and was strategically an important Turkish defensive stronghold.

The initial British contingent was centred around the 29th Division, which was made up of approximately 17,000 men under the command of General Hunter-Weston. The make-up of the division was very limited in terms of regular army units and there was a heavy reliance on dominion armies to make up its battle strength. This division was the only one that had not yet been engaged on the Western Front, and the volunteers making up its ranks had little time thus far to fully complete their basic training. Even so, Kitchener had made it clear that the Division was "only on loan" and should be returned as soon as possible for service on the Western Front after the objectives were achieved. The 29th would land at five beaches, officially named S,V, W, X and Y, on the toe of the peninsula at Cape Helles and would move up the Kilitbahir Plateau under the covering fire of the navy, towards the forts at the Narrows. The French committed a Division of approximately 16,500 men under the command of General d'Amade. They would land on the Asiatic side of the Dardanelles as a feint to tie up Turkish troops, diverting them away from the main landing on Cape Helles. Following their landing, they would be withdrawn soon after to the peninsula to support the British advance. A second diversionary attack would be made by the Royal Navy at the Gulf of Suros to the north, where there was a large buildup of Turkish forces, the 5th and 7th Divisions of the Turkish Army.

The Anzac contingent was commanded by General William Birdwood and consisted of two infantry divisions: The First Australian Division commanded by Major General Bridges (three Brigades – 1st, 2nd and 3rd AIF) and the combined New Zealand and Australian Division commanded by Major

General Godley (two Brigades – 4th AIF and the NZ Brigade of Auckland, Canterbury, Otago and Wellington Battalions). These Divisions would make a secondary landing on the west coast of the Gallipoli Peninsula about 25 kilometres north of the British at Z beach and advance across the peninsula to Maidos (present-day Eceabat) to prevent Turkish reinforcements being sent to the Cape Helles front and cut–off Turkish troops being driven back by the British. This would be a classic pincer movement from the north to assist the British attack on the Narrows coming up from the south.

On the 20th February, 1915, Kitchener had warned Lieutenant–General Maxwell (Commander in Chief, Egypt) that the main body of the ANZAC forces should be ready to depart Egypt from the 9th March, however, a Brigade was to go to the island of Lemnos immediately in case the Allied fleet did break through. As General Bridges had already chosen the 3rd Brigade to be the first to go into action, it was accordingly decided to send this Brigade immediately to Lemnos. From Alexandria, the 9th and 10th Battalions embarked on the *Ionian* and the remainder of the Brigade on the *Suffolk*.

General Birdwood directed that the 3rd Brigade be specifically trained in landing and re–assembling, adding a hint that landing places should resemble those on the toe of the peninsula. There was much speculation among the men and officers of the Brigade as nothing had been revealed until the captains of the transports opened their sealed orders after departure, which revealed they were bound for Lemnos, although this was the generally expected destination.

The 9th Battalion arrived at the island of Lemnos on 4th March, 1915, however, due to the limited water supply on the island, which could only cater for a few thousand men, it was considered necessary to keep nearly the whole force in the transports. To decide which Battalion should go ashore (it should be noted that the men were in very cramped conditions on the boat and all were eager to get on to land again) it was agreed to toss for it. Lieutenant Colonel Lee of the 9th Battalion was successful and it was the 9th Battalion that won the right to leave the ship and go ashore. During their first evening ashore there was a severe thunderstorm and the camp was flooded. Lieutenant Ross writes that they were all very damp the next morning, however, on taking a short march into the township, the population was very happy to see the men for two main reasons; first to make money out of them, and second that they were going to kill Turks.[69]

Of interest, prior to the Australians landing on Lemnos, the British had to effectively occupy the island. Although the island was in the possession of Greece (a country allied to the British), the island was actually claimed by the Turkish Government, and therefore when the 9th Battalion set up camp, they could be considered at that time to be occupying enemy territory.[70]

Before the 9th Battalion had been long at Lemnos, it became known that the Battalion was to make a landing at the Dardanelles, and on 19th March the news passed around of the unsuccessful attack by the navy on the Straits the day before. On the 18th March, just before dark, some of the men had seen a four-funnelled cruiser come into the harbour with one mast shot away and three-fourths of a funnel missing, but no particulars of the engagement were heard until the following day.

The men during their time on Lemnos endured many more storms and had a bird's eye view of the very crowded Mudros Harbour, bristling with ships of all different types and sizes. Most days for the Battalion were spent building a road and a pier for disembarkation on to the island for troops and horses from the moored ships. During a stormy night on the 21st March, a French torpedo boat ran aground and Lieutenant Colonel Lee sent off a party of 150 men to aid the surviving crew after a call for help was received. One Frenchman had been killed in the accident and it was the band of the 9th Battalion that played the music during the funeral service. As a side note, a handwritten letter of appreciation was sent by General d'Amade (Commander of the French Eastern Expeditionary Force) to the Battalion commander for assisting his men and for the band's attendance at the funeral service. This letter is on display at the Brisbane Enoggera barracks in the 9th Battalion Museum.

Lance Corporal Neal was one of the men selected to help the French sailors, and as Australian soldiers were known to do, he states that he was able to obtain from the wreck a blue and white flag along with a cartridge and other articles for mementoes. On the way back, he stopped in the village and had a glass of cognac, and further on towards home, had breakfast at a Greek's home on the hills. It was a fine "junket" as he describes it. He goes on to state that a machine-gun from the wreck was presented to C Company of the 9th Battalion.[71]

One of the main training exercises undertaken by the Battalion was disembarking from the ship into smaller boats by the men and then practising rowing and controlling the smaller boats. Most exercises were carried out in daylight hours, although there were a number carried out at night. On the 23rd March, Sir Ian Hamilton, the commander in chief of the Mediterranean Expeditionary Force, came ashore and inspected the 9th Battalion. The Battalion made a sham attack, including a bayonet charge, and Hamilton's comment on this was that it was very fine, but every man taking part would have been killed on account of not taking cover while advancing. This is an amazing comment in the light of what was to happen many times throughout the impending Gallipoli campaign. It was a shame that he was not around when many men lost their lives due to orders for them to charge over ground that had no cover at all!

Of interest was the fact that the troops also spent a lot of time landing on beaches and then charging up a number of hills around the island until they were exhausted. While the hills were unlikely to be as challenging as those they were about to scale rising up from Anzac Cove, it did provide them with some useful training that would have no doubt assisted them in the preparation for the landings on the 25th April. Most importantly, it provided them with the fitness they would need to move inland so quickly over steep terrain. These exercises were usually carried out at Talikna Point, a rugged part of the harbourside a couple of miles from the Mudros camp.

The Battalion War Diary entry by the Commanding Officer, Lieutenant Colonel Lee, indicates that at the end of March 1915, the 9th Battalion strength was 34 officers, 1023 other ranks and 61 horses. This would have been the approximate strength at the time of the landing a few weeks later.

On the 4th of April, the 9th Battalion started embarkation on to the SS *Malda* and by the 8th April all troops from the Battalion had left the island. The longer stay of the 3rd Brigade at Lemnos was due to it having to wait for the arrival of the 29th British Division and the French troops, who would also play a critical part in the opening days of the Gallipoli campaign.

The troops then spent time on board the SS *Malda* right through until the 24th April, the day before landing. Lieutenant Ross indicated in his diary that conditions on board were very stale and the men wanted to get off the ship and stretch their legs.[72]

Troops practise landing from boats in Mudros Harbour on Lemnos Island. (AWM P00821.005)

The 2nd reinforcement for the 9th Battalion arrived on 9th April, 1915 and its arrival just prior to the men moving up to the front fulfilled the requirement that the Battalion had its first two reinforcements go with it to the front.

On the 15th April, a letter was read out to the men from General Birdwood, which exhorted the troops to do their best in carrying out a most difficult operation, landing on an enemy's coast in the face of opposition. It ended with the words, "You now have a chance of making history for Australia". Hence from that point onwards, a spotlight and the hopes of a nation had been put squarely on the shoulders of these men from the 3rd Brigade, who would lead the attack as the covering force for the landing of the two Anzac Divisions.

On the 19th April, the practising ceased in most Battalions. The slouch hats were withdrawn and a flat-topped, peaked British field service cap was issued in an attempt to confuse the Turks over whether the soldiers of Australian and New Zealand were part of Hamilton's order of battle. Also around this time, small, rectangular colour patches were issued. They were worn on the sleeve, just below the shoulder of each Australian soldier, and their objective was to distinguish the different units. In the AIF infantry units, the Brigade was denoted by the lower colour and the Battalion by the upper colour; for example, the light blue was the basic colour for the 3rd Brigade, and the black was used to distinguish the first Battalion in each Brigade. Hence the black over light blue became the colour patch of the 9th Battalion.

It was not until the 19th April that 3rd Brigade headquarters received some preliminary operational orders, and the Battalion's Commanding Officers in turn were then provided with verbal instructions about the operation, which was then slowly filtered down to the troops. On the 20th April, however, much more detailed operational orders were provided setting out each Battalion's objectives.

The actual time for the landing had been fixed for 23rd April and the first departures from Mudros were to have taken place two days earlier, however, the weather turned and a gale blew, which forced the postponement of the scheduled landing time. Therefore the preliminary movement of troops between various transports in the harbour did not start until the 23rd April and the landings were pushed back to the 25th April.

Had the landings occurred soon after the failed attempt of the naval bombardment and attack on the Narrows by the British and French Navies, they may have caught the Turks far less prepared. The Turks themselves had expected the Allies to invade following the failure of the naval attack on the Narrows on the 18th March, however, more than five weeks were effectively lost in further administration decision-making about the landings, the need to complete unloading and repacking of transports ships arriving from Alexandria that had been loaded incorrectly, and other administrative duties. During this time the Turks took the opportunity to vigorously strengthen defences on the peninsula, and within a week the Turks had reinforced the two Divisions of troops already on the peninsula with two more and a third was brought up soon after. By the Turks' own admission following the war, if the Allies had attacked after the first naval attack on the straits on the 19th February, the landings would have been successful and the Straits would have fallen.[73] But true to its very nature, events take place during war that create both opportunities that are taken for advantage, and as in this case, opportunities that are lost.

The other interesting fact to note about the change in dates was that it had the effect of reducing the time from moonset (darkest part of the night) to dawn by almost two hours. This was important in that it was considered crucial for the men in the initial wave of the landings to make the most out of the darkest part of the morning and gain a surprise advantage. The change to the 25th April gave the men just one hour of complete darkness from 3am. This meant that the battleships would be visible to the Turkish defenders sometime prior to landing, and as noted below, the first tows were planned to hit the beach at 4.30am, which would be half an hour after the first light of dawn.[74] Thus, even before a man was landed on the beaches the crucial element of surprise had been lost and the mission started to be compromised.

Following the 18th March attack in the Dardanelle Straits by the navy, another division of Turkish troops arrived and now there were 80,000 troops in place to defend the Dardanelles. Believing the naval strength of the British would make landings of troops difficult to stop, General Otto Von Sanders (Head of the German military mission in Turkey) and the commander of the Turkish 5th Army concentrated the Turks inland so that they could counterattack in strength once Hamilton had shown his hand on where the landings would take place. However, as discussed in the writings of Lieutenant Colonel Sefik Aker, Commander of the Turkish 27th Regiment after the war,[75] he indicates that before the 5th Army was formed the Turkish Commanders that had responsibility for the defence plan for the Straits had a very different view and were effectively overruled by General Von Sanders' strategy. It is interesting to note that the opposing strategy determined that due to the fact that the tactical ground that commanded the Maidos area was close to the beaches i.e. the high ground of Second Ridge, the defence around the points dominating Ari Burnu and similar landing zones should be made strong and it would be here that the enemy would be engaged on the beaches.

The Turkish 5th Army Group had 5 Divisions (5th, 7th, 9th, 11th and 19th) and added another Division (3rd) under the control of General Von Sanders just prior to the campaign starting. The Turkish infantry of the 7th and 9th Divisions making up III Corps, in particular, were considered among the best available at that time in the Turkish Army given their battle experience during the Balkan Wars of 1912–13. In fact, they had more experience than most of the Allied troops involved in the campaign.

Von Sanders, with some 150 miles of coastline to defend, decided to split his six Divisions into three groups:

- 5th and 7th Divisions were sent to Bulair – Bulair is situated in the north at the neck of the Gallipoli Peninsula, at the narrowest part, which is only a few miles wide. Von Sanders was concerned that if this area was taken by the Allies in conjunction with occupying the Sea of Marmara the 5th Army could be cut off.

- 11th and 3rd Divisions were sent to the Asian side of the Dardanelles to protect Besika Bay and Kum Kale. There were a number of critical artillery batteries on this side of the Dardanelles that he believed would be attacked by the Allies.
- 9th Division, under Colonel Sami Bey, had its headquarters located on the Kilitbahir plateau, and the 19th Division under Mustafa Kemal was headquartered at Bigali, inland from Anzac Cove. Essad Pasha, Turkish Corps Commander, was in charge of both these Divisions. These Divisions were charged with guarding against landings at Cape Helles and Gaba Tepe. The 9th Division was spread over both areas, but the 19th Division was essentially held in reserve at Bigali, within sound of the gunfire at Anzac Cove.

It is interesting to note that while the Germans sent considerable goods, ammunitions and money to Turkey in recognition of the country's support, their commitment to providing German soldiers to the Turkish fronts was minimal. This was especially the case during the Dardanelles campaign, in which there were only a few hundred Germans involved, and most of these men were in leadership positions. While only making up a very small proportion of the men facing the Allies, there were many from this German contingent that lost their lives during the ensuing campaign.

Von Sanders told his Divisional commanders to hold their troops together and to send only security detachments to the coast. Therefore, wherever the British landed, the Turkish defences would be light, however, close to each landing spot, the main bodies of each Division would be camped ready to move when required. Von Sanders was effectively working on the principle that says he who tries to defend all, defends nothing.[76]

The key Turkish Division in the context of the initial Anzac landings on the morning of the 25th April was the 9th Division. Of the three regiments of the 9th Division, the 25th Regiment was in reserve at Serafim Farm on Kilitbahir Plateau and could be diverted north to Gaba Tepe or south to Cape Helles. The 26th Regiment was located in the Helles area and the 27th Regiment was based at the Anzac area. The 27th Regiment was mostly focused on opposing a landing at Gaba Tepe, rather than Ari Burnu, but had spread Battalions thinly along the coastline and had two Battalions in reserve near present-day Eceabat. Specifically, the 2nd Battalion of the 27th Regiment had its four companies located around the Anzac landing area as follows:

- 6th Company holding the southern area at Gaba Tepe;
- 7th Company holding Brighton Beach;
- 8th Company were north of Ari Burnu; and
- 5th Company was held in reserve behind Gaba Tepe.

From Hamilton's perspective, his forces had clearly lost the element of surprise and thus he sought to fool Von Sanders as to where the main landings would take place by having as many men going ashore in multiple places before the Turks could work out where the main landings were taking place and counterattack. The plan was for the 29th Division (British) to land on five small beaches at Cape Helles, the ANZACs would land near Gaba Tepe and the French would land at other locations, mainly the other side of the Dardanelle Straits at a place called Kum Kale. The intention was that at all locations, a covering force would go in ahead of the main body. The covering forces would be landed from warships and the main body of troops would then be landed from transport ships. The troops would actually be taken to shore on each of the ships cutters, which were in turn towed by steam pinnaces. The cutters would be cast off near the shore and rowed to the beaches.

Hamilton and his staff planned their attack on the basis that the Turks would contest the beaches, then shrink away at the sight of the Union Jack flags waving in the breeze and the large numbers of British and Allied soldiers landing in waves on the beaches. In fact, they had tended to underrate the Turks throughout most of the planning, assessing them as a second-rate opponent. One of Birdwood's staff officers commented,

> *It will be grim work to begin with, but we have good fighters ready to tackle it, and an enemy who has never shown himself as good a fighter as the white man.'*[77]

Carlyon[78] indicates that the British forgot two important things. First, the Turks had a long brutal military history, and second, while they had little of the ingenuity of their forebears in attack, what they were good at was defence. The Turkish soldiers from the local Anatolian villages were fatalists raised on hardship. Most were illiterate. They did not expect much from life and were used to being misused by corrupt leaders. They knew how to hang on and to endure in the face of pain and death. Most importantly, they were not trying to hold on to an old conquest. They were fighting for their heartland, homes, families (which in some cases were not far from the battlefields), the capital and their identity. Failing to take these people seriously was a tremendous error of judgement made by the Allied strategists that would play out over the next eight months.

Von Sanders wrote in 1928 that,

The preparations of the enemy were excellent. Their only defect being that they were based on reconnaissances that were too old and that they underestimated the powers of resistance of the Turkish soldier.

For the most part, the German officers had great respect for the Turkish soldier. While most were poorly educated, not well trained and often poorly clothed and equipped, they lacked little when it came to courage and their ability to resist in defence and survive in the most difficult circumstances. They had no fear to die and the Germans, in fact, often referred to the "oriental fatalism" of the Turkish soldiers.[79]

Fortunately, even the British conceded that it was clear that there would be stiff resistance from the beach positions in the beginning and that the soldiers who would be first to land would bear the brunt of the Turks. The 9th Battalion at the outset was going to be in for some trouble.

Bridges had already decided that the 3rd Brigade would be the covering force and therefore first ashore, largely because of his faith in Sinclair-MacLagan, who was a trusted friend as well as the most experienced of the senior officers. Another factor was the toughness of the troops making up the 3rd Brigade, many of them were outback men and miners, although in the case of the 9th Battalion, only a reasonably small number of the men within the Battalion had this background.

Colonel Sinclair-MacLagan, along with General Bridges and the Battalion commanders, had seen the Gallipoli Peninsula's coastline from the *Queen Elizabeth* on the 14th April, all having been dressed in naval attire to avoid being recognised as soldiers. During this assessment of the landing area moving north to south down the coast, the officers were mainly interested in the topography of the coastline from Fisherman's Hut in the north through to Gaba Tepe in the south. Looking at maps of this coastline it seems clear now, and would have be clear during the assessment, which areas were most suitable to land and then to enable troops to move quickly inland. The most rugged and formidable part of this stretch is clearly Anzac Cove below Ari Burnu, as Carlyon indicates no army would land here on purpose. The officers, knowing this, concluded that they would land somewhere in a two kilometre frontage between Hell Spit (just south of Anzac Cove) and a point one mile north of Gaba Tepe. The sandy beach to the north of Gaba Tepe, which was in this landing zone, looked so pleasant that the English named it Brighton Beach. The banks on this beach are a mere five feet or so and the coastal plain behind ran for 50 to 200 metres before the ground rose. The centre of the landings should be roughly opposite a hill that became known as Bolton's Ridge. The country here was noted to be hilly and rougher than around Gaba Tepe without being steep, with a few kind valleys. The headland at Gaba Tepe had also been fortified with wire and earthworks, therefore better to take it from the flank rather than the front.

The key to securing this area of the peninsula was to take the heights of Chunuk Bair and Hill 971 and a landing at Bolton's Ridge would link the troops up to the Legge Valley, which leads to these heights at the northern end of the Third Ridge. In contrast, at Anzac Cove, the troops would have to go cross-grain against the ridges. Many writers speak of three key ridges that run out of the Sari Bair range and down to the sea between Ari Burna and Gaba Tepe that define the area where the Anzacs fought. Particularly during the first few weeks of the campaign these ridges were the focus for the initial landing forces. The first was Bolton's Ridge, the second Pine Ridge and the third was Gun Ridge. Over the months that followed, as the stalemate became more evident, the front extended well to the north of Bolton's ridge, past Ari Burnu right up to inland from Fisherman's Hut where there is one very steep ridge that dominates the landscape leading straight up to the heights of Chunuk Bair.

It is, as Carlyon states,[80] true that the Third Ridge from Chunuk Bair through Scrubby Knoll and on to Anderson Knoll was everything in this battle. To command the Maidos Plain, which lies way to the south on the peninsula leading towards the Dardanelles, you need to have guns on the Third Ridge. Mustafa Kemal, the Turkish Divisional Commander, knew this and the first thing he did when he reached the Anzac landing area was to head for Chunuk Bair. The importance of the Maidos Plain was that this stretch of land runs across the peninsula from behind Gaba Tepe from the base of the Sari Bair range, across to Maidos just above the Narrows of the Dardanelles. The British had planned to storm north up the peninsula towards the Maidos

Plain, link up with the Anzacs and head for the key Turkish gun installations and forts along the Dardanelles, in particular those at Kilitbahir at the Narrows (the narrowest point of the Dardanelles). The navy would want these guns silenced to help ensure their success in future attacks.

As mentioned, the Third Ridge meant everything and was the central piece of the objectives for the 3rd Brigade during the first few days in which speed, surprise, striking deep inland and securing ground well away from the coastline was paramount. Therefore, it was planned that the 9th Battalion would land on the right side of the initial landings, two of its companies would clear Gaba Tepe of guns and the other two would head for Anderson Knoll at the seaward end of the Third Ridge, the far right flank a mile from the beach. The 10th Battalion would land in the centre, capture the Turkish guns on 400 Plateau (part of the Second Ridge) then cross Legge Valley and occupy Scrubby Knoll on the Third Ridge. The 11th Battalion would land on the left and seize Chunuk Bair at the top end of the Third Ridge. The 12th Battalion would be held in reserve.

After the covering party of the 3rd Brigade had occupied a line stretching from Gaba Tepe to Chunuk Bair, the left flank of the men from the covering force would be secured by the landing of the 2nd Australian Brigade, which were to arrive very soon after the second wave of the covering force had landed. Their objective was to extend the line northwards to the summit of Hill 971, about two kilometres distant, and out along North Beach to Fisherman's Hut.

Next to land would be the 1st Australian Brigade, which was to be held in reserve near the beach. If the landing was successful, this reserve brigade and the 4th Australian Brigade and the New Zealand Brigade would leapfrog through the newly captured positions and from the south capture Mal Tepe, which lay about 10 kilometres inland from the landing. From this position at the northern flank of the Kilid Bahr Plateau, the Turkish communications with Helles could be threatened and perhaps cut off altogether. It might also prevent the Turks from sending reinforcements to assist in repelling the attack by the British at Cape Helles.

Following his viewing of the coastline and after assessing information provided by aerial reconnaissance, Sinclair-MacLagan stated that if Gaba Tepe is strongly held, it will be almost impregnable for his men. Several gun emplacements were noted on the promontory and a further four behind it.

On the basis of the limited intelligence received about enemy positions and strength, it was clear that the landing boats would be shelled on the way in and then taken in enfilade on the beach. Therefore, to counter this threat and obtain maximum benefit of surprise, Birdwood decided that the covering force would land silently before daybreak to conceal their approach without naval barrage. As mentioned earlier, he was now limited by the lunar settings and had only an hour of darkness. The moon would set at 2.57am and the first streaks of dawn would appear about 4.05 am and the sun would be up at 5.15am. The ships needed to limit their time in approach towards the coastline while the moon was still up, lest the Turks see their silhouettes.

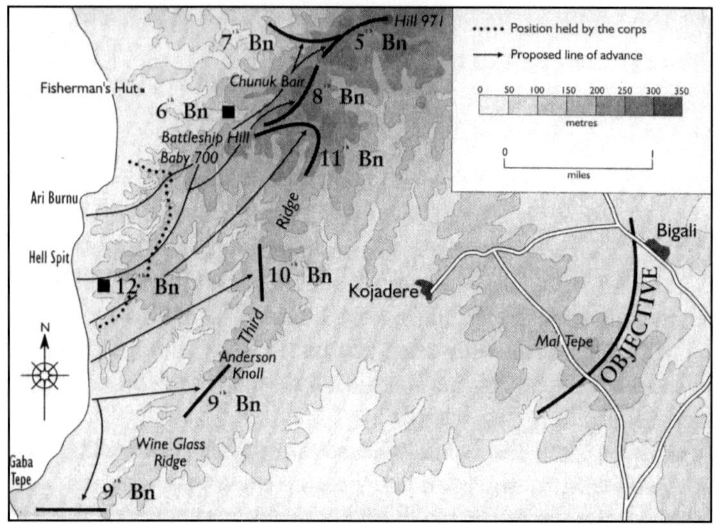

The Anzacs' objectives during the first few days. (Carlyon)

All this meant the best he could achieve would be for the first wave of soldiers to hit the beach at about 4.30am. With luck the troops might be on the guns before the Turks had time to act. From the scattered trenches, Birdwood knew that there were only isolated posts on the shore north of Gaba Tepe. Landing as much of the 3rd Brigade as possible simultaneously on a wide front and quickly reinforcing it would allow the attack to penetrate inland, even if one or more of these isolated posts managed to pin down parts of the line. It would also reduce the effects of shelling on the men landing from the Turkish guns at Gaba Tepe.

The order of landing for the covering force would be as follows; the first wave of 1500 men would be made up of 500 men from the 9th Battalion (A and B Companies), and 500 each from the 10th and 11th Battalions of the 3rd Brigade. They would disembark five miles off the coast from the battleships *Queen* (which held men of the 9th Battalion), *London* and *Prince of Wales*, into 12 "tows" each consisting of three lifeboats towed by a small steamboat and carrying about 120 to 130 men. The battleships would proceed with the tows beside them as far as they could go without being seen by the enemy, and then stop, while the tows made a dash for the beach. Off the island of Imbros, 15 miles from Gaba Tepe, the second wave consisting of another 2500 men, being the balance of the 3rd Brigade (including the remaining 500 men from the 9th Battalion i.e. C and D companies) and the whole of the 12th Battalion, would transfer from their transports into seven destroyers towing more lifeboats, this time trying to get them as far into the shallow water as possible and then cast the lifeboats off. Then the occupants of each boat would row independently to the shore where they were to land straight after the first wave.

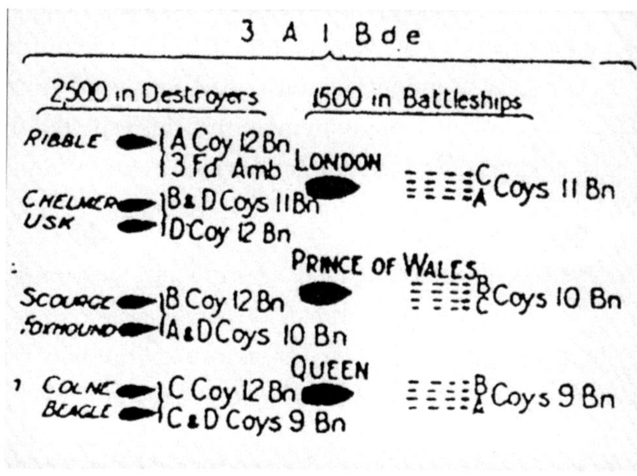

The warships involved with landing the men from 3rd Brigade AIF. (Wrench)

The 1st and 2nd Brigades AIF, some 8000 men, would then approach the shore to land at around 5am on the 25th April.

As Pedersen outlines,[81] the plan itself was nothing if not bold, with surprise, speed and the expectation of weak Turkish resistance its outstanding features.

However, given the terrain and the distances from the beach, the objectives set were very ambitious. The battle plans were nonetheless reasonably well thought through given that the senior officers had such little time to prepare and such limited knowledge of the landscape and effectiveness of their enemy. The key weaknesses in the plans were associated with not understanding the terrain, inadequate preparations for casualties and the limited consideration of the difficulty the tows would have in getting men ashore during the darkest part of the night with the effects of current, and for the most part under fire. It is interesting to note that even 30 years later with better landing craft and more sophisticated navigation equipment, the American troops landing at Omaha beach during the D-Day landings of World War II missed their landing objective by some two miles.[82]

The men were not briefed until 10 am on the morning of 24th April after a church parade. The 3rd Brigade commanders on each of the troopships called their men to parade and read a special order from their Colonel, Sinclair-MacLagan. Sinclair-MacLagan, a natural pessimist, thought that while it was an honour to have his 3rd Brigade spearhead the landing, he knew full well that it might well lead also to its destruction. He reiterated to the men that they needed to conserve ammunition and warned against Turkish artillery. "We must expect to get shelled, but remember that this is part of this game of war and we must stick to it no matter what the fire". He went on to state in a rather chilling matter-of-fact way via his written address:

> *It is necessary you should understand that we are to carry out a most difficult operation. There is no going back. Whatever footing we get on land must be held on to at all costs, even to the last man… … You may get orders to do something, which in your position seems wrong and perhaps a mad enterprise. Do not cavil at it but carry it out with absolute faith in your leaders…. Some pieces have to be sacrificed to win the game and it is to win the game that we are here.*[83]

The 9th Battalion was under no illusions. The Colonel was preparing them for the worst and they knew they were in for a fight that many would not return from; moreover, they were to follow orders no matter what the cost.

Within the Colonel's address there were a number of clear directives for the men and some practical advice, among other details:

- Forward is the word, until on our position, when Hang On is what we have to do, until sufficient troops and guns are landed to enable us to push on;
- You will need to drop your packs; but carry tools (entrenching tools) forward as far as you can, it may mean saving lives later in the day;
- Keep your food and water very carefully; we don't know when we shall get any more;
- After taking out a charger, shut the cartridge pocket. Once ashore don't be caught without a charger in the magazine; and
- Don't show yourselves over the skyline and give your positions away, if you can avoid it.

The requirement to move quickly inland was drummed into the men, especially those in the initial wave of the landing. It seems that the officers were well informed of their objectives and provided with some idea of the terrain anticipated on landing, namely Brighton Beach. This, in particular, must have created much uncertainty and confusion for these same officers when confronted with a totally different terrain when they eventually landed.

The dangers ahead were bluntly acknowledged by other commanders such as Lieutenant–Colonel Johnston (11th Battalion), who indicated to his men that the General had informed him that it will take several battleships and destroyers to carry our Brigade into Gallipoli; a barge will be sufficient to take us home again! However, the relief for the men now that the incessant waiting was over, combined with a keenly felt sense of anticipation, kept morale very high. The 11th Battalion greeted Johnston's grim news with cheers. Lance Corporal Mitchell wrote "We are delighted beyond words at the prospect of such a chance at proving our mettle". "Every man was bursting to get a go at the Turks", wrote Private Arthur McGuirk of the 3rd Battalion. [84]

As the troops from the 3rd Brigade boarded, Colonel Sinclair-MacLagan continuing in his pessimistic outlook, said good bye to General Bridges in the *Prince of Wales* and boarded one of the destroyers.

"Well, MacLagan," said Bridges as they parted, "you haven't thanked me yet."

"Yes, sir, I do thank you for the great honour of having this job to do with my Brigade," was the reply. "But if we find the Turks holding these ridges in any strength, I honestly don't think you'll ever see the 3rd Brigade again."

"Oh, go along with you!" said Bridges, laughing. [85]

Those 9th Battalion troops from A and B companies, which included Private Nelson Scrivener, involved in the first wave of the attack boarded the *Queen* at 2pm on Saturday, 24th April and headed for Imbros where they would drop anchor and wait for the moon to sink. By 8pm the second wave (balance of the 3rd Brigade) in four transport ships arrived at Imbros also. They had already started on their first preparations for the landing the next day and the platoon commanders were inspecting each man's pack.

As well as his rifle, which had to have empty chambers as no shots were allowed to be fired before daybreak, and 200 rounds of ammunition, each man's pack contained:

- Two empty sandbags rolled around his entrenching tool handle. The sandbags would also be used to throw over any barbed-wire barriers that may be encountered and then later be filled with dirt to help build parapets wherever the troops were entrenching;
- Two or three waterbottles, whose contents had to last for three days;
- Tin of bully beef, small tin of tea and sugar and a number of very hard, coarse biscuits for the same period;
- Greatcoat and towel; and
- Change of underclothing, socks and other personal gear.

All these items were stuffed into packs looped for quick release if a boat were sunk.

The men of the second wave dozed on the decks of their transports huddling together for warmth against the cold. Endless cleaning of rifles and checking of gear betrayed the nervous excitement that made sleep impossible. One officer doing his rounds indicated that moving among them one could see a look of determination in every man's face. They were silent. Many were the prayers offered that night by the men awaiting battle and most would have thought of loved ones and friends at home. All were anxious about how they would behave during the onset of action as they knew the reputation of Australia was in their hands. It was a solemn voyage.

The C and D companies of the 9th Battalion, which included stretcher bearer Corporal Frederic Scrivener, were transferred from their transport ships into the destroyer *Beagle* at 11pm. Each of the companies involved in both the first and second waves were asked to assemble for inspection at their allocated numbers painted on the ship's decks, from which they would disembark into the tows the next morning, and ordered to put their packs down on the deck where they could find them again in the dark. Night had fallen by 7pm.

The men of the first wave were by this time sleeping on the mess deck and the crew had given them their sleeping quarters in order to give them the chance to rest. However, at midnight they were woken and provided with a hot cup of cocoa and tots of rum as well as cigarettes and tobacco from the ship's canteen. Lieutenant Ross, with the A and B companies of the 9th Battalion, writes that "There was little conversation, each breast beat high and talk seemed of little importance. At last we are moving towards the real thing. While the men had their cocoa or rum, the boats for the landing were being lowered".[86]

Major Miles Beevor of the 10th Battalion, who was escorted to the wardroom of the destroyer *Foxhound* noted later:

> *From sundry aspersions dropped by several of the naval officers, I gathered that they did not expect any of us to survive the morrow. This may have been the reason for the bright hospitality, which handed over the key of the refreshment locker.*[87]

Conflicting thoughts gripped each man. On one hand, Staff Sergeant Laseron, 13th Battalion, observed that it is always the other fellow that is going to get shot. The fact that a bullet might get oneself is somehow inconceivable. On the other, the possibility had to be accepted and many men wrote off short letters to their loved ones just in case.

Major Hamilton of the 6th Battalion was thinking of his wife and little daughter and apologised to his wife for being a brute and leaving them both for this life of danger. (Hamilton was among those that died the next day).

Private David Mills 8th Battalion wrote:

I have kissed dear little Nan's photo goodbye. May God have mercy on my soul and care for them I have left behind.[88]

He would die in three days on the Gallipoli Peninsula.

At 1am the ships were stopped on the sea between Imbros and the peninsula, five miles off Gaba Tepe. Bean writes in his diary that the moon was still high and the shape of land was at times visible to the east. The hulls of the battleships lying near one another on the water motionless were difficult to pick out except through glasses.[89]

At 1.30am on Sunday, April 25th, the tows were all formed up alongside the battleships. Two tows each of three rowing boats had been placed on either side of the troop-carrying battleships. The men started scrambling down the rope ladders, sleeves rolled up to distinguish them from the Turks. Figures silhouetted in the moonlight one minute and lost against the water the next, the menacing outline of shore, whispered orders, the occasional clang of a rifle butt, shuffling boots and muffled curses as footing was lost all coalesced into a tremendously eerie scene.[90] The boats were loaded all within about 40 minutes.

So quiet was the embarkation that Admiral Thursby was surprised when told at 2.35am that it had been completed. "Cast off and drift astern" came the command and the two tows on either side of the battleship dropped back behind it to join the steam tow–boats also awaiting their role.

While the Anzac ships were assembling, Turkish troops under Captain Faik (2nd Battalion – 8th Company Commander), who were responsible for defending the area around Ari Burnu, had spotted the massed convoy of ships out to sea. The 250 men of Captain Faik's Company (2nd Battalion 27th Regiment) who were positioned around Ari Burnu that morning and dispersed over a large area were specifically within either of three platoons:

- Platoon No. 1 – Landing area around North Beach (entrenched at Fisherman's Hut) – Commanded by Second Lieutenant Ibrahim-Hayredin;
- Platoon No. 2 – Main body entrenched at Plugge's Plateau covering the landing area of Ari Burnu (Anzac Cove), smaller sections of men were

at Hell Spit and lower down on Ari Burnu headland – Commanded by Second Lieutenant Muharrem; and

- Platoon No. 3 – Main body in reserve on Second Ridge with a section of men south at Clarke Valley – Commanded by Sergeant Suleyman.

Captain Faik at about 2am contacted his Battalion Commander, Major Ismet, by telephone and then by written report, indicating that he and some of his men from the reserve platoon had spotted many enemy ships through his binoculars straight in front of his position but a long way out to sea. He could not tell whether they were moving or not. Major Ismet told him that there was no cause for alarm. At most the landing will be at Kaba Tepe (Gaba Tepe) and to continue to watch the ships.

At 2.30am at another location Captain Faik, by this time quite anxious by the number of ships he can see, then contacted Divisional Head Quarters. He was asked how many were transports and how many were warships and replied that it was impossible to tell in the dark, but there was a large quantity of them. With that the conversation ended. The Turkish Command was not stirred into action and they waited for news of a landing at one of the more expected of locations. Soon after, the moon sank below the horizon and the ships became shrouded in darkness. It was 3am on the beaches and the battleships/destroyers were now creeping towards the shore. For the Turks, fortune favoured the Allied Command. Had it not been for the setting of the moon at that time, Captain Faik may have been able to identify the types of ships and confirm that they were moving towards the shore line, possibly with tows extended behind. He would then have had a stronger argument for sending reinforcements forward immediately to his position and potentially changing the dynamic of the first day's landing. Some degree of both fate and planning had worked in the favour of the Australians, especially the 3rd Brigade, and some preservation of the element of the surprise landing had been kept intact.

At 2.53am, the battleships *Queen, Prince of Wales* and *London* started pulling the tows containing the troops strung out behind them on either side slowly towards the shore at about five knots. By this time the destroyers with the men of the 3rd Brigade, second wave, were at the same location and had arranged their tows likewise. The destroyers also moved along behind them.

At 3.30am in complete darkness, when the battleships were supposed to be two miles offshore they stopped and Thursby ordered "Land armed parties" and the steamboats cast off and the twelve tows of the first wave leapt forward. The sailors on the decks waved their caps in the Navy's silent cheer. They would have been well aware that many of these men would not see the day out.

The four steam tow boats that pulled the rowing boats carried no troops, but a naval officer and a senior officer in each. Each troop-carrying row boat carried 30–40 troops, a coxswain and four seamen whose duty was to cast loose the line and get out the oars. There was a midshipman in the last boat of the tow. The senior company officer often sat with the midshipman at the tiller. The direction of the tows was the responsibility of the naval officer.

The 9th Battalion's moment of glory was fast approaching!

Troops from the 10th Battalion line the deck of the battleship *Prince of Wales* as it leaves Mudros Harbour, 24th April, 1915. (AWM A01829)

Chapter 5

The Landing at Anzac Cove

At Gallipoli on April 25th, 1915, romance and realism met on the battlefield. As it always does, romance lost, states Carlyon in his Gallipoli epic.[91]

With the time for action now upon them and the infernal waiting over, the men of the 3rd Brigade being in the first wave of the landings, now in the boats that would take them into battle, take them into Anzac Cove, started to move off for the beach. You can almost imagine the tension in the air, the anxious anticipation of action and the strong bonds with the men around them that had formed over the past few months. They were now personally dealing with their inner thoughts and emotions, hoping that they would not let their mates down and that they would prove brave enough when the time came to go into action. Would they live to see another morning?

Private Percival Young, A company, 9th Battalion (killed in action 7th August, 1915 with 8th Battalion), a lawyer who lived in Albion, Brisbane, writes:

> *At midnight we were assembled on deck (HMS Queen), and we clambered down the ship's side to the boats below. With as little noise as possible, the boats left the side of the warship and no-one who was in those boats will ever forget the silent cheer that the men of the British Navy gave to the Australians as the boats drew away. A frantic wave of their arms, nothing more, but enough to assure us that they were proud of their Australian brothers in arms, the 9th Battalion of Queenslanders.*
>
> *With scarce a ripple, our boats drew towards the shore, 200 yards, 100 yards, and then there was the tightening of belts and fixing of equipment. Nearer and nearer we drew.*[92]

The boats themselves were not much bigger than a surf boat and many were commanded by teenage midshipmen. One of the original landing craft is on display in the Australian War Memorial (see appendix 2).

It was very quiet out on the water, just the slap of the waves on the sides of the boat could be heard by the men. The wind had died down by this stage, although a cold chill sent tingles down the men's arms. The time was 4.30am. The sea was described as a pane of glass and a thousand stars winked above Plugge's Plateau. It is, as Aspinall wrote of the 25th April, 1915, as if the elements are holding their breath. It was also very dark, on account of a thick mist, and the men in the boats could hardly distinguish the tows on either side of them. No-one spoke a word above a whisper, and barely heard was the splash of the boats as the little waves lapped at their sides. The suspense in the crowded boats was very trying; "I was shaking all over with nervousness and excitement", wrote one man.[93]

The total journey to the beach would take about 50 minutes. The destroyers carrying the second wave of men from the 3rd Brigade were waiting behind the battleships and were not expected to move forwards until 4.15a.m.

George Combs (11th Battalion) later stated that:

> *All the time we were moving in the boats not a man whispered or coughed or stirred, all that could be heard by those close to the pinnace was the very gentle tick–tick of the engine, no louder than that of a watch.*[94]

Hearts leapt into mouths when a pencil of light from a Turkish searchlight in the Narrows arched upwards, a second beam joined in and then both abruptly vanished. Many men were wondering as they went closer to the shore whether the Turks would be surprised or would they be alert and waiting.

The Turks, however, had known what was planned in some form and at 2am the Turkish coastal patrols had reported to Captain Faik atop Ari Burnu (Anzac Cove), that they had sighted many ships.

The time is 6am and Australian soldiers leave the transport ship by means of rope ladders for the landing at Anzac Cove. (AWM J05589)

Four boatloads of Australian soldiers are towed by steamboat towards Anzac Cove on the morning of the 25th April, 1915. As it is full daylight and there is a transport to the right of the photo, they are most probably from the 2nd Brigade. The 3rd Brigade by this time was already pushing inland. (AWM P02194.003)

Lieutenant Waterlow (naval officer) riding in the southernmost tow and the flotilla leader, Commander Charles Dix, in the northernmost one, between the two of them they guided the tows into the beach. Keeping the tows together and in line for the targeted landing spot was difficult, in fact just prior to the lifeboats casting off they were not heading for the landing beach, but running diagonally across the face of it. At about 4am the silhouette of the shore could be made out, which faintly showed the Ari Burnu headland. At this moment Waterlow realised that the tows were being taken too far to the north, so he made several efforts to correct the course. The other naval officers, realising they too were off course tried to correct the mistake at the last moment before casting off the life boats, which led to some mixing of battalions and the bunching of the tows that occurred on landing rather than being spread out over a wide front as had been planned.

At 4.25am, muffled oars dug into the water as the 36 lifeboats cast off from the steam tows about 100 yards out and the boats from the first wave of the 3rd Brigade were now nosed towards the base of the Sphinx. This was not where they were supposed to be.

Breaking the silence, Commander Dix knew for sure that all had gone wrong when the boats were within 50 yards of the shore and shouted:

Tell the Colonel that the damn fools have taken us a mile too far north![95]

Indeed he was right and the boats made the shore at Ari Burnu about a mile to the north of the intended landing place.

Many explanations have been put forward as to why the landings occurred at Anzac Cove rather than on Brighton Beach. One explanation for the error was the effects of a strong northerly current, however, the currents inside the Dardanelles are fierce, but in the Aegean off Anzac Cove they were not significant and moreover there was no wind that morning.[96] Another offered was that the Turks had moved a marker buoy placed off–shore by the Royal Navy to provide direction for the landing fleet further north.

There is the argument that the battleships anchored too far north and so the tows heading east from them were bound to end up where they did, due to the limitations of navigation at that time and large margin for error. Not to mention that even if the battleships were on course, the steamboat compasses on which the tows were to rely were notoriously unreliable.[97]

One theory that is supported by a number of historians is that the intended landing site had always been Anzac Cove and therefore intentional rather than a mistake. This is hard to believe as there is no indication that either senior naval or infantry officers were aware of this plan. It is inconceivable that the Commander of the 3rd Brigade, which would lead the landings that morning, would not have been told. In fact, General Birdwood wrote prior to the landing, while contemplating the potential effect of the Turkish guns on his men following daybreak;

> *If I find that the firing is too heavy on the ships off the beach, I shall move the whole landing further north, up near the Fisherman's Hut; but the country there [around Anzac Cove] is so very difficult and broken that it is impossible to attempt a landing there while it is dark.*[98]

Clearly, General Birdwood, who was a critical part of the planning for the campaign, was not contemplating landing around Anzac Cove, especially the initial covering force landing in the dark.

In addition, it seems that Colonel Sinclair-MacLagan was confused by where the landings occurred and clearly expected to have landed to the north of Gaba Tepe, but south of 400 Plateau, and declared soon after coming ashore that they had landed at the wrong beach.[99] One of the main objectives for the covering force, in particular the 9th Battalion, was to capture the guns and defences of both Gaba Tepe and Anderson Knoll. It therefore does not make sense to land the men three kilometres away from these objectives and force the men to advance through unmapped and rugged terrain, which meant crossing a number of steep spurs in order for them to be in a position to attack. It is true that after the covering force had landed, the designated landing zone became Anzac Cove rather than Brighton Beach, however, it seems this may have been much more good fortune than foresight. After a beachhead had been obtained and secured, it was clear that Anzac Cove was a reasonably well sheltered enclave for landing troops. It was away from the direct line of site of the Turkish gun emplacements at Gaba Tepe and was far less hazardous than the original landing zone.

The most logical and well supported of the explanations is indeed a simple one. A naval midshipman by the name of J. Metcalf, who was in command of boat no. 2 (carrying 9th Battalion men) for the first wave of the covering force, had mistaken the Ari Burnu headland for Gaba Tepe headland. Although these landmarks by day are very dissimilar i.e. there was nothing like the Sphinx at Gaba Tepe, at night viewed by men who were in complete darkness and looking at landmarks as silhouettes on the skyline, there could certainly have been some confusion and anxiety. In fact, it is interesting to note, that almost 60 years after the landing took place, Metcalf indicated that he believed he was responsible for the change of course and the mistaken interpretation of the critical landmarks. As the lead boat no. 1, had fallen behind and Metcalf's boat was now leading the landing flotilla he had to take over responsibility;

> *A few minutes later I looked astern again, as it was very dark and I had no idea how far we were from rocks or sand. About a quarter of an hour later I realised that we were heading very close to the northern side of Gaba Tepe, which because of its height is very conspicuous. Knowing that there were many Turkish troops there and we would get enfilading fire along the starboard side as well as from ahead, I was confident that we must be heading for the wrong place. There was no–one to consult, I felt the lives of the men I was towing were my responsibility. Without any delay I altered course two points to port to get away from Gaba Tepe. After a quarter of an hour, finding that the other tows to port of me had conformed, I again altered course a point and a half to port.*[100]

Lieutenant Commander Waterlow of the Royal Navy later confirmed Metcalf's account. All of the other 11 steamboats were required to keep in line with his boat as they made their way into the beach. He too had seen the headland looming out of the darkness, but also they noted that there was another prominent headland just further to the north from their position (Ari Burnu) and there was some confusion. All the tows were now heading due north effectively along Anzac Cove. Waterlow indicated that he was then convinced that they were not heading for Gaba Tepe, but a position well north of it. He tried to alter the course southward by going down the line of boats astern to draw the boats with him, but it was too late, they were already too close to shore and had no other alternative but to dash straight for the cliffs that were in front of him. This is why they were all so bunched and mixed up on landing rather than spread out in some Battalion order that had been planned.

General Birdwood interestingly in a later interview noted a positive aspect to the landing in that had they landed anywhere else, they were likely to have needed to evacuate because the men would have been shelled heavily. The beach near Gaba Tepe, which had been originally selected for the landings, was noted later to have been strongly defended by barbed wire, some of which had been laid in the water. Certainly as Birdwood indicated, the strong Turkish post there and the exposure to artillery fire from the Turkish guns firing from batteries at Gaba Tepe would have made the landing very difficult, perhaps impossible, and would certainly have resulted in a very heavy roll of casualties far greater than that actually encountered.[101] Anzac Cove, due to the steepness of the cliffs, provided some level of immunity from shell fire and given the difficulties of the terrain, was probably the least guarded landing place by the Turks.

Now back to the landing. A dazzling yellow light glowed for half a minute from Hell Spit. "Seen" hissed a soldier in one of the 11th Battalion boats, but still the shore was silent. "Look at that" yelled Captain Ray Leane, 11th Battalion. A man was silhouetted against the skyline. A shout in Turkish, then a rifle cracking from the top of Ari Burnu.

Turkish Private Adil Shahin (16 year old shepherd boy from a local village of Buyuk Anafarta before the war) in the 2nd platoon of the 27th Regiment was asleep on Hell Spit when the sentry started shouting:

There's something unusual, get up! Then the squad commander ordered us all to move up into the trenches... There were very few of us in the squad... we looked and saw there were lots of them [soldiers] pouring out of their boats and we opened fire and they lay down on the sand with their guns in their hands.[102]

The Turkish No. 8 Company's 250 men were all that opposed the Australians in the first instance and they were under strict orders not to fire until the boats grounded.

Private Percival Young, 9th Battalion, states:

Bullets splashed all around the boats and tore through the woodwork. The pack upon my back was torn with bullets, but I was untouched. We pulled with all our might for shore: men cried, laughed, prayed and swore, and still the bullets tore through the boats throwing all into confusion. A midshipman in the pinnace towing the boats, a little chap of about 14 yelled, "Get ashore men and get at them!" A seaman seized an oar to push the boat further in, and, as he pushed, fell dead, shot through the head.[103]

The crisp smack of bullets striking flesh began to be heard in many of the landing boats, followed almost immediately by a moan as the unlucky casualty slid to the bottom of the boat. Lance Corporal Mitchell, 10th Battalion (survived Gallipoli, Western Front and died in 1961), wrote, "Some men crouched, some sat up nonchalantly, some laughed and joked, while others cursed in ferocious delight." Another unnamed Australian soldier dryly remarked, "They had better cease all that shooting or someone is going to be killed!"[104]

The first few boats to hit the beach shortly before 4.30am were those of the 9th Battalion and fortunately many of their boats reached the shore just before the first shots were fired. For the boats following, however, after the alarm had been raised and the first rush of bullets rained down, there was an urgency for the remaining boats to get to the shore anywhere regardless of the position. Some boats were grounded on the seabed a little way off the beach, immersing the soldiers leaving the boats up to their waists in water. In some places offshore, the stones on the bottom were round and slimy, causing men to slip and fall into the water. There were also a few who exited their boats in deep water, and held down by the weight of their packs and equipment, were drowned. Turkish bullets sent sparks flying from the shingle as the remainder of the first wave of the AIF hurtled across the beach, which was no more than half a cricket pitch wide.

The 9th and 10th Battalions had landed in a cluster around Ari Burnu, but the seaward face of the knoll defiladed them from the Turks on top. Therefore, they were still relatively unscathed when they reached the beach. Grounding 300 yards north of it, the boats of the 11th Battalion were hit by many bullets as they rowed past Ari Burnu headland and were then tormented by a machine-gun positioned near Fisherman's Hut further north as they jumped from the boats on landing.

At Fisherman's Hut, Second Lieutenant Ibrahim–Hayreddin and his platoon of 60 to 70 men first saw the invasion force approaching via the fading light of the moon:

> *[We] occupied the trenches and waited ... [We] saw the landing craft carrying the first landing forces coming straight towards [us]. [We] waited for them to approach before opening fire, but the craft veered of in the direction of Ari Burnu. [We] saw that as they approached Ari Burnu both sides began firing in the dark ... the landing forces who tried to approach north of Ari Burnu (11th Battalion boats) were coming directly towards us. As they drew near [We] continued to fire at a number of enemy troops who*

were desperately trying to get ashore and compelled them to flee under cover in the direction of Ari Burnu.[105]

Many of the officers and men had been briefed prior to disembarking that what was expected of the terrain and the initial assault immediately following the landing was 10 or 15 yards of sand and a low cliff about four or five feet high, and upon dropping packs on this small ridge they would need to form up and then rush across 200 yards of open ground to the first hill. This was a very good brief, if they had indeed landed at the anticipated strip of level ground of Brighton Beach. Instead a precipitous slope rising up to Plugge's Plateau lay directly ahead of the 9th Battalion. This was not what was expected. Some of the officers thought it must have been Gaba Tepe and others did not think so but had no idea where they were, which led to some initial confusion. Fortunately, as mentioned earlier, the Turks had limited fortifications in this area due to its unsuitability for landing and only a few trenches had been dug.

Private Nelson Scrivener, A company, 9th Battalion, had a terrible start to his Gallipoli adventure. He was shot in the thigh while getting out of the boat on landing and was fortunately looked after by probably the 3rd Field Ambulance (that had landed with the 3rd Brigade at 4.30am) on the beach before being evacuated later that day to Alexandria. It is interesting to wonder whether Corporal Frederic Scrivener (stretcher bearer) was aware that his brother had been shot at that stage, given the stretcher bearers worked closely with those from the Field Ambulance and would certainly have been in the area. Given the confusion at that time, the thick scrub and the high number of casualties very early, it is hard to say with any certainty that the two would have had news of each other.

The Keid family also would have one of its boys among the first of the Australian casualties. Harry, landing in the initial wave of the 9th Battalion, was shot in the pelvis, although he maintained that it was a ricochet rather than a direct hit, and lay on the beach wounded for several hours as he awaited medical treatment. The wounded in that initial wave would have to wait. Hampson[106] indicates that Harry lay quite conscious on the beach unattended for about eight hours, at all times very exposed with the war raging on around him. While he maintained that lying in the saltwater for some time before crawling up the beach had helped prevent infection setting in, his injuries must have been quite serious, because when he was picked up, he was transferred to the ANZAC Base Hospital in Weymouth in England rather than Lemnos or Egypt. Hampson suggests that it would also be nice to contemplate that Guy Keid of the 3rd Field Ambulance, who also landed that morning, had been the one to attend to his brother.

Private Henry Cheney of the 10th Battalion (survived Gallipoli, but was killed on 2nd April 1917 with the 50th Battalion) writes that the machine-guns in the bows of the steamboats clattered away, covering the dash to the beach, which he describes as a baptism of fire:

> *I scrambled ashore as best I could, holding my rifle well above my head, but it is not a sandy bottom on that beach, it is cobblestones and so made our progress very slow. The first act ashore was to fix my bayonet, second to divest myself of my pack. Everything was disorder now, excitement running very high.*[107]

The machine-guns that Cheney refers to were located on the bow of each of the steamboats and could only be used if the senior officer on board ordered it into action. At least one of the steamboats, which had landed the men of the 9th Battalion, reversed out to sea in order to enable its machine-gun to fire at the Turkish rifle flashes coming from the Plateau (Plugge's) above. The machine-guns wounded the Turkish Second Lieutenant Muharrem within the first rounds of firing, shot in both shoulders and then when he was withdrawing, he was again shot, this time in the arm.

Scrambling ashore, the men ran across a narrow stretch of beach until brought up by a sandy bank that was about 10 feet high. Here they lay on the ground, took off their packs and laid them down and fixed bayonets. Some had vainly attempted to fix their bayonets while in the water. The orders that were given pre–landing had been very clear that no shots were to be fired until daylight. These orders were for the most part carefully observed by the men, despite the fact that a few men on first landing lost their heads in the excitement and began to fire into the darkness. It is said that of the Australians killed or wounded before daylight on the day of the landing, none was found with a cartridge in his magazine and every one had the cut–off of his rifle closed, as instructed. This indicates the high state of discipline that existed among the troops.[108]

Private Young states:

Those that were able sprang into the water, helter skelter out of the boats. The water was up to our necks, but stumbling and wading we reached the shore and rushed for any bit of cover that was available.[109]

Young goes on to state that the first man ashore was Lieutenant Chapman of the 9th (killed at Pozieres in August 1916), closely followed by Colonel Lee, Major Robertson (killed on 25th April, 1915), Major Salisbury, Captain Ryder, Dr Butler and the other 9th Battalion men of the leading boat.

Private Tom Usher, 9th Battalion, stated:

You're up to your neck in water – and a lot of them got drowned too, with the weight of the packs and that – then scramble ashore and take shelter as quick as you could. You're only looking after yourself, you couldn't worry about the other bloke, you had to get ashore as quick as you could – just keep your rifle above your head and keep it dry ... I could see these cliffs and I ran for it. You didn't care who you were with as long as you could get away from the fire ... I remember one bloke, he got hit in the mouth – he lost part of his tongue I couldn't understand what he was talking about.[110]

What Private Usher outlines above is a clear indication of the mindset of the men of the 9th Battalion was as they landed on the beach as part of the first wave under fire in a foreign and foreboding landscape.

The Australian soldiers then rushed into the hills full of verve that belongs to young men that have not seen much of death.[111] The men remembered the instruction from their officers to go forward inland with all haste and not to get stuck on the beaches, however, there was little organisation when they landed and a lot of confusion. This was especially the case given that Battalions were mixed even from the moment that they set foot on Anzac Cove, and they were shocked at the sheer climb that faced them. Rifle fire seemed to be coming from all directions and the terrain was extremely confusing and difficult to negotiate. All communication had broken down between the remaining officers and few men knew where the forward parties were, moreover, there was no concentration of force, but many smaller leaderless parties who rushed ahead, scrambling up the face of the headland and yelling, carried away by the adrenalin.

Hardly any of the Battalions were where they should have been, and given that there were so many volunteers that had not been under fire before, this added to the level of confusion and disorder that existed.[112]

Major McNicoll, who was the commanding officer of the 6th Battalion (2nd Brigade) that landed after the 3rd Brigade, stated that:

As soon as the boats keel hit the stoney shore, men jumped out up to their waist-belts in sea water to the detriment of the rations of biscuits in their haversacks. So intent were our minds on the business ahead of us, that no–one seemed to notice his wet condition for an instant, nor can he remember when and how he dried out.[113]

Despite their bewilderment at where they were and what lay immediately ahead of them, the men of the covering force knew they had to push on and went swarming up Ari Burnu in uniforms that were heavy with water, and pushed through waist-high scrub that had thorns an inch long that shredded clothing and skin.

Private Cheney hardly noticed and stated:

We were at fever point and just made as much noise as we could… … I was lost in the wild mob, in the wildest of charges that I think was ever made. Everybody had taken leave of their senses and was certainly not accountable for their actions. Although I know well enough what fear is, it left me completely in that charge. Straight up that rugged, rocky precipice we went.[114]

Private Young of the 9th states that:

In the darkness before the dawn, men gathered on the beach beneath the cliff. Packs were thrown off and bayonets fixed. All this time a machine-gun on the cliff above us had been pouring a hail of bullets into the landing parties. Dr Butler had lost some of his stretcher bearers in the deadly fire and this made him very angry. "Come on men, we must take that gun," he cried and started climbing the cliff, his revolver in hand. We stormed up behind him. Sergeant Fowles and Patrick Courtney were on either side of me as we climbed the cliff and both were shot dead. We rushed the gun and bayoneted the Turk gun crew. We smashed the gun so that it could not be used again and dashed forward to storm the next trench, the line growing stronger as the boys rushed up to reinforce. On and on we went right up the cliff to the summit, where we had to pause for sheer want of breath. Looking below we saw the British ships shelling the Turkish positions, while the Turks replied by shrapnel all over the landing place. Boat after boat was smashed under our eyes and the occupants mangled or drowned. The sight maddened us. "On Queenslanders!"came the cry, and with bayonets fixed we rushed the Turkish position. [115]

Sergeant Herbert Fowles of A company, 9th Battalion, a 22 year old school teacher from Gatton, Queensland, who had climbed up the first cliff with Private Young, was fatally hit in the back by rifle fire from Australians climbing from behind when he had reached the top of Plugge's Plateau. "I told them," he said as he lay there dying in the Turkish trench – "I told them again and again not to open their magazines." A Red Cross Wounded and Missing Enquiry Bureau file indicates that an enquiry was made into the circumstances of Sergeant Fowles' death and noted that there was no suspicion of foul play and he had been shot in the back by one of his own men. Private Walker, who knew Fowles well, was later interviewed in a Cairo hospital and stated that the Sergeant's last words to him were "Hard luck being hit by one of your own men!". Fowles was attended by a 9th Battalion stretcher bearer, Private Henry Mahaffey, at the place where he was shot and admitted that he did not expect Fowles to make it back to the beach alive given his wound.[116]

Private Patrick Courtney, who is referred to in the paragraph above by Private Young in his account, was actually Private Thomas Courtney, 9th Battalion, per Australian War Memorial records. Private Courtney was a 19 year old engine cleaner from Rosewood, just outside Brisbane on enlistment and was recorded as killed in action on the 2nd May, 1915. He is now buried in Plugge's Plateau cemetery.

In regard to that first climb, Charles Bean noted how steep the slope was the men had to deal with through the following descriptive passage. "Those who were wounded rolled or slide down it until caught and supported by some tuft or scrub. Here and there a man hung over a slope so precipitous that Butler [Captain A.G. Butler – 9th Battalion Medical Officer], going to his help, had to cut steps in the gravel face with his entrenching tool in order to reach him".[117]

Of Captain A.G. Butler, much is written about his outstanding service to wounded men of the 9th Battalion and his conviction to duty throughout the first day. Butler was certainly one of the first men ashore on the 25th April, 1915. As Butler stepped from the boat, a British seaman who was in the act of handing him his medical satchel fell back shot through the head. After attending to several wounded men on the beach, Butler led forward a number of men (as referred to by Private Young above) and even stopped to dress a wounded Turk at the top of Ari Burnu knoll. When his supply of bandages ran out he used his puttees, and even ripped his shirt into strips to bind up the wounded. "I can still picture him," said a stretcher bearer many years after the war, "as I saw him on the 25th April, practically in rags, here, there, and everywhere, looking after the wounded and organizing parties to take them back to the beach."

On the southern side of Ari Burnu, where Major J.C. Robertson of the 9th Battalion landed, there was a steep bank as high as the wall of a room, and those attempting to climb quickly slipped back to the base again. Then someone found a rough track leading around it, and by this means they reached the top of the knoll. Besides being very steep, the hillside was covered with scrub. This was mainly composed of small bushes of prickly dwarf oak, about three feet high, with leaves like a small holly. In some places the scrub was so close and thorny that even a strong man had difficulty forcing his way through it.

Once up the first slopes, the soldiers realised that they were in an even worse climbing predicament than they had first thought, as the topography is not simply a steep climb, but is broken by deep ridges, curving narrow valleys and eroding soil, forming crumbling red gullies. The gravel outcrops formed perfect cover for the enemy, who had time to plan their defensive positions to be most effective within a battlefield that forms the ideal setting for snipers. In some cases, Turkish snipers who were in positions on the higher ground were concealed so effectively behind natural camouflage they were often inadvertently run past by the frantically climbing Australian troops.

As they climbed the Australians cheered, swore and joked, which is hard to imagine with men dying all around and bullets flying there seemed little thought of self-preservation. Such was the adrenalin that was pumping at the landing. One of the men said afterwards, "The swearing that went on, as well as the jokes, was marvellous." When they encountered any of the Turks they chased the enemy with shouts of "imshee yalla", "eggs–a–cook", "oranngees" and any other expressions that they had picked up during their stay in Egypt.[118]

The first troops from the 9th and 10th Battalions soon reached the top of Ari Burnu Knoll to find that most of the Turkish platoon there had withdrawn to further up Plugge's Plateau. They went straight on after them, climbing slopes so steep they resorted to digging in their bayonets to pull themselves up. After 20 minutes, they climbed over the lip of Plugge's to see soldiers from the 11th Battalion appear at its northern edge. One of these men was 40 year old Captain W. R. "Dick" Annear, C Company, 11th Battalion, who is shown with his other fellow officers in the photo of the whole Battalion on the Great Pyramid of Cheops during training at Mena Camp. He had climbed up from the beach with the first wave of men. Annear was lying on the parapet of an unoccupied enemy trench when Turkish fire from the direction of MacLagan's Ridge found its mark, hitting him in the head and killing him instantly. Captain Annear has the unenviable record of being the first Anzac officer to be killed at Gallipoli.

About half an hour after they had come ashore men from A and B companies of the 10th Battalion were organised and sent down from Plugge's towards the 400 Plateau, moving across Shrapnel Gully following the retreating Turks.

Ignoring the fire from the machine-gun near Fisherman's Hut, the 11th Battalion's two companies rushed Ari Burnu when they saw the others climbing it. As more Australians arrived the Turks withdrew across a deep gorse–covered valley towards the Second Ridge 500 yards away. The young Turkish soldier Adil Sahin later stated that it was all very confusing at the time:

> *We didn't know anything about this invasion. We were very scared and retreated to the Second Ridge, firing as we went. I was very frightened.*[119]

In the growing light, the Australians laughingly fired at them and others scampering over MacLagan's Ridge, which linked Plugge's to Hell Spit. It was just before 5am and the battle seemed over, as the Turks seemed to be in full flight.

During the next half-hour, the men that were on Plugge's Plateau, which included some men of both A and B companies of the 9th Battalion, were sorted into Battalion groups corresponding to the formation that the advance was originally planned. It was at this time that the men heard for the first time during the landing the burst of shrapnel from the Turkish guns on Gaba Tepe into what was termed Shrapnel Valley.

Those from the 10th Battalion had formed up in the centre and headed towards Johnson's Jolly, now clearly visible 100 yards to the south, from where they would go on to the Third Ridge. Those from the 9th Battalion on the right pursued the Turks towards Lone Pine, which the 9th had to cross in order to secure the right flank on the Third Ridge, which was their original objective. With the intention to strike out for Baby 700, the men of the 11th Battalion re–formed on the left of Plugge's.

The 9th men were without senior officers as Lieutenant Colonel Lee, Commanding Officer of the Battalion, had been shot in the hand and had not reached the plateau. Major J.C. Robertson had received a bullet wound to the chest and Major S.B. Robertson had gone far to the left with a few of his men towards Baby 700. Therefore the junior Major, A.G. Salisbury, accordingly assumed command of the Battalion and with his men climbed the steep Razorback Ridge, meeting only scattered fire, reaching the far side of the 400 Plateau a little north of the head of Owen's Gully. The Major was to continue to lead the Battalion for the rest of the day. On reaching the Plateau, he took charge of the 9th's position on the right of the 400 Plateau and handed the left over to Captain J. Ryder.

Many men, especially those from the 9th Battalion that had made good progress inland immediately following the landing and had not stopped with the others on reaching the top of Plugge's Plateau, were by this time widely scattered. These men were operating in small parties moving forward independently of officers and were soon separated from the larger groups of the 3rd Brigade. Private Young was in one such group.

> *We pressed forward till we seemed we would drop from exhaustion. Then we saw the Turks coming up in force. Taking advantage of every bit of cover available, we emptied our magazines into them again and again. The Turks fell like leaves, but still more came on. Men dropped, and our numbers began to weaken, Where are the others? Have we come too far? Were questions in the minds of all. Then the order came to retire steadily, bullets flicked all around us and many of the boys fell and we had to leave them. Slowly and steadily we fell back to the shelter of the captured trenches.*

The landing of the second wave occurred at about 4.50am, with the remaining 2500 men from the 3rd Brigade who had been on the destroyers storming the beaches with as much vigor as the first wave. This wave included men from C and D Companies of the 9th Battalion, who at about 4am had been ordered to get into rowing boats from their respective destroyers. The destroyers carrying the 9th Battalion men were the HMS *Beagle* which carried C Company and the HMS *Colne* carrying D Company. The rest of the second wave spread across the other destroyers were the remaining two companies of the 10th and 11th Battalion and all of the 12th Battalion, which was held in reserve.

The HMS *Beagle* was allotted the southernmost position of the British destroyers landing troops during the initial landings. On the first alarm, the Turks at Gaba Tepe at once sighted the *Beagle,* which was positioned just off Brighton Beach, and opened up on the destroyer with every rifle and machine-gun in the defensive line. The range was long, but one machine-gun in particular had the ship accurately within its sights. Its shots pattered on the high bows of the destroyer like hail on a roof, and the water through which the boats had to move was whipped to spray by bullets. Slowing to a halt 200 yards off the beach, each of the destroyers pulled their tows alongside and started disembarkation at 4.40am.

The second wave of the 3rd Brigade covering force met heavy fire from the slopes either side of Ari Burnu, and many of the boats were under fire all the way into shore. In some cases, all the rowers in a boat were hit and the bodies had to be pushed overboard so that others could take over. The battleships *Triumph, Majestic* and *Bacchanti* which had accompanied the troop-carrying battleships, which were given the responsibility of bombarding the Turks as soon as the landings had been made, were firing at the Gaba Tepe guns, but could not silence them as they had been effectively sheltered within a quarry.

The outline of Turkish soldiers on top of Plugge's Plateau could still be seen by the men as they approached the beaches, along with the constant rifle fire that was raining down on the soldiers of the first wave as they made their way up to the Plateau. At this stage, the men of the first wave had yet to capture the top of Plugge's.

Turkish artillery was not reported to have started shrapnel fire until about 5.10am, which was about 40 minutes after the men of the first wave of the covering force had landed and about the same time as the second wave of the 3rd Brigade were landing. Therefore, many of the men brought on to the beaches aboard the destroyers were under artillery fire throughout the whole of the journey towards the shore, especially as it became easier for the Turkish artillery based at Gaba Tepe to see the landing boats on approach

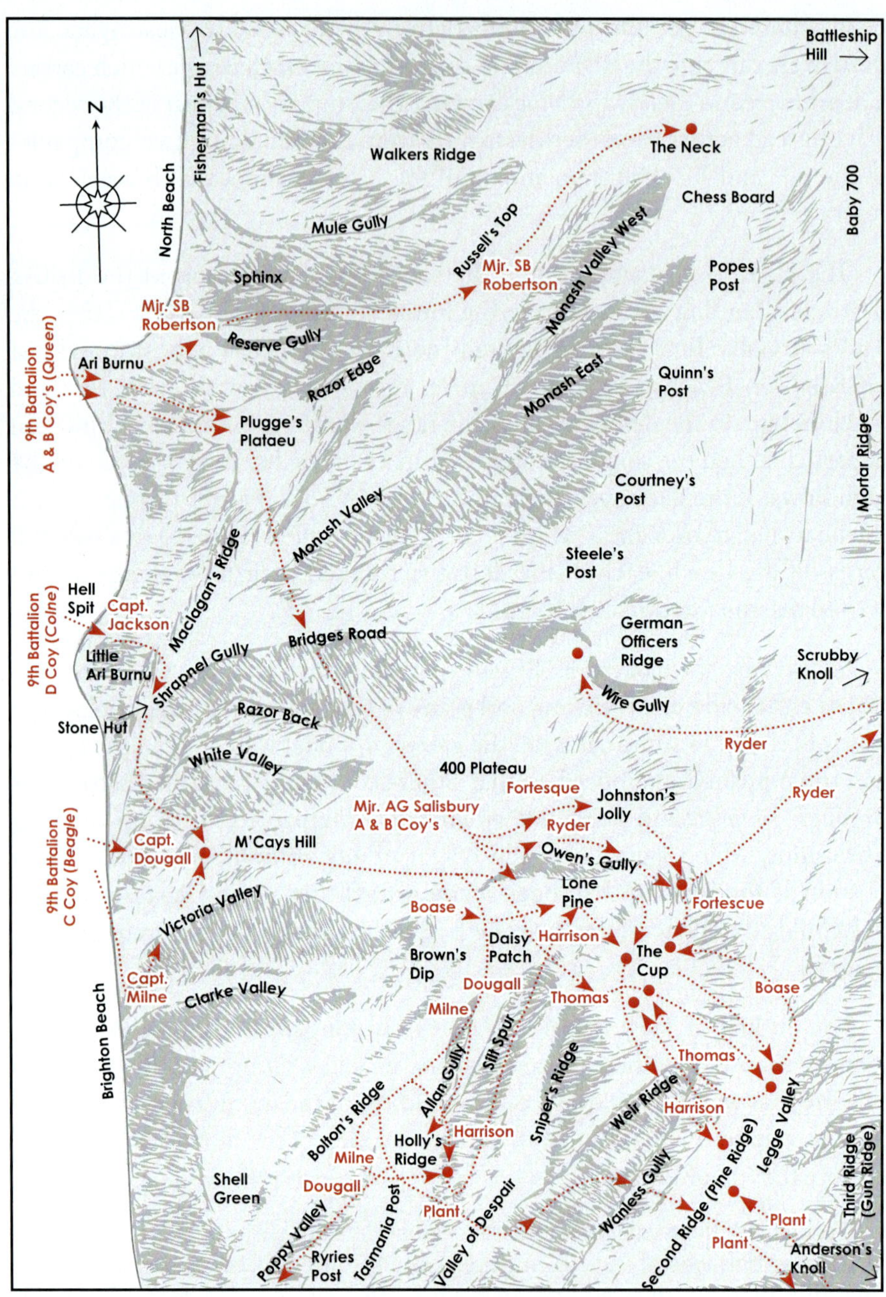

The movements of the companies of the 9th Battalion on the morning of the first day.

and landing the men on the beach with the increasing light of sunrise. The 2nd Brigade, landing as part of the main body of troops from destroyers later that morning, were shelled on approach, on the beaches and then the gullies as they advanced on to the First and Second Ridges.

The main round fired by the Turks on the Gallipoli Peninsula was shrapnel shell. This type of shell had a time fuse and the idea was to have it burst over the enemy, preferably five metres above the ground, so that the 250 shrapnel balls it contained would rain down on the target. Shrapnel fire was especially effective on soldiers out in the open, as were the Anzacs during most of the first day. Later in the campaign when both sides were well dug in, high explosive shells fired from the Turkish heavy howitzers with a much higher trajectory was found to be more effective.

The C company of the 9th Battalion landed between Hell Spit and McCays Hill, which ran from the southern side of Shrapnel Valley, where the 400 Plateau sloped down to the sea. Part of the company under Captain Milne landed just opposite the mouth of Victoria Gully and others reached the shore a little farther south still, near the entrance to Clarke's Gully. This was the furthest landings on the right-hand side of the battlefield there would be that day. This was very much in line with the original plan to have them on the right flank, and it is interesting to note that they were only just north of the allocated landing area of Brighton Beach.

Captain Milne and his men had landed just to the north of Turkish Platoon No. 3, commanded by Lieutenant Hakki (2nd Battalion), positioned north of Gaba Tepe, along the Bolton's Ridge spur. In addition, there was also a section of Turkish soldiers located at Clarke Valley much closer to Milne's landing spot. Both Turkish positions opened fire on C Company, 9th Battalion, and after dumping their packs, the Australians immediately charged the nearest Turks which were those located at Clarke Valley.

After cleaning up the Turks located in the initial beach defensive positions and moving past machine-gun fire from the direction of Gaba Tepe, halfway to the top of the first hill (McCays Hill), part of Milne's C company met a portion of D company, 9th Battalion (possibly half the company) coming up from the other side. D company under Captain Jackson had landed just to the north of Hell Spit. (This is close to a place later referred to as Queensland Point, named as such by Queenslanders who landed in this area, and a cemetery was later established that became known as Beach Cemetery)

The 3rd Brigade's Commanding Officer, Colonel Sinclair-MacLagan and Captain Ross, his staff Captain, had also come ashore with the first tow of Captain Jackson's D company and immediately climbed the ridge above the beach, the southern shoulder of Plugge's Plateau.

Meanwhile, D company had charged, cheering as they ran, over Little Ari Burnu and then began to move south. Going down the far side of the hill through scattered rifle fire into Shrapnel Gully they found a small stone hut, in which amazingly, half-a-dozen Turks were sitting by a fire with a pot of coffee on it. These Turks were bayoneted, and as the story goes, the Australians took some time off from the war and drank the pot of strong black coffee that was brewing.[120] Soon after leaving the hut however, Jackson was wounded and command of D company was passed to Captain Dougall. The company then moved to the top of McCay's Hill, whereby meeting up with C Company.

Instead of moving further inland across 400 Plateau, like most other 3rd Brigade men, most of the men with Milne and Dougall turned in a southerly direction towards Gaba Tepe, which was after all their objective, moving down Bolton's Ridge towards the Turkish trench line that was occupied by Lieutenant Hakki and his men. The exception was that two of D Company's platoons under Thomas and Boase were ordered to move directly across 400 Plateau in pursuit of the Turks that were retreating from the beach.

With Milne's men moving down the ridge from the seaward side and Dougall's on the landward side, the Australians were soon spotted by Hakki's platoon, who forced them to ground with scattered fire. Soon after, Milne was wounded and ordered Corporal Harrison to work his way to the left behind the Turkish trench. "Go for it, Corporal, clean the buggers outta there". Harrison and his men crept up close to the trench unseen and then charged up the slope yelling and screaming at the Turks. Within seconds it was over. They had captured the Turkish position, although Hakki and most of his men had managed to escape with one killed and two wounded. The wounded Milne took a breather in the captured trench and stated, "They've taken more than a couple of bob off this uniform". Soon after, other members of the 9th Battalion under Lieutenant Plant arrived at the trench with Milne. They did not stay long before moving across Bolton's Ridge and down into the valley heading for Anderson Knoll, which was part of their objective.

Harrison and the wounded Milne eventually headed up towards 400 Plateau to rejoin both Thomas and Boase. Dougall and the remainder of the

9th Battalion that was with him from D company, continued down Bolton's Ridge until they reached Harris Ridge. They occupied a Turkish trench and awaited further developments. It would not be long before they saw advanced elements of Lieutenant Colonel Sefik Aker's 27th Regiment, those that had been held in reserve at Maidos, making their way towards Anderson Knoll.

It is interesting to note that the advance of many of C and D company men of the 9th Battalion was so swift that they reached the 400 Plateau before many of their mates who landed in the first wave. This was mainly due to the fact that the men from A and B companies, which had landed just north of Hell Spit, had been working against the ridges and scaling Plugge's Plateau under fire, effectively slowing their advance.

One of the significant actions of the 9th Battalion that day was the taking of the Turkish Mountain Battery located at the Cup, which was a key objective that morning on the way to taking possession of the Third Ridge. The key characters in this action were Lieutenant Thomas and Corporal Harrison, who in particular had just successfully led men of the 9th Battalion to take a Turkish trench on Bolton's Ridge.

Lieutenant Thomas, who had arrived at the edge of Owens Gully (southern side of 400 Plateau) earlier with his platoon of approximately 50 men, had noticed down into the ravine to his right what he thought was a machine-gun post given the freshly turned earth. He cautiously headed down in that direction towards the Turkish position. By this time, Corporal Harrison and his men who were following in Thomas's footsteps, were forced to ground following Turkish machine-gun fire being directed at them while they crossed 400 Plateau. They continued to crawl through the scrub until they reached the edge of Owens Gully and caught sight of Thomas and his men moving towards the Turkish machine-gun site and followed them. Harrison had also noted a number of tents and smoke from camp fires rising up into the sky down in the valley and his plan was to head towards these and attack.

Thomas looking back saw them to his right approaching the Cup and attempted to warn them that they were heading straight towards what he believed were Turkish machine-guns and trench positions. However, every time Thomas's signaller stood up to "semaphore" the message with his arms one of the Turkish machine-guns fired at him. Harrison could not understand the full message, only the last word "guns". Harrison and his men had managed to crawl up to the bottom of a wall of freshly turned earthworks unseen and found themselves not below a machine-gun pit, but below the muzzles of two Turkish howitzers from the battery located at the Cup. Harrison gave orders for each of his men to target a Turk and be prepared to attack.

At the same time, Captain Sedik and his men who were operating the guns were aware that their position was in danger and Sedik began ordering his men to withdraw the guns back to Third Ridge. He was, however, too late Harrison yelled for his men to fire and most of the Turks manning the guns in the gun pit fell in the first fusillade. Captain Sedik was killed at the entrance to the pit by Harrison as he tried to fire his revolver. Harrison and his men stormed over into the position and fired upon another group of Turks who were frantically loading the machine-guns on to mules and it was not long before they had shot or bayoneted the few Turkish survivors still remaining. Joining them soon after came Thomas and his men. A quick survey of the battery site was undertaken to assess for any useful intelligence and the men came across a small roofed shelter that had a lot of stores and ammunition. The men also tried to disable the guns, but the guns were useless as the Turks had managed to take the breech blocks before they left. Orders were given to light up pipes and rest for 10 minutes. The time was around 6.30am. Unknown to Thomas, one of the guns had been saved along with the battery's spare parts and as the men took their break they noticed some of the Turkish survivors with this gun making their way back to Third Ridge in the valley below.

Lieutenant Boase and his platoon had crossed the 400 Plateau south of Owen's Gully and came across a 100 metre square of level ground that consisted of green grass and poppies. This area would from then on be referred to as the "Daisy Patch". They continued along the southern edge of Owen's Gully until they came across Thomas and his men.

Sinclair-MacLagan, landing at Anzac Cove at 5am, stood on Plugge's at 5.30am and watched parties from the 9th and 10th Battalions which had recently left, heading for the 400 Plateau. As Brigadier Chris Roberts wrote, Sinclair-MacLagan's Brigade was still in reasonable shape to reach its objectives. With the assault on Gaba Tepe no longer feasible, the 9th Battalion had at least three companies within striking distance of Anderson Knoll instead of the two originally allotted. Most of the 10th was close to the Third Ridge, and the 11th was on or around Plugge's, 800 yards nearer to Scrubby Knoll and Battleship Hill than anticipated.

By about 6am, Plugge's Plateau had been secured and parties from the 9th and 10th Battalions had captured the undefended 400 Plateau and had begun to probe towards Third Ridge. Small groups of men dashed down the inward ridge that became known as Pine Ridge and into Legge Valley and then towards Third Ridge, the final objective of the covering force. It could be said that at this time the landing and move inland was going reasonably well. The Turkish resistance had not been as strong as first thought and groups of Australians had driven the Turks from First and Second Ridge, and the leading groups of men were nearing their final objectives for the 3rd Brigade.

Carrying picks and shovels, Australian soldiers, most probably from the 1st Brigade, are crossing Plugge's Plateau around noon on 25th April, 1915. Stray bullets from the fighting on the far side of Shrapnel Valley are whizzing overhead. The foremost men are crouching in the scrub to avoid them. This photo, one of the few of troops under fire at Anzac, was taken from a captured Turkish trench. (AWM G00907)

Lance Corporal Neal of the 9th Battalion, who was part of the second wave, states in his diary that they disembarked from the destroyer and:

Pulled for the beach under heavy rifle fire. Assisted in rowing. Some of our chaps shot whilst going over. Very strong tide to pull against [which may help confirm the theory that the ships were landing on the wrong beach due to strong currents]. Heavy fighting going on to our left. After reaching the beach Turkish fort on the right point of Saros Bay shelled beach with shrapnel, rid of our packs and chased Turks who ran for their lives. Retired at 8am to take up position on hill and entrench. Saw last of my company here and made my way right up and with the party who captured their two field guns. Remained in trench with Captain Daley who was shot in the knee and made cover for shrapnel fire. Took care of wounded and stayed there to defend them. Several chaps around and by me are hit by bullet, machine-gun and shell fire. Saw Mr. Hayman in front of this position also Major Steele a little in front with machine-gun. Captain Daley sent me on right wing to look for snipers. Was cut off and forced to retire to line of trenches held by our men for the night. Heavy firing all night and rain set in.

Private Arthur Blackburn of the 10th Battalion, a lawyer from Adelaide, wrote in a letter to his brother that his boat came under fire when he was 50 yards from the shore and bullets were whizzing in all directions. The men crouched low in the boats. One bullet clattered into a mess tin on a soldier's back, but amazingly no–one in Blackburn's boat was wounded. He then started swimming and half wading towards the shore. Three times he went right under as he landed near the centre of Anzac Cove.

The beach was very rocky and it was not the easiest thing on earth to clamber over big slippery rocks. All this time bullets were whizzing all around us and men were falling here and there. I rushed across the shore to the shelter of a small bank and there shed my pack and fixed my bayonet then to drive the beggars away. The way our chaps went at it was a sight for the gods; no one attempted to fire but we just went straight on up the side of the cliff, pushing our way through thick scrub and often clambering up the steep cliffs on all fours.[121]

Blackburn reached the top of the First Ridge and came under fire from fleeing Turks on the ridge ahead looking down on where they were. Two men were hit on his right and one on his left. Dawn was breaking and the Turks could see them very well and were on the higher ground (as they were throughout the first day), and out on the right where Blackburn was, the Turks had the sun behind them.

> *The country suited them beautifully for they could crawl forward in front of us through the scrub, firing all the time and we could hardly see them.*[122]

Blackburn and his mate Lance Corporal Phil Robin (who was killed on 27th April, 1915), an accountant from South Adelaide, crossed Shrapnel Gully and went up to 400 Plateau.

Blackburn writes further:

> *Up until the time I met up with Phil Robin when he was about to go down into the valley too, I had seen no one that I knew as the battalions in our Brigade were completely mixed up. Travelling across this valley was a decidedly lively time as the scrub was full of snipers and every little while a bullet would come closer than was pleasant. However we got to the top of the ridge in safety and there found several other chaps but no–one in charge. Just at that moment Captain Herbert came up and he decided that we should entrench there. Phil and I went out to watch the valley on his front and flank while he did this. We stayed out there until driven back by the enemy, who were coming to the attack in force.*[123]

From Blackburn's further letters and the writings of Bean, it can be concluded that Blackburn and Robin had crossed Legge Valley and climbed the Third Ridge north of Scrubby Knoll, giving them the deepest penetration inland that morning. Scouting southward they passed beyond the crest of Scrubby Knoll, circling what was later to become Mustafa Kemal's headquarters that day, until they saw Turks approaching from a valley to the east of their position. Both men retreated back to their Battalion on Johnston's Jolly and reported their sightings.

Blackburn had also seen Australians off to the south-west. They were a party under Lieutenant Noel Loutit, also of the 10th Battalion, which had also reached the Third Ridge south of Scrubby Knoll.

From the southern end of the Plateau over the spurs that jut out southwards from that end of it, most likely being Snipers and Weir Ridge, a party of about 20 men of the 9th Battalion under Queenslander Lieutenant Eric Plant going very fast, reached the Third Ridge south of Anderson Knoll at about 6.30am. At this point they had a good view over the country behind the ridge. In the distance they could see water, which they took to be the Sea of Marmora.

However, there was danger of being isolated and they noticed a large formation of Turkish infantry approaching the ridge, which were likely to have been the advanced parties of the 1st and 3rd companies of the 27th Turkish Regiment. As his small party was heavily outnumbered, they retreated back to Pine Ridge.

A little later, Lieutenant Ralph Prisk of the 6th Battalion led a platoon with a few stragglers from the 9th Battalion from 400 Plateau into Legge Valley with the aim of also reaching the Third Ridge. He too noticed a large number of Turkish troops moving in his direction whereby he also moved back to Pine Ridge, however, he was then forced to retire back again because of friendly fire from Australians to his rear that were now established on 400 Plateau and mistaking his party for Turks. The Turks arrived at Scrubby Knoll on the Third Ridge at 8am and for the rest of the campaign this hill just three miles from the Narrows became Turkish Headquarters. Indeed there were many men of the 9th Battalion that morning who had pushed on and actually achieved the objective set, but were not supported, unfortunately along with their comrades in the 10th Battalion. Many of these Queenslanders were killed out in no-man's- land, cut-off and left fighting to their death holding the ground where they stood, picked off by snipers. Their bodies became lost in the small gullies and thick scrub, covered spurs of 400 Plateau, most never to be recovered. This area on Third Ridge would soon fall into Turkish control and remain so throughout the campaign.

This was the furthest in on the right flank the Australians would get for the rest of the Gallipoli campaign. After these early rushes by the Australians had been repulsed and groups of isolated Australian troops had been cut-off because there was no force coming up from behind to occupy and defend the ground, the remnants of the men who had landed in the first few hours on the 25th April were to fall back and dig into positions such as Johnstons Jolly and Russell's Top. These would become the front-line trenches for the rest of the campaign.

Lieutenant–Colonel William Malone, Wellington, NZEF, who landed later that day, commented:

> *The Australians had carried the heights surrounding the bay, but instead of being content with that and then digging in hard and fast had scally–wagged for miles into the interior, some three of four miles, got scattered and so became prey to the Turks ... their troops encamped at Bijuk Anafarta and*

Koja Dere were brought against the scattered Australians and slaughtered them.[124]

Lance Corporal Harry Rydon (9th Battalion) landed with the second wave of men from the 3rd Brigade. Harry was a 23 year old farmer from Bowen in Queensland and noted:

Later I was in a Turkish gun placement we had captured the same day when a sniper got me with an explosive bullet. I felt for a few seconds as if I'd been blown in two. It caught me just on the left side of the backbone, above the hips, and burst as it came out higher up on my right side, leaving a deep cavity. Two of my comrades carried me into a roofed dugout, where I lay for about four hours. There were no stretcher bearers, I think most had been shot. It was certain death to show oneself outside of the trench. We were on the extreme right flank and threatened from all sides. Then a machine-gun came to our rescue and surprised the Turks halfway up the hill. You could hear the moaning quite close below us. I think the machine-gun ran out of ammunition, anyway it went, I could only guess what was happening. It was getting dark, suddenly I saw two figures rush past. Next moment there was a scuffle just behind me, somebody shouted "It's a Turk" Bang Bang! He was a dead Turk then. The other fellow disappeared, I think they were snipers who did not know that we still held the trench. When it was dark we received orders to retire. There were only 11 left and six wounded. They got me on to a canvas sheet and four men helped to carry me. We hadn't gone too far when one of them dropped stone dead, and the man next to him fell wounded by the same bullet. It was enough to break a man's heart.[125]

Led by Lieutenant Noel Loutit, the vanguard of the 10th Battalion chased some Turks, probably coastal sentries, south into Shrapnel Valley where they linked up with men from the 9th Battalion. When the 10th Battalion men caught up with the Turks they tried to surrender and like so many of the earlier clashes, the Australians were without pity. No doubt angry and frustrated about their mates becoming casualties from Turkish snipers who were hard to find, effectively taking "pot shots" from concealed positions on selected Australian targets. It must have been very frustrating for the men as they made their way inland after the initial confrontation with the Turkish coastal sentries that had held their ground around Anzac Cove and the heights of Plugge's Plateau. The objective of these small pockets of Turkish resistance was to stem the roll forward of the 3rd Brigade, create panic and pin down the Australians until fresh Turkish reserves were able to reach the front-lines. Therefore, when Australians did catch up with a Turk or identify a sniper's position it was really payback time. Bean reported that as the Australians got in among them the Turks threw down their rifles, but they were too many to capture and were consequently shot. When later in the day the Turkish reinforcements started coming through from inland positions to reclaim the ground lost in the first few hours, they did the same to the Australians.[126] Groups of Australian soldiers on Baby 700 to the north and Pine Ridge to the south were cut–off and never seen again. When Australians returned after the war in 1919, they found skeletons of their countrymen, scraps of uniform and webbing still attached, lying in little semi–circles where they fell, the ground around them littered with .303 shells.

When daylight came, the officers and troops of the main body on the transports could not gain much information on the progress of the landings, but could see, especially those with telescopes or field glasses, what was going on. The men who were still landing and those climbing the First Ridge of hills were visible along with those fighting along the sides and on the tops of those hills. Activity beyond the First Ridge was for the most part, out of sight.

General Ian Hamilton, who was aboard the HMS *Queen Elizabeth* wrote in his diary:

> *By 5.35am the rattle of small arms fire quieted down; we heard that about 4000 fighting men had been landed; we could see boatloads making for the land; swarms trying to straighten themselves out along the shore; other groups digging and hacking down the brushwood. Even with our field glasses they did not look much bigger than ants. Wave after wave of the little ants press up and disappear. We lose sight of them the moment they lie down.*[127]

It is presumed that the General had been watching the landing of the 2nd wave of the 3rd Brigade (4000 men formed a Brigade).

The men of the main body had certainly noted the flare and heard the initial rifle fire following the first wave of the landings while onboard their ships. Many also indicated they could hear faint cheering and shouting. Certainly the British Admiral Wemyss was very impressed with what he saw and said to an Australian Officer afterwards:

> *Your men are not soldiers, they are fiends. I have seen many famous regiments charging, but I have never seen fighting like this. Your men will do me. It would give me great pleasure to lead them into action at any time.*[128]

Distributed across all seven destroyers, the 12th Battalion was to assemble at the foot of the 400 Plateau as the 3rd Brigade's reserve. Half of the Battalion got ashore with the 9th and 10th Battalions, but the other half landed under Lieutenant Colonel Lancelot Clarke with the 11th Battalion on the northern flank. Landing on this northern flank near Fisherman's Hut was tough and they were engaged by machine-gun fire and also by Turks positioned up on Russell's Top, the ridge leading to Plugge's. Losses were heavy. Clarke directed a platoon of his men to silence the gun and ordered an advance of the others to the crest of Russell's Top. Captain Tulloch (11th Battalion) led 60 men up Walker's Ridge, the northernmost of the two spurs that jutted seawards from Russell's Top. When Tulloch got to the top, he saw Clarke lying dead. Along with 50 men under Lieutenant Margetts (12th Battalion), the 57 year old Clarke (a Tasmanian shipping manager) had achieved an unbelievable feat. Facing the unclimbable second spur, called the Sphinx, they crawled on hands and knees up the marginally less sheer cliff alongside the Sphinx and surprised 30 Turks. The Australians charged, pausing at the Nek, over which the Turks had fled; Clarke was at that time shot through the heart. As the fire died down, Tulloch's and Margetts' groups linked up and were met by some 12th Battalion men under Captain Joseph Peter Lalor (grandson of Peter Lalor of the Eureka Stockade revolt fame). Knowing that the 12th Battalion was supposed to be in reserve, he resisted the urge to press on. His men dug in just short of the Nek. Those from the 11th with Tulloch set off for Battleship Hill, which had been their objective. Later that afternoon at about 3.15, Captain Lalor in an effort to find out where Turkish fire that was being directed at his position was coming from, stood up and said, "Now then, 12th Battalion", and was immediately shot dead by a Turkish bullet. Lalor had left behind his famous family sword, which was reputedly used during the Eureka rebellion, at the Nek before he went forward. It was later reportedly found by at least two other Australians, but lost again in ensuing battles. Its resting place on the Anzac battlefields is one of the enduring mysteries of the campaign.[129]

In an interesting sidenote, Captain Tulloch survived both the Gallipoli campaign and the remainder of the war only to be murdered by a burglar at a guesthouse in East Melbourne in May 1926.

While much of the fighting on the northern aspect of the battlefield has not been outlined due mainly to the fact that this was not the area where the 9th Battalion was active, the fighting for control of the high ground around Baby 700 and the Nek was hard fought. The high ground around Baby 700 changed hands on numerous occasions that day, attack and counterattack, with both Australian and Turk strategically trying to take the initiative from the other and hold on to any ground taken. The Australians had to constantly ensure that their flanks were secured, and where possible, defensive positions could be linked without gaps in fire and a firing line was established along the northern end of the Second Ridge.

Given the strategic importance of the high ground, the fighting in the Anzac northern sector was considerably more desperate as both Australian and Turkish commanders came to realise how critical it was to control the heights.

The fighting in the northern sector early on the first day involved mainly the 12th and 11th Battalions of the 3rd Brigade, however, as the casualty rate climbed other men from the 2nd and 1st Australian Brigades on reaching the heights started taking over lead roles and filling gaps in the firing line. Later in the day, many of these positions were then being filled by New Zealand troops, which formed part of the Australian and New Zealand 4th Brigade. Throughout the course of the day's fighting, as men from recently landed Battalions made their way up on to Plugge's Plateau or started along Shrapnel Gully, they were diverted to either the northern sector of the battlefield to help secure the heights and to join loosely formed firing lines to defend against Turkish counterattack or to the southern sector around 400 Plateau.

Back at Anzac Cove, the 2nd Brigade's landing began disastrously. With tows still having not yet returned to pick up the troops of the first Battalions of the 2nd Brigade, at 4.45am the Captain of the *Galeka* anchored 600 yards from Ari Burnu. When the ship started being hit by shrapnel, he decided that they could not stay long and ordered a landing from the ship's boats, which started embarking the 7th Battalion. As the 2nd Brigade was supposed to be on the left of the 3rd Brigade, they rowed towards the left of the rifle flashes and unknowingly headed straight for Fisherman's Hut, where a Turkish machine-gun and well-defended trenches were located. This was the machine-gun that Clarke had requested a platoon under his command to silence, but unfortunately had not yet been reached by his men. It opened up when the boats were 200 yards offshore. Private Bert Heighway remembered smelling the burning paint as bullets riddled his boat. Nearly every man in his boat was hit. Finally, as the platoon under Clarke's orders approached the entrenched positions at Fisherman's Hut, the Turks withdrew to the higher ground. Of the 140 men of the 7th Battalion in the first four boats, less than

40 were unscathed, the rest lay in the boats or on the beach, dead or dying. A passing steamboat towed the last two boats into Anzac Cove. By the time the survivors had rejoined the rest of the Battalion, only 18 remained.

Fisherman's Hut is today, as it was in 1915, marked by a small stone hut that is sited on the position of the original "Hut" and is still owned by the same family who originally lived there in 1915.

After this incident off the coast of Fisherman's Hut, Anzac Cove became the main landing area for the whole Corps throughout the remainder of the morning and over the next few days. While the Cove was out of sight of the Turks, because they knew the Anzacs were concentrating their landings there, the beach was never without shrapnel fire. During the morning of the 25th April, the fire was also supported by the Ottoman battleship *Torgud Reis,* which was moored in the straits between Maidos (present-day Eceabat) and Cannakale. It had been firing over the peninsula unmolested into the Allied shipping that lay off the coast of Ari Burnu until it was observed by aircraft carrying out reconnaissance and was moved on due to the menacing presence of the HMS *Triumph*. Later, after returning to its earlier position to continue with shelling the Anzac landing area, the Turkish battleship suddenly withdrew completely. This may have been due to the warning that the Australian submarine *AE2* was in the area and had managed to make its way through the minefield.[130] It is interesting to think that the *AE2* may have contributed in some meaningful capacity, among other achievements, to help their countrymen during their landings that day and reduce casualties.

Now back to the 3rd Brigade. Sinclair-MacLagan had decided that the Third Ridge was too big and distant to capture. He halted on the Second Ridge, sending some men from the 11th Battalion and a company of the 12th Battalion who were with him at that time to occupy Baby 700. With what he believed to be limited manpower and fearing a counterattack at any time, he ordered his men to dig–in on the seaward side of the 400 Plateau and up along the ridge towards the head of Monash Valley. The positions along this ridge soon became purpose made strong posts named after Australian officers Steel, Courtney, Quinn and Pope. Sinclair-MacLagan wanted to consolidate until the 2nd Brigade arrived and then resume the advance. However, he was ignoring the need to reach the Third Ridge as quickly as possible and that little real resistance had occurred so far, not to mention the fact that he was effectively leaving those men of the 9th and 10th Battalions who had made good progress and were now at the Third Ridge awaiting reinforcements to their own devices, which for many became their ultimate death sentence. At that time, in no great strength, the Turks had been driven back and the way ahead lay open for the Australians.

By 6.30am, the Australian 3rd Brigade, 10th Battalion on the left, those remaining of the 9th on the far right and bits of the 12th intermingled were digging in across 400 Plateau as Sinclair-MacLagan had ordered. Reinforcements were needed to advance further, but few were coming forward at that time. The 12th Battalion, which was supposed to be held as the Brigade in reserve after the landing, had become broken up. This was not helped by the spreading of the Battalion across all seven of the destroyers. Landing with the second wave of the covering force, under fire and being caught up with the confusion and enthusiasm of the advance, they committed themselves in small groups to whatever advance or fighting was happening in their immediate vicinity.

On the Turkish side, the two companies of the 2/27th Battalion that faced the landing had denuded their fringe outposts to try to contain the Australians advance. This greatly helped the company located to the north of Ari Burnu, as only a few men could easily hold the narrow frontage leading to Battleship Hill while others came up. The Turks who therefore withdrew from Russell's Top (just below Battleship Hill) were reinforced when Tulloch's men met them just short of Battleship Hill. The southern company under Captain Faik, however, which caught the full force of the landing, disintegrated before help could arrive.

Loutit's party was another one of a number of groups who had pursued the remnants of the Turkish coastal sentries across Legge Valley to the Third Ridge and were now left effectively in no-man's land due to Sinclair-MacLagan's orders. "We had trouble keeping up," Loutit later said. Only when Loutit stopped on the Third Ridge to await promised reinforcements did the Turks he was chasing stop. At 8am he went with two men to the summit of Scrubby Knoll and saw the Narrows three and a half miles off. Rejoining the others when fired upon, he noticed a group of Australians digging in on the 400 Plateau 1200 yards rearwards on the inland slope of Lone Pine. He sent back again for help, asking for men to come forward over to the Third Ridge and protect his southern flank. This group was Captain John Ryder and a platoon of the 9th Battalion who had come along with Salisbury from Plugge's. As the order to dig in on the Plateau and not advance any further had at that time not yet been made by Sinclair-MacLagan, they rushed over and lined up on Loutit's right around 9am, however, the Turks began pushing past them soon after. The pause had given the Turks time to regroup with men coming up from Gaba Tepe. The group of men under Loutit and Ryder found themselves under very heavy fire, and with mounting casualties sent further messages back asking for support. One of Ryder's Sergeants reached the main line on a horse found in the Legge Valley, while some men under Captain Peck of the 11th started forward to support their position. To Loutit's annoyance, although they had reached the objectives set for the covering force, as they were about to be outflanked by greatly superior numbers of Turks, Ryder's men withdrew at 9.30am, forcing Loutit and his men to follow. Of the 32 men with Loutit who had started out towards the Third Ridge, 11 were able to reach the Australian line, digging in as an outpost overlooking Wire Gully and German Officers Ridge beyond it.

Like many other crucial times during the campaign an initiative had been lost. The digging in by a large portion of the 3rd Brigade across 400 Plateau had given the Turks time to regroup and attack along the Third Ridge, taking back ground that had been reached by numerous bands of men in smaller groups of the 3rd Brigade, such as those led by Loutit and Plant.

Many men from both A and B companies of the 9th Battalion that had been taken up under the command of Major Salisbury on Plugge's Plateau had now started crossing 400 Plateau. They were soon stopped and ordered by Major Charles Brand (3rd Brigade Headquarters staff) to fall back and dig in to help form a defensive line just to the south of the 10th Battalion. Given that his position would have been just forward of the 10th Battalion and fearing the potential for his flank to come under pressure, Salisbury ordered a platoon under Lieutenant Fortescue to remain forward and act as a screening force at the northern head of Owen's Gully.

On the southern edge of Owens Gully, Major Brand also ordered Thomas and Boase and their platoons to move out on to the very edge of 400 Plateau near Lonesome Pine (later renamed Lone Pine) so they could get a better view of Third Ridge and form a screen, but not go too far, and if attacked to fall back to the main firing line. By this time, which was around 8.30am, both Sinclair-MacLagan and Brand had agreed that pushing on to the Third Ridge with the limited number of men they had available to them was reckless, especially with the buildup of Turkish forces they could see and that had been reported, which were now reaching the Third Ridge.

By this time also, Captain Dougall with men from D company of the 9th Battalion, who had earlier entrenched at Harris Ridge, decided that he should move from his current position and join up again with the Australians he could see moving across 400 Plateau.

As the morning progressed, Sinclair– MacLagan became more and more concerned by the number of Turks he could see massing along Third Ridge as part of a developing counterattack. The sound of fighting could be heard along the southern flank of Third Ridge by the outlying small groups of men, many at this stage scrambling to make their way back to the front-line or making desperate stands against waves of Turkish soldiers of the 1st and 3rd Battalions of the 27th Regiment. At about 9am, MacLagan ordered Salisbury's men forward (and parts of the 10th and 7th Battalions) in sections to the landward edge of 400 Plateau to meet the expected attack and support the men already forward as part of the earlier screen, which included Thomas and Boase's platoons. Sinclair–MacLagan was also concerned that if the Turks attacked in force and were able to force back the men of the forward covering screen, it might start a general retirement of those also holding the very thin line further back on the Plateau. By this time Captain Milne's company of 9th Battalion men had joined up with Salisbury. The men stopped digging and put their equipment back on for an advance as ordered.

When men of the 9th Battalion started moving in sections through the waist-high gorse just beyond Lonesome Pine, almost immediately after they reached the open area a shattering fusillade erupted from Turkish machine-guns and rifle fire located on the Third Ridge and swept across the Plateau. It was as if a giant scythe had swept across the field as men dropped below the scrubline, dead, wounded or trying to take cover. Those that were not killed immediately scattered seeking cover. Quickly realising his mistake, Sinclair-MacLagan attempted to rescind the order, but by this time the sections of the Battalion were fully dispersed across the Plateau. It was a disaster for the 9th Battalion. At this time, only the 10th Battalion on Johnston's Jolly was holding the line on the Plateau, and the void left by the 9th Battalion was now slowly filled by the 2nd Brigade.

A commander of the 27th Regiment's Turkish Machine-gun Company positioned on Third Ridge witnessed the advance of the 9th Battalion:

A cover force that was advancing continuously on Kanli Sirt [Lonesome Pine] caught the eye of our machine-gun company. The area where we suspected this force was hiding among the brushwood was immediately kept under heavy fire. The sight and movement that we saw through our binoculars indicated that our machine-guns had caused a terrible and touching tragedy in that area.[131]

Following this action, while there were still a number of groups of 9th Battalion men in forward positions spread between Bolton's Ridge and Third Ridge, as Bean[132] indicates, the 9th Battalion ceased to exist as a cohesive unit. The men that had landed that morning had been decimated on the battlefield and would be operating as a support unit in the firing line for other Battalions spread around 400 Plateau. This was especially the case over the next few days, given the reduced number of men at arms available until the next contingent of reinforcements for the 9th Battalion arrived.

At about this time, to make matters worse for the men on the 400 Plateau, salvos of shrapnel also started to burst on the Plateau with great fury from the Turkish batteries located just behind Gaba Tepe. For the men ahead in the forward parties to retire now would mean crossing the 400 Plateau, which was being swept by shrapnel, rifle and machine-gun fire, so it was better for them to stay where they were.

Against the Turkish artillery there was little or no defence (with the exception of an Indian gun that had set up and provided some fire cover for a few hours) and these batteries fired away with almost immunity. By midday there were four Turkish batteries in action on the Third Ridge (henceforth called Gun Ridge). Nowhere did the shrapnel fall more heavily than on 400 Plateau. With each burst 10 to 15 feet above the ground, a hail of pellets lashed the defenceless backs of the Australians trying to dig in. The cries of the wounded were terrible and the site of the dead ghastly. Men were getting used to the "sickening thud" that signaled the man alongside had been hit. No stretcher bearer could approach the position without being shot down.

Corporal George Mitchell of the 10th Battalion described what it was like having to make a short advance under fire and then lying in an exposed position on 400 Plateau:

A scramble, a rapid pounding of heavy boots and clattering of equipment, a startled yell and a crumpling body which has to be leaped over, a succession of slithering thuds, and we are down in the bushes forty yards ahead .... In this little advance Alec Gilpin has been fatally wounded in the stomach. All day he begged to be shot. We settled down to a necessary duel. The sharp smacking sound of an impacting bullet caused me to look around sharply. Alf Crowther gleefully showed me his cap which had a bullet hole drilled through in the brim. "Well you're not born to be shot", I said. But it was a rash prophecy. The men began to get hit, a terrible cry was wrenched from the bravest as the nickel demon ripped through flesh bone and sinew … [Nearby another] fired a few shots and again I heard the sickening thud of a bullet. I looked at him [Crowther] in horror. The bullet had fearfully smashed his face and gone down his throat rendering him dumb. But his eyes were dreadful to behold. And how he squirmed in his agony. There was nothing I could do for him but to pray that he might die swiftly. It took about twenty minutes to accomplish this, and by that time he had tangled his legs in mine and stiffened. I saw the waxy colour creep over his cheek and he breathed freer.[133]

Of the 1st Division's 12 Battalions, most were involved in fighting on the 400 Plateau and its surrounds. For most of the day, however, just two Battalions of Turks opposed them, 1st and 3rd Battalions (along with the remnants of the 2nd Battalion) of the 27th Regiment under Colonel Halil Sami Bey's 9th Ottoman Division. When their initial attacks were repulsed, the outnumbered Turks simply fired from the Third Ridge and Legge Valley at the Australians, who were constantly moving over the plateau. Private John Gordon of the 9th Battalion stated:

Their machine-guns never seemed to tire and they poured belt after belt into us. Occasionally I would have a few shots but we had no target to shoot at, and it was bringing trouble to those near one to make too much of a show.[134]

As standing up to dig was fatal, Private Cheney lay on his stomach and scratched a "molehill of earth" in front of him with his entrenching tool along with most others.

By about 1pm, the tide of the battle turned definitely in favour of the enemy, and by 2pm the Australians were gradually falling back to what was to become their permanent line until the August offensive on 400 Plateau. At this time the line, although established, was dangerously thin and in many places not continuous. Turks from the 1st Company of the 27th Regiment were already on the inland slopes of the Plateau, and were infiltrating forward, sniping at any movement they could see. Both the 2nd Brigade and most of the 3rd Brigade had been swallowed up into the line already, and elements of the 4th Brigade were now also starting to become committed to the fighting.

This line now snaked to the west of Johnston's Jolly on 400 Plateau. Very few of the Turks though reached the 400 Plateau, and those that did were swept off by fire nearly as deadly as their own had been.

Both Thomas and Boase's platoons continued to move slowly forward and inland until they were right above Legge Valley. Just beyond they could see Third Ridge where they saw Turks digging in along the Ridge. The Australians sniped at the Turks digging and also at the steady stream of Turkish soldiers advancing along the ridge toward Scrubby Knoll. Thomas ordered some of his men to climb down into Legge Valley, but they did not get far before they were met with a concentration of rifle and machine-gun fire, and many of these men were killed or wounded.

It was not long before both Thomas and Boase could see Turks advancing towards their isolated position. Both flanks were exposed and the Turkish advance threatened to cut them off. They agreed to withdraw in stages of about 50 metres with each platoon covering the retirement of the other. Thomas had sent a runner back to Major Brand to inform him of their withdrawal, ask for support and advise of the Turkish advance. This message was never received.

Of the men of the 9th Battalion that had earlier made the ill-fated advance and survived, about 50 men managed to link up with Thomas and began to take up positions just forward of the Cup.

One of the men that may have been part of this group was Corporal Frank Loud, 9th Battalion who was a 23 year old farmer from Mitchell, Queensland, who managed to survive the rest of the war:

> *On reaching shelter in the shape of an old trench, I followed it down and along another narrow communications trench I came upon a gun shelter ... ... I think it was built for about six guns. There was two field guns there in the shelter and another with a couple of dead horses alongside ... apparently the gun had been removed when our chaps advanced as there was a plentiful supply of shells in each funk–pit. There must have been about 60 of our lads in the trench also a machine-gun which was doing excellent work until put out of action by a shell.*[135]

The trench with the guns that Loud refers to were the same guns found by Corporal Harrison and his men as described previously, earlier in the morning of the first day.

Corporal Harrison at this time was forward and further to the south of Thomas and his men and could see them withdraw back towards the Plateau. Harrison and his remaining men were now also in great danger of being isolated and surrounded and were now well in front of the Australian lines.

Lieutenant Fortescue and his small group of men of the 9th that were earlier positioned at the head of Owens Gully had been forced down into the Valley due to the intensive shrapnel and machine-gun fire that was being directed at the Plateau. A Captain of the 8th Battalion ordered Fortescue and his men to move to the right across the southern part of the 400 Plateau to join the firing line of the 9th Battalion that was near Lonesome Pine. In doing so his men suffered a number of casualties before they met up with Lieutenant Costin, and a number of men from his machine-gun section. Costin indicated that he had no idea where the firing line was, but believed that a number of 9th Battalion men were now positioned in a gully to the left of him (the Cup). Fortescue and his surviving seven men joined up with Thomas, Boase and their remaining men. By this time the Turkish counterattack could be seen driving past their positions on the northern flank; the main attack seemed to be directed at Johnston's Jolly.

Salisbury and Milne of the 9th Battalion had also begun to withdrawn their men back towards Lonesome Pine. Milne, who had by this time been wounded five times, was ordered back to the rear area. Salisbury came across about 20 men from the 2nd Brigade in Brown's Dip and with these men moved back towards Costin's machine-guns and other men of the 9th Battalion. The bombardment of Turkish shrapnel that rained down on this position at this time was almost beyond endurance, and one by one Salisbury's officers and men around him started to be killed or wounded in the scrub. Salisbury's runners sent back for reinforcements did not get through and no other support was received except for other isolated parties on the Plateau searching for the firing line. Salisbury himself made three or four trips back to Brown's Dip to look for reinforcements, bringing with him small groups of men from the recently landed 2nd Brigade, which was now replacing the casualties of the 9th Battalion in the firing line.

Private Gordon of the 9th Battalion (who went on to join up with the Flying Corps in June 1917) wrote later:

I was lying next to a chap when he disappeared, having been struck by a percussion shell. How it missed me I don't know. Chaps were hit all sides and I was the only person alive out of a dozen either side of me.[136]

The question asked by many of the men was where were the Allied guns to suppress the Turkish shelling? The morale of the men on 400 Plateau was taking a real beating.

Sometime after 3.30pm, Thomas's shoulder was smashed by shrapnel and he was forced to leave the position under the command of an officer from the 2nd Brigade. (Fred Thomas was a 22 year old labourer, living in Milton, Brisbane, at the time of the war. He went on to survive the war and returned to Australia in 1918.)

Corporal Loud wrote in his diary:

We were there the whole afternoon under a hot fire coming from three directions. Several of our lads were killed around me and a few wounded. It was sickening to watch but one soon gets callous and takes no notice of wounds. One man on exposing himself to get a shot had his jaw shot away – you could see the bone hanging from the flesh. On someone calling him into the trench for shelter he coolly stooped down for his rifle and walked in, whilst another helping me drag a man hit in the shoulder into shelter, was hit in the back. On examination we found the bullet had only gone through the muscle on one side ... making a clean fresh wound while still another was hit in the cheek four teeth smashed and out the other side, without touching the jaw bone. Late in the afternoon some of the slightly wounded left us and made their way back to the main body to ask for reinforcements as we could not leave in a body.[137]

Lieutenant Boase and his men had already been forced to retire from their advanced positions towards the rear of the Plateau and back to the main firing line. (Allan Boase was 20 years old when he enlisted, his occupation is shown as a soldier and he lived in Caboolture. He had achieved the rank of a Major when he returned back to Australia in 1918.)

Meanwhile Corporal Harrison and his men were also being attacked by Turks further south and after having defended their position for most of the day, they were forced to retire to the Australian lines at the rear of 400 Plateau. (Percy Harrison was 23 when he enlisted and his occupation is shown as a fireman, living in North Lismore, NSW. He is shown to have returned to

Australia in October 1915, which was towards the end of the 9th Battalion's Gallipoli campaign, so we can assume that he may have been badly wounded or badly affected by disease or sickness that would not allow him to be recuperated and then returned to the front-lines again.)[138]

The main body of the 1st Division comprising the 1st and 2nd Brigades had been delayed in their landing, which was originally intended to be at 5.30am. This had been caused by the late arrival of the pinnaces back from landing the initial waves. The last of these Brigades, being the 1st, did not get fully ashore until 1.00pm. The two leading Battalions of the 2nd Brigade, 6th and the remainder of 7th Battalion that had not come ashore disastrously at Fisherman's Hut, landed around 6.00am. Frank Brent of the 6th Battalion wrote of boarding the landing boats from the ship *Galeka:*

> *We were all done up like sore toes with rifles, shovels, ammunition and packs. How we got down those rope ladders I just don't know, what with the nervousness and the excitement of not knowing what was in front of us. I just felt washed out. As I got into the boat there were about three chaps of the 9th Battalion who had been killed and they hadn't had time to lift them out so we had to walk gingerly over these blokes ... [on landing on the beach after coming under rifle and shrapnel fire] there were dead and wounded of the 3rd Brigade all around. We scampered as hard as we could to a little bit of shelter and dumped our packs, shovels and picks. We'd had enough of those. Then somebody said: "Well, up you go" and away we went up the slope.*[139]

As soon as the 2nd Brigade men were ashore, Sinclair-MacLagan ordered them to the right of the line instead of putting them, as per the original orders, to protect the left flank and to advance north. Sinclair-MacLagan was able to convince Colonel James McCay (2nd Brigade Commander) that the original plan could not be carried out and he must divert his entire Brigade to guard the right flank. He was concerned that if a Turkish counterattack came about from the direction of Gaba Tepe as was expected, and the Turkish forces being in larger numbers, the remainder of his 3rd Brigade on the right would not hold. McCay was recorded as saying "It is a bit stiff to disobey orders first thing", but reluctantly he accepted.

With over 1000 men on a 600 yard frontage along the Second Ridge and the 7th Battalion arriving, they were in loose touch.

The wounded who managed to be evacuated faced grim prospects. Hospital ships were limited and the only one stationed off Anzac Cove was the *Gascon,* which was available to take up to 300 serious cases. In addition, there were another two transports (*Clan MacGillivray* and the *Seang Choon*) with rudimentary equipment available, but they were only suitable to help lightly wounded men. Within hours of the landings the *Gascon* had become full of wounded and dying men and so too the two other transports. On one of these transports there were three doctors attending 659 badly wounded men. Medic Peter Hall indicated that many of the wounded men sat all night unable to speak, but with awful appeal in their eyes imploring you to bring a doctor to see them. Smaller boats and lighters went from ship to ship with their bloodied cargoes trying to hawk wounded on to the larger ships.

Being shelled by the Turks with impunity (the only Allied battery, which landed at 10.30am and engaged Gun Ridge, was almost annihilated and soon after had to retire) increased the stress already felt by men who were mostly fighting leaderless in small groups and unaware, because of the scrub, of what was happening to their mates often only six feet away. There was certainly a lack of artillery. Although some 26 of the available 36 Australian field guns were landed, most had been re–embarked because no suitable gun positions could be found for them and coupled with the concern that they may be captured, decisions were made to hold them back from the action. Fire support from the warships anchored offshore during this first day was of limited effect against scattered enemy troops in broken cover and due to the fact that Australian soldiers were for most of the morning scattered across the battlefield.

Understandably, some wavering of the men started, especially on the 400 Plateau where the fire was heavier than elsewhere. Unwounded men started trickling back from about 1pm towards the beach. Bean thought that by nightfall there may have been 600 to a 1000 stragglers on the beach. Most sought instructions and returned to the front-line, some helped with the wounded to get some reprieve before moving back to the front. The weaker sort, Bean indicated, would skivy off to safe dugouts.[140] Captain Gellibrand of the 1st Division's staff said afterwards that the number of men that retired from action altogether was negligible. This I believe would have been the case given the general character of the men at that time. To be seen as a coward was a label to be avoided at all costs, and most wanted nothing more than some direction and leadership so that they could return to their units after being separated for most of the day. Of the 9th Battalion specifically, there were about 200 men collected and returned back to the front-line from the beach.[141]

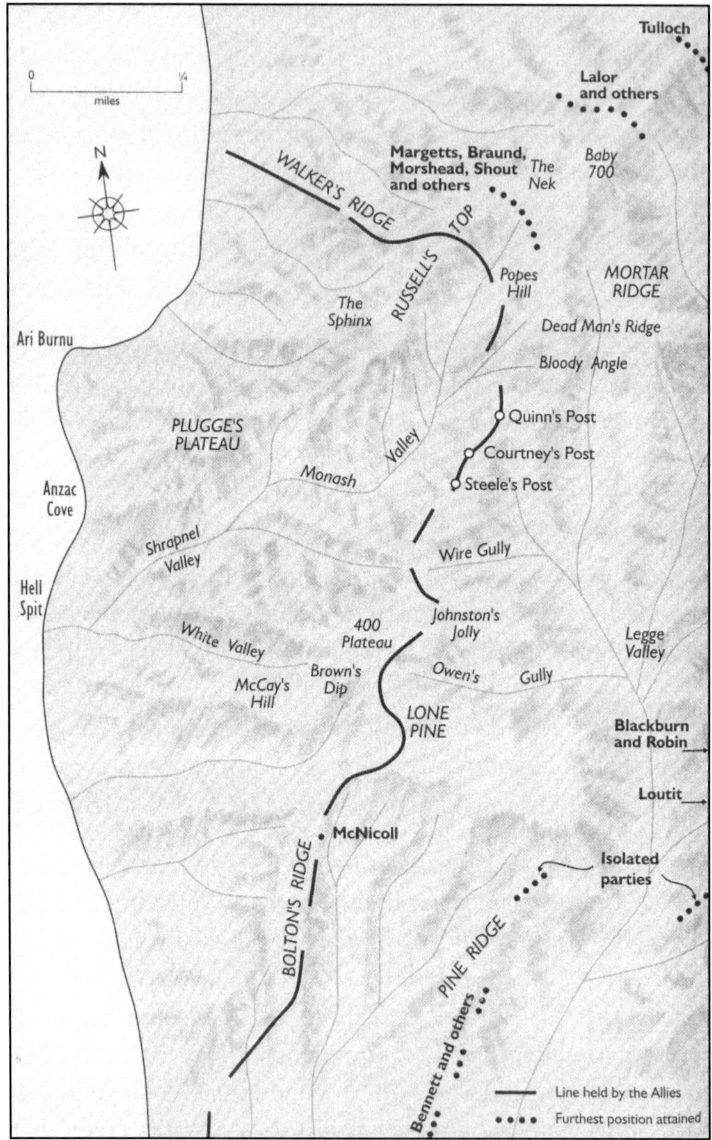

The Anzac positions at the end of the first day's fighting. (Carlyon)

Private R.G. Hamilton was with the first wave of the 9th Battalion and was wounded on the first day, although he was lucky enough to have been evacuated that same day. He describes his brief stay at Gallipoli in a letter to his family:

> *Just a line to let you know that I am still numbered among the living ... I will try to give you an idea about our landing though I don't suppose it will interest you much but you see I have nothing else to write about ... . When we got ashore we fixed bayonets and charged their first line of trenches, but they would not stay and cleared back to their main body which was about two miles away and we only got a few. After a short respite of about half an hour they opened fire again, also their artillery and land batteries and our gunboats, talk about an inferno, well I'm deaf yet from it, then shrapnel fell around us like hailstones, however we kept at it all day fighting against fearful odds but being continually reinforced, thereby holding the ground we had gained during the early part of the day, but at an awful costs that you will see when the casualty list come out.*
>
> *I am glad to say ... I was in the firing line all day with the exception of a half an hour when I helped one of our wounded officers back to the dressing station. It was terrible to see your comrades shot down around you, shattered to pieces with shells and shrapnel others shot or wounded ... with bullets. I had some very narrow escapes, once while digging a small embankment in front of me with my entrenching tool a machine-gun turned on to me, I had the tool in front of my head and four or five bullets hit it in less than a second, but one missed and hit my puttee leaving a hole ... and only grazed the skin, the machine-gun then shifted to the next man and shot him instantly.*
>
> *It was very late that evening when I did get hit .... We lined the top of a ridge and was told to hold it at all cost, the hail of bullets that were fired at us was terrific, another machine-gun found me but I was behind a small bush, it stripped all the leaves off the bush and caught me in the foot smashing the bone and going right through the bottom of my boot, I had to go back then and was eventually sent on to the boat at about eleven o'clock that night. Well, I won't tire you with anymore news right now, you will be bored before you get half through this, and there is no other news to tell you.*[142]

I find it amazing that he could have believed anyone at home could have thought that Private Hamilton's letter would be even remotely boring, especially given that it described how he had cheated death and that he had been wounded. I am sure that they would have been on the edge of their seats worried about what he would say in the next paragraph and what his condition was. But again in the true style of that time, he did not want to make a fuss about himself or what he was doing, in fact he writes as if it is all in a good day's work!

Barges evacuating wounded from Anzac, while those able to stand or sit leave on the steam launch *Keraunos*. The number of wounded swamped both the evacuation and medical plans. (Alexander Turnbull Library, Wellington New Zealand – F–8784–1/4)

Robert Hamilton went on to to bigger and greater honours as a soldier. He attained the rank of Lieutenant and was awarded the Military Cross during action with the 9th Battalion at Meteren in July 1918 having rushed a German post and captured a number of Germans and a machine-gun. When his Company Commander was wounded he took charge and led the men through the remainder of the operation. He returned to Australia in October 1918.[143]

By 6pm, the 4th Brigade had started landing and moved up to positions from Pope's Hill right down to Second Ridge and 400 Plateau, which helped to fill the gaps that had emerged during the day.

Most of the troops in the line, such as the 9th Battalion, had been digging in for hours. At sunset, the Turkish artillery ceased and the infantry rifle fire became inaccurate. Able to move about, the men quickly got below ground even as the Turks continued to attack. Given away in the darkness by cries of "Allah! Mohammed!", fierce Turkish assaults on Walker's and Bolton's Ridges were halted with significant Turkish casualties by the Australian soldiers.

The beach at dusk on the 25th April, 1915 looking north to Ari Burnu. A wounded Australian lies in the foreground, while medics wearing Red Cross armbands tend other casualties. (AWM PS1659)

From 7pm, the first talk of a possible evacuation started to be discussed. Some of the senior staff officers were demanding immediate re–embarkation. Birdwood was less certain. He reported to Hamilton at 8.45pm that the position was not very satisfactory, the country was difficult and the shelling and casualties were severe. Moreover, some of Hamilton's subordinates were far more negative and were painting a worse picture of the scenario. Roused from a deep sleep, Hamilton read Birdwood's message. Bouyed by the news that the *AE2* had penetrated the Narrows and sunk a Turkish ship, Hamilton encouraged Birdwood in a reply that enjoined him to appeal to his men for a supreme effort to hold on. "You have got through the difficult business, now you have only to dig, dig, dig until you are safe". It is interesting to note that at that time, the Anzac forces that had landed still outnumbered the Turkish troops almost two to one. There were approximately 15000 Anzacs ashore compared to about 8000 Turkish troops. The big difference was that the Turks still were in control of the high ground.

Those Anzac soldiers who were not wounded were organised into carrying parties to take ammunition and water upto the front-line, while the wounded were cared for as best possible on the beach. Morale was taking a dive among the exhausted men and it began to get cold, with a steady, drizzling rain falling across the battlefield, adding to the misery of the men, especially those men lying wounded awaiting attention. For these wounded men, assistance was unlikely for some time, if it came at all.

All they could do was to hold on and wait for the British advance from Helles, although most feared that an all-out Turkish counterattack would occur at any moment. One soldier wrote:

> *There was no rest, no lull, while the rotting dead lay all around us, never a pause in the whole of that long day that started at the crack of dawn. How we longed for nightfall! How we prayed for this ghastly day to end! How we yearned for the sight of the first dark shadow.*[144]

By 3am on 26th April, more than 1700 casualties had been evacuated from the beach south of Ari Burna, now known as Anzac Cove. The 9th Battalion's Medical Officer, Captain Butler, describes the 25th April as "stretcher bearers day". For his own actions that day and his special service to the wounded, Butler was awarded the Distinguished Service Order (DSO) and his actions are best described by an article in the *Canberra Times* written by an unnamed soldier:

> *One can see him clearly during that famous landing, from the time that he stepped out on the beach dressed like a veritable Christmas tree ... until several days afterwards when he was on the point of collapse from sheer exhaustion. His energy, bravery and devotion to duty were an inspiration to all with whom he made contact during those anxious days. After a diligent search by some of the officers, he was located in a possie in Shrapnel Gully, still carrying on his good work, having had no rest and little to eat or drink during this period.*[145]

Private Young of the 9th Battalion states that:

All through the night the awful din continued. Water was scarce, wounded and dying men were all around us, and our rifle barrels grew red–hot with the continuous firing.[146]

Corporal Frederic Scrivener, being a stretcher bearer, was in great demand that first day and over the next few days with the high number of casualties that were being sustained. He was also in constant danger and many stretcher bearers were becoming casualties themselves from sniper and shrapnel fire, trying to reach wounded men and moving up and down the supply routes bringing their cargoes of wounded and dying men back to the aid posts. A New Zealand Colonel, Fred Waite, noted that the stretcher bearers were very brave and stated that a man without a load could dash for cover, however, the stretcher bearers with their human loads had to walk steadily on, ignoring sniper and hostile gunners.[147] From the front-line it took about two and a half hours to get a patient to the makeshift hospital on the beach.

Private Fred Symonds, a stretcher bearer with the 5th Battalion, wrote:

The stretcher bearers are absolutely unable to cope with the casualties; some of the wounded have been lying out for 24 hours, and may be here for another 24 hours by the look of things ... Went on stretcher bearing this afternoon; a cry came up for spare men to volunteer, as a whole line of men had been enfiladed by an enemy machine-gun, and were lying under fire. It was frightful work getting the poor fellows down those hills; it took five men in some cases to get one wounded man out, and a lot of bearers are being shot; we have lost 10 out of 40 already.[148]

Frederic's work over the next few days was noticed and added to a list of men "having performed various acts of conspicuous gallantry or valuable service during the period 25th April to 5th May, 1915". While he was not decorated on this occasion, possibly because there were so many men doing much the same in those first few days, his recommendation reads:

While under heavy artillery fire, Sergeant Scrivener bandaged and carried in wounded men. In one case he had to double across a considerable distance under heavy fire to get assistance from a medical officer for one of his comrades.[149]

Throughout the first day and then indeed over the next few weeks, the Turkish sniper ruled the Anzac area. Nowhere was safe, and in some cases there were accounts of Turks dressing in Australian uniforms in order to ply their trade. In all the confusion of the first few days, the Turkish snipers took full advantage of the landscape, which formed the perfect arena for the sniper. The Anzac area in many places became almost an amphitheatre for Turkish snipers operating from the high ground, observing the movements along the supply routes of the Anzac troops. On the first day there were many men killed by hidden gunmen, waiting for an Australian to come along a chosen route, sometimes firing from well behind the Australians' line of advance. Given the thickness of the scrub, the Turkish snipers were very hard to locate and had considerable success in creating confusion, casualties, fear and slowing progress throughout the first day. Once a sniper was located, however, they were rarely given any quarter. Even though offering to surrender, the Australians were quick to shoot or bayonet the Turkish sniper.

The Turkish snipers were in many cases well prepared with food, ammunition and were often well camouflaged, constantly assessing their position for exposure and moving around when they thought their position had been compromised. Often they took up positions where they could observe and snipe at men moving supplies or moving up to the front in long lines. One of the early favoured routes was Shrapnel Valley, which became one of the main supply and troop access routes from the beach landing site up to the front-line at Quinn's, Courtney's and Steele's Posts. The valley ran along a dry creek bed up, starting from just south of Hell Spit and winding up between MacLagan's Ridge and Razorback Ridge up towards Second Ridge where it became known as Monash Valley. For the Australians, Shrapnel Valley was to be known as the Valley of the Shadow of Death. The Turks named it Kuruke Dere, or the Valley of Fear.[150] The Turkish snipers were especially active in the morning when the sun was behind them, and it became common for 20 or 30 men to be hit by sniper fire each morning in the Valley.

There was no official Anzac action to negate the sniper threat for several weeks until trenches and dug–outs had been completed and sandbag walls constructed, especially along Shrapnel Valley. Engineers worked hard to build high sandbag barriers five feet thick at intervals along the Valley route, placed alternatively on the left and right sides of the roadway, with rough signs painted with words or arrows to indicate the best route between the sandbag island shelters.

However, the most effective response was a group of volunteer Anzac snipers who started to take the fight back to the Turks and began going out at night to hunt enemy sharpshooters who were observed in an area during the day. As Ashmead–Bartlett stated, "it became necessary to hunt out and kill off these pests one by one." Then after a few weeks, specific groups of Anzac marksmen were identified by a New Zealand officer, Major William Malone, and by Colonel Harry Chauvel of the first Australian Light Horse Brigade, and given the task of forming sniper parties, tasked with reducing and removing the stranglehold that had been created by the Turkish snipers. From this point on, the threat of sniper casualties, especially on the supply routes, was sufficiently reduced and the Anzac snipers began to take the initiative away from the Turks. Men like Private Billy Sing, a Queenslander who enlisted as part of the 5th Light Horse Regiment. Billy Sing, known as "The Assassin", became a legend among the Anzac troops fighting at Gallipoli and he was formally accredited with 201 confirmed Turkish kills. The real number, however, was probably many more.[151]

The consequence of a sniper's bullet finding its mark could be best described as being both sudden and horrible. A diary entry by Trooper Jack Idriess, 5th Light Horse Regiment, highlights this fact:

> *A man was shot dead in front of me. He was a little infantry lad, quite a boy, with snowy hair that looked comical above his clean white singlet. I was going for water. He stepped out of a dugout and walked down the path ahead, whistling. I was puffing the old pipe while carrying a dozen water bottles. Just as we were crossing Shrapnel Gully he suddenly flung up his water bottles, wheeled around, and stared for one startled second, even as he crumpled to my feet. In seconds his hair was scarlet, his clean white singlet all crimson.*[152]

Dawn came on the 26th April, the sky had cleared and the sun rose and revealed the battle scars across the beachhead. Digging across all areas of the front-line trench positions and reserve areas was continuing in earnest by both Turk and Australian alike, each trying to take some advantage and strengthen their defensive positions and filling gaps in the line. Most importantly, the expected Turkish counterattack which was to happen on the following day, did not take place. Both sides had by the second day fought themselves to a virtual standstill.

The anxiety in the aftermath of the landing was greater than at any other time during the campaign. Kemal had to drive the Anzac forces into the sea before they became established; the Anzacs had to establish themselves before the Turkish onslaught fell. On the 26th April their task became easier. Naval gunfire knocked out some of the Turkish guns and Ottoman losses and exhaustion precluded the expected counterattack. Only "accidental collisions or attempts by a local commander to gain some particular vantage point" took place that day.[153]

On Monday, 26th April, Lance Corporal Neal's luck runs out:

Queen Elizabeth shelling enemy over our heads. Enemy shell the ridge on which I was entrenched. Received a shrapnel wound in the backside about midday. Crawled some distance then helped by two comrades who took me to the Red Cross. Conveyed to beach and sent to Alexandria per a German liner.[154]

Private Young informs us through his diary entries that:

On Tuesday afternoon the enemy renewed attack with vigor, and things looked very black for us. We had been without sleep for nearly sixty hours and the water was all gone. We felt the end was near and many of us shook hands as we thought, for the last time. There was no word of retiring, we were resolved to die where we stood. All this time we were pouring a rapid fire into the advancing Turks. Fate was on our side; the Turks faltered, and then fell back. Had they known what a thin line held the trenches it would have been good–bye for all of us.[155]

On Tuesday 27th April, the Turks launched an all–out counterattack against the Anzac perimeter in what could be described as the climax to the battle of the landing. However, dispersed by the broken terrain, the fresh regiments had arrived late and the Turkish soldiers who were already in the line were tired and demoralised, and the push degenerated into disjointed assaults devoid of any punch. The counterattack by the Turks had been a failure. Those Turkish soldiers that got close to the Anzac trenches were driven off at very high cost. The naval fire throughout the day had been devastating on the Turks, and from then on they always tried to avoid attacking in daylight, especially where the ground was exposed to naval fire.

Private Young again:

On Wednesday we managed to move some of the wounded to the beach, but it was risky work for the stretcher bearers and many of them fell beside their stretchers as they tried to cross the beach towards the hospital ship. In the afternoon, word came that the Australians were to be relieved and never a message was more welcome. About two o'clock on Thursday morning a large force of British marines took our places. Staggering with weariness, some crawling on hands and knees, others unable to move without assistance of their mates, we reached the beach, threw ourselves down and slept for hours.[156]

After four days of nonstop fighting, the Anzacs were physically spent. Many had only two decent meals, and most men had no sleep since landing and their nerves were frayed from the constant blasts of exploding shells. Relief for these men was essential.

Lieutenant C.F. Ross of the 9th Battalion indicates in his diary on the 29th April:

Now the fifth day of hell and the loss of sleep and the continual rattle of guns and rifles is very nerve racking. Marines are taking the place of our men who are getting a little spell.

On the 30th April he writes that:

The marines relieve our party and we leave to look for the 9th, arriving back in the afternoon and go on to the beach for a rest. Young Payne of A company is killed by a shot from the mountain battery.[157]

On the 1st of May, Lieutenant Ross developed very bad dysentery and is ordered off to Alexandria in the evening. "Some shrapnel flying about on the jetty and one of the bearers is wounded while putting me aboard the boat. There are about 300 sick and wounded aboard." He indicates that "he is sorry to leave the "scrap" and won't feel satisfied till we get back".[158] While in hospital recuperating, his diary entries indicate that he is constantly looking for other Queenslanders and every day he expresses a desire to get back to his men at the front. He remained in Alexandria until mid June 1915 when he was returned to Gallipoli. Lieutenant Ross survived the war and ended up as the last Commanding Officer of the 9th Battalion.

On Wednesday, April 28th, the 3rd Brigade had been ordered into reserve at the southern end of the beach, and its members who were still in the trenches were gradually relieved. They made dugouts for themselves near a spot where the first dead were buried. This place, which afterwards became quite a large cemetery, was in a dangerous spot, at the entrance to Shrapnel Gully, near a turning known as Hell Fire Corner. On Wednesday 28th, as more men came in, another reorganisation of the 3rd Brigade was made on the beach. By this time the men were bearded and their uniforms ragged. Even though ordered to the rear in reserve due to their condition, the men of the 9th were still called on from time to time to return to the front-line to assist. One example of this was when a post manned by some of the relieving British marines was lost to the enemy and they began to fall back. Parties from the 3rd Brigade had to return to the line to push the Turks back. On one occasion Captain Dougall, with Lieutenants Fortescue and Ross and 100 men of the 9th Battalion, were sent back to MacLaurin's Hill. Most returned to the beach the next morning, but 20 under Ross had a longer stay in the front-line.

At the landing, the 9th Battalion lost heavily. It is not possible for any precise figure to be given, for it was not until the 3rd Brigade had been recalled to the beach in reserve on the 27th and 28th April that any assembly or roll call had taken place. The parade state of the 9th Battalion at 9am on Saturday, 30th April, just above Victoria Valley, shows there were 10 Officers and 419 other ranks. The total casualties up to noon that day were 19 officers and 496 other ranks. These were the heaviest casualties of any Battalion, with the exception of the 7th Battalion at the Anzac landing, the 7th having received a further 26 casualties, up to that time. The 7th Battalion lost a large number of men on the way into the beaches off Fisherman's Hut in their landing boats before even setting foot on the peninsula.

In terms of officers, the 9th Battalion was seriously handicapped from the outset, losing the three senior officers i.e. Commanding Officer Lieutenant Colonel Lee (shot in the hand on the first day and then spraining an ankle while making his way down to the beach for roll call – see also appendix 1), the second-in-charge Major J.C. Robertson, had received a bullet wound to the chest on the landing and was evacuated, and the Senior Company Commander, Major Sydney B. Robertson, was killed in action on the first day. Sydney Robertson, who was 29 when he landed at Gallipoli with the 9th Battalion, was a law student and worked as a lawyer's clerk, living in Ipswich, Queensland (although born in Sydney). Robertson was killed close to Baby 700 central Anzac on 25th April while rising from behind the cover of shrubs where he and the remnants of his small group were taking refuge. This was during the heavy firing from the Nek brought upon them by Mustafa Kemal's 57th Regiment, that had pushed the Australians back from Battleship Hill and Baby 700. Kemal had identified early that it was imperative to hold the high ground in the Anzac theatre and therefore crucial to stop the threat posed by the Australians who were advancing up the ridge towards Chunuk

Bair. It was at this point that Kemal had ordered his troops in the now famous manner:

> *I do not order you to attack; I order you to die. In the time that it passes until we die other troops and commanders will take our places.*

Initially it seemed strange that Major Robertson was killed so far away from the rest of the Battalion, however, he had been separated from the 9th Battalion along with a few of his men after his boat had drifted further north than the others and had beached itself somewhere near the Sphinx. Robertson had then joined up with Captain Lalor of the 12th Battalion. They had then dug in just short of the Nek. One of the 9th Battalion's scouts, 29 year old Sergeant Frederic Coe, returning from the direction of Baby 700 with a number of Captain Tulloch's scouts found Robertson and some of Lalor's men at the Nek sitting down smoking and eating as if on a picnic. "Good god, sir," he said to Major Robertson, "aren't you preparing for the counterattack?" Stunned Robertson replied, "What counterattack?" and told him that the Turks were coming on in their thousands. Robertson said, "I did not dream that they'd come back". As predicted, the Turkish troops arrived at the Nek before the line was set and Robertson and his men were hurled back, while a Turkish mountain battery on Scrubby Knoll drenched the Nek area with shrapnel.

There was a lack of leadership because of the fact that there were 19 officers listed as casualties from the 9th Battalion by the 30th April, 1915. This would have been a key factor why the 9th Battalion and other Battalions of the 3rd Brigade were in so much confusion throughout the first day. Across the 3rd Brigade, the total officers listed as casualties by the fifth day of fighting were 62. The 9th Battalion had approximately 29 officers, assuming that the other three Battalions had much the same in number then overall casualty rates among officers of the 3rd Brigade after five days of battle was approximately 53 per cent, slightly more than one in two. One reason for this high casualty rate may have been due to the bravado of the officers and their need to lead by example, to the point where they took non-essential risks. As one soldier from the 10th Battalion noted, all our officers were recklessly brave. Most men crouched to minimise the size of the target on the way into shore in the boats, however, most of the officers sat upright and some were killed or wounded. Another soldier describes their actions as "reckless abandon". The loss of so many officers early in the action would certainly have reduced the Brigade's usefulness in larger scale operations over the following weeks after the landing. Until suitable officers could be brought in to replace the officers lost or wounded officers following recuperation made their way back into the Battalion. For some of the men it also meant an opportunity for them to be promoted in the field.

Captain Alfred Salisbury's A company of the 9*th* Battalion suffered in particular on the first day, through the loss of a number of officers who were fighting around Brown's Dip and the Cup on 400 Plateau after the mad run from the beach. Bean noted that:

> *The fire upon the crest of Lone Pine was now almost beyond endurance… … one after another of Salisbury's officers fell. Captain Alexander Melbourne [Qld University lecturer aged 26] was badly wounded in the head, Lieutenant Chambers was hit [draftsman from New Farm, Brisbane, who would go on to the Western Front battlefields only to be killed in action in August 1916] and some distance from them Lieutenant Joseph Costin, bravely holding his isolated position on the crest, was killed by a shell that destroyed one of his machine-guns.*[159]

Many of the officers wounded or killed fighting on 400 Plateau were hit because they had to keep standing up to try and see where their men were.

The one man I was most interested in from this party was Joseph Costin, mentioned by Bean above, who is listed as being born in 1891 in Graceville, Brisbane, the same suburb that I grew up in and know very well. He went to Brisbane Grammar School and was an electrical engineer working in Paddington, Brisbane at the time war broke out. He enlisted in the 9th Battalion when he was 23 and sailed on the SS *Omrah*. During the first days of fighting by the 9th Battalion on 400 Plateau, Lieutenant Costin displayed greats acts of courage as outlined below by Private James Millar (9th Battalion, 23 year old labourer from East Brisbane who went on and survived the war and ended with the rank of Captain and had been mentioned in dispatches for action at Pozieres in August 1916):

> *At about 12 O'Clock, I came across the Queensland Machine-gun section of the 9th Battalion. They were putting up a magnificent fight, and drawing fire of guns and machine-guns on to themselves all morning. There were only Bob Luckett and Lieutenant Costin left in the section when I joined it, and if ever two men deserved the DSO then those two did. Luckett was alone working the gun, and Lieutenant Costin was range–finding for him, and keeping up the supply of ammunition. I saw Luckett knock over 50*

or 60 Turks at 1400 yards in one "bang" so Costin must have got him the exact range. Then Luckett was wounded in the leg, and Costin took the gun himself until he was wounded. [In actual fact, Lieutenant Costin had been killed at that time][160]

Corporal Bob (Joseph) Luckett never recovered from being wounded and later died of his wounds sustained that day at sea on the 2nd July, 1915. He was a blacksmith, born in Grafton, but enlisted with the 9th Battalion at Enoggera, Brisbane.

Lieutenant Joseph William Costin (AWM P08743.001)

When Costin fell, his Sergeant at the time, Alexander Steele, continued to fire the machine-gun and then carried the only remaining gun to Lieutenant Frank Haymen's party in their gun pit. Steele was awarded the Distinguished Conduct Medal for his actions that day and was promoted to 2nd Lieutenant at Gaba Tepe on 28th April, 1915. Steele (born in Mt Gambier, SA, enlisted in the 9th Battalion at Enoggera and was posted at that time to the Battalion's machine-gun section under Costin) was wounded in action not long after on 19 May, 1915 and evacuated to hospital in Egypt. He rejoined the Battalion on 9th August, 1915 and was again wounded on 31st August, 1915 and evacuated to Helopolis. He rejoined the Battalion in Lemnos when it had been withdrawn for rest on 9th December, 1915. He was killed in action on 7th October, 1917 while with the 11th Battalion, having been made second-in-charge of the Battalion and rising to the rank of Major, at Ypres on the Western Front.[161]

The other officer involved in this action was Lieutenant Frank Haymen of the 9th Battalion (born in Toowoomba, the 23 year old surveyor was still studying at Queensland University at the time he enlisted and lived in Kangaroo Point, Brisbane) whose men were in a nearby gun pit when Sergeant Steele joined them. Haymen was killed later that day at the Cup which was on the Lone Pine Plateau just inland from the 400 Plateau. Like the other men mentioned above, they were part of the advanced covering party who were isolated on the lip of Lone Pine, 300 yards ahead of where the rest of the 3rd Brigade were digging in on 400 Plateau.

The 9th Battalion machine-gun section lost over 80 per cent of its personnel at the end of the first day, most on or around 400 Plateau.

Sergeant Alex Steele, in a letter back home to his mother, describes some of the fighting he was involved in on 25th April, especially the action that afternoon at the Cup;

> *The section, or what is left of them, get into action but we soon lose 13 out of our fifteen, three of whom are killed, and so I have to get into a Turkish trench among some field guns we captured and start to use a rifle. We stuck there all day and I got three or four Turks off my rifle at ranges under 600 yards. One man spotted with a telescope while I dropped 'em. They attacked us heavily at dusk and I got two more at 200 yards, we then got orders to fall back to the main line which was fairly well entrenched by this time. We were nearly a mile ahead of this line and were in great danger of being cut–off …… I covered the retirement and collection of wounded and must have got many Turks as I didn't spare the ammunition and they were very close. We took nearly three hours to fall back to the main line so you see Mr. Turk didn't hurry us.*[162]

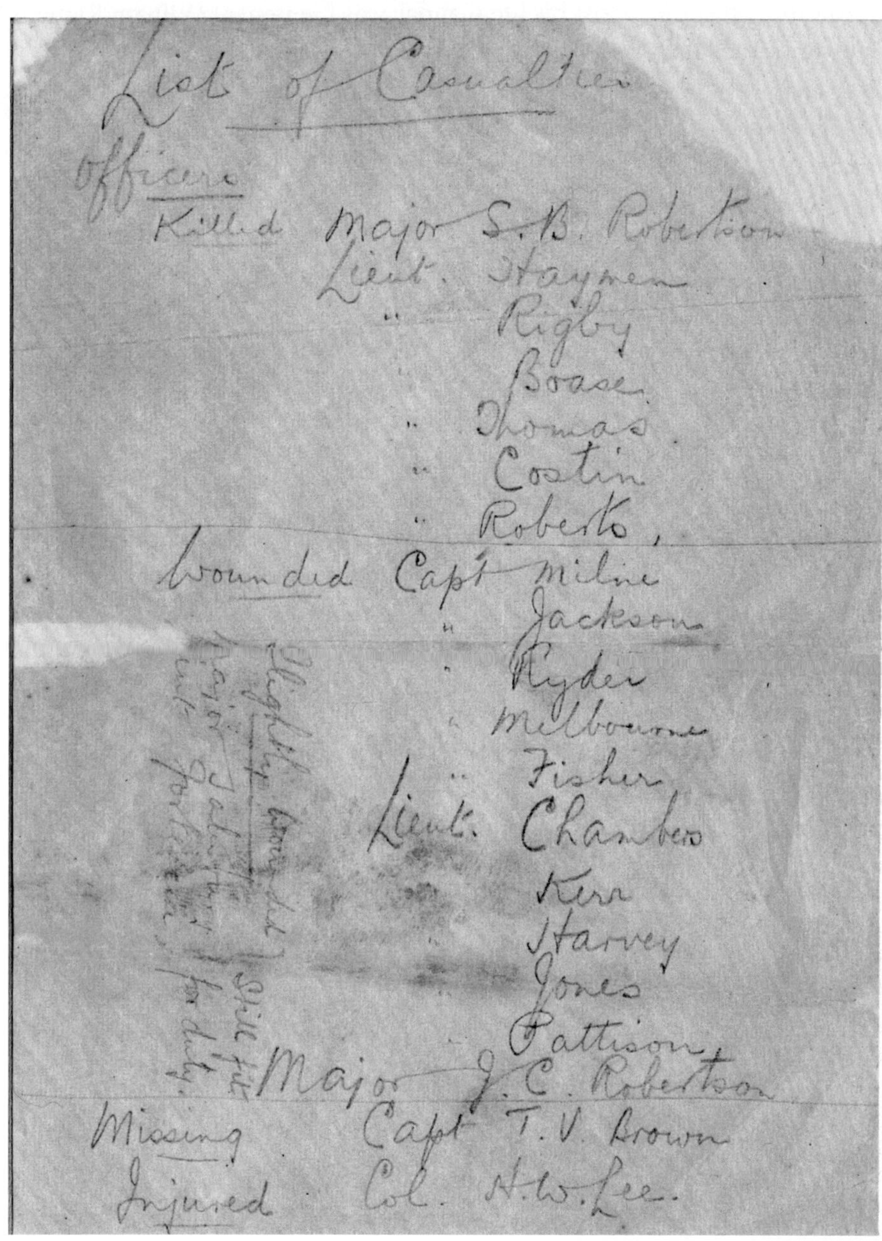

List of Casualties

Officers

Killed Major S.B. Robertson
Lieut. Haymen
" Rigby
" Boase
" Thomas
" Costin
" Roberts

Wounded Capt Milne
" Jackson
" Ryder
" Melbourne
" Fisher
Lieut. Chambers
Kerr
Harvey
Jones
Pattison
Major J.C. Robertson

Slightly wounded
Still fit for duty

Missing Capt T.V. Brown

Injured Col. H.W. Lee

A portion of the casualty list sent by the signal officer to the medical officer during the first few days at Anzac. Lieutenants Boase and Thomas had been wounded, but not killed as the list indicates. (John Oxley Library, State Library of Queensland, Australia).

Another officer who lost his life that day was Lieutenant William Rigby B Company, 9th Battalion (a 22 year old insurance clerk who lived in Yeronga, Brisbane), who was killed at Baby 700, part of the small group of 9th Battalion men who were with Major Robertson fighting on the left flank. The Lieutenant had been ordered to "carry on" by Major Robertson just before he died while rising from the cover of scrub. Moments later, moving forward, Rigby was also killed.

Of the 496 other ranks of the 9th Battalion, just under half were listed as missing. It was noted some of these men were found to have been wounded and taken to the hospital ships without notification reaching the unit. Many others were killed in action and their bodies not yet recovered at the time of the roll call. Given the rush forward on the first day and the subsequent fall-back, many casualties had to be left behind. Many bodies of Australians killed on the first day would not be recovered for the entire campaign. The fact that many wounded had been evacuated without notification reaching unit headquarters was understandable, given the low number of officers and the confusion that occurred in the first few days.

Almost one in two of the troops of the 3rd Brigade were casualties in the first three days of fighting at Gallipoli. Roughly 2000 Australians died in the first day's assaults. A large proportion of them would have come from the ranks of this Brigade.

Private Young indicates that:

On the Friday we had a muster and the roll was called. The diminished numbers of the 9th were enough to sadden the stoutest heart. Stragglers who came in from time to time were greeted with cheers and hearty handshakes.[163]

Private Grant of the 1st Battalion states that the men stood glassy eyed in ragged rows while the officers called the roll:

This was the most touching sight I ever witnessed. Everybody was congratulating everybody else on their good fortune to escape injury or death.[164]

Lieutenant Margetts wrote after the 12th Battalion gathered that, "We were all surprised to see each other." All too often at the roll calls, which occurred for each of the 3rd Brigade Battalions as they were removed from the front-line trenches into the reserve areas, men found that mates they had hoped to see again were absent.

The first hospital ship to evacuate wounded from Anzac was the *Gascon* and it reached Alexandria, Egypt on the 29th April, 1915. Of the 548 casualties it carried on board, 14 died on the voyage, which took one and a half days. The casualties aboard from Gallipoli were taken to the No.1 Australian General Hospital, at Heliopolis in Cairo. Sister Constance Keys, of the Australian Army Nursing Service, who sailed with the men of the 9th Battalion on the SS *Omrah* wrote;

> *I don't know if the news is known in Queensland yet but the greatest number of men we came over with are either killed or wounded. The whole Battalion (sic 9th) was practically cut to pieces. The hospital train came in right behind the Palace – nine long carriages painted white with the Egyptian Star and Crescent on the side.*

The first roll call of the 9th Battalion above Victoria Gulley, a few days after the landing. (AWM J06121)

For Lance Corporal Neal, who had been wounded on the 26th April, he sailed from Port Suez with about 750 wounded men bound for Australia on 15th August. He states that they reached Fremantle, Western Australia on September 3rd:

> *Boys received great reception. Anchored out from wharf to disembark WA wounded. Sailed Saturday about 4pm. Reached Melbourne on 10th*

September, great reception for the boys. Left Sunday from No. 6 dock Melbourne. Passed Wilson's Prom. 6.30pm.[165]

While the attack at Gallipoli Peninsula by the Anzac forces in the first few days did not meet the objectives set as had been planned and was certainly an unimaginable tragedy, it was by no means a failure as some historians have indicated.

One significant reason why the original strategy was not carried through successfully in the first few days of the campaign was the lack of time for proper preparation and planning. This lead to, among other things, a limited understanding by Hamilton and his staff officers of the difficult terrain the men would have to deal with in order to achieve their objectives.

Hamilton and his aides had very little time to enlist the help of experts to provide advice in regard to even some of the more basic needs of an army, such as the provision of resources like fresh water and the nature of the ground conditions. For example, while it was essential in the plans for the infantry to be supported by artillery pieces during the attack, it was certainly not properly understood whether artillery could be brought up from the beaches into effective positions around the Anzac area. It was rumored that a lot of the information they were able to gather and read about the Gallipoli Peninsula was sourced from shops in Egypt, in particular a 1905 handbook of Turkey.[166]

In regard to understanding the terrain, there was not even a good map of the peninsula available to the officers who would be leading the men at the time of landing. A map of the Gallipoli area was provided to Hamilton during his briefings in England before leaving for the campaign, however, it proved very inaccurate. While some reconnaissance was made from naval ships traveling along the coast prior to the landings, Alan Moorehead in his book *Gallipoli* explains that, "none of these measures succeeded in conveying any real idea of the difficulties of the country, and the maps which were supplied to the officers were incomplete, if not downright inaccurate ... the Kaba Tepe region, where the Anzac troops were to land, was unmapped and almost wholly unknown". The first accurate map of the Anzac area was obtained about four weeks after the landings from the body of a Turkish officer killed during the 19th May attacks along the Anzac front-line. Bean also noted in his writings that this map was used together with others captured at the Cape Helles battlefield to compile a good map, which was subsequently issued to all Allied forces. Even with a good map it would have been very difficult to direct troop movements around the Anzac area given the topography of high ridges, the winding maze of valleys and steep cliffs. It was very easy for individuals and even larger groups of men to become hopelessly disorientated and confused. This was particularly the case during the first week before tracks and paths were cleared through the thick brush and signposts were erected.

In addition, the inability to keep the proposed operations from the enemy beforehand meant that to some degree, the element of surprise had been lost many weeks prior to the landings taking place. This was a critical point in ensuring that it was difficult for the Turkish/German command to determine the numbers of Allied troops involved, when the landings were to take place and therefore where to establish defensive positions to repel the invasion forces. The intentions of the Allies had been well advertised by the naval attacks on the Dardanelles in February and March 1915, which had been accompanied by a number of small-scale landings of men attacking a number of gun emplacements. There was also a sudden mass purchase of small boats in most ports throughout the Mediterranean, a significant buildup of troops in Egypt and then the relocation of troops on to the islands such at Lemnos off the Turkish coast. Certainly the grand armada of ships that had formed up in the Mediterranean in the weeks leading up to the invasion was duly noted and reported by enemy spies and the odd German spotter plane on patrol. The news of transports in most of the main harbours, military units on board, approximate size of the force and its movements was also freely reported by Egyptian reporters. The Turks expected an attack of significant scale, but they did not know exactly when or where it would occur along their coastline.

When looking back on most battles throughout history and reflecting on the decisions taken by commanders before and during the fighting, with the benefit of hindsight we can determine where opportunities were missed, initiative was not taken and assumptions flawed that may have changed the course of the battle. The fighting on the 25th April, 1915 in the Anzac area is no different. The first well discussed and debated point is that had the Turkish Command acted earlier on reports of the start and suspected locations of the landings, the results of the first day may have been very different for the Anzacs. In the early hours of Sunday morning a series of communications between Turkish commanders was taking place.

Captain Faik, a Turkish company commander with the coastal sentries of the 2 Battalion, 27th Regiment, situated up on Second Ridge, had observed through his binoculars silhouettes of many Allied ships offshore from his position at about 2.30am and reported this to his Battalion Commanding Officer, Major Ismet. The Major reassured the Captain that if there was to be a landing then it would be at Gaba Tepe and not at Ari Burnu.

Soon after the Australians had actually begun to land at Anzac Cove, Lieutenant Colonel Aker (Commander of the Turkish 27th Regiment), situated at his headquarters back at Maidos, heard the distant sound of gunfire and made enquiries of his officers on the coast. He was informed that the enemy was indeed landing troops in large numbers at Ari Burnu. He made ready to force march his 2000 men held in reserve towards the Ari Burnu/ Gaba Tepe coastline. However, he was told to await further orders as the Chief of Staff–Sefik Bey, was still not convinced that the landings occurring at Ari Burnu were any more than a feint for the real landings that would take place elsewhere. These orders took some time to come through. All the while Lieutenant Colonel Aker could hear the battle raging to the west, his frustration growing with the knowledge that his thinly spread men at the coastal defences would now be under extreme pressure and wondering when the support would come for them. Aker exclaimed:

> *Hulusi Bey, our comrades are burning there under fire. How much longer are we going to wait? I am waiting for a movement order ... for goodness sake please hurry!*[167]

At 5.45a.m, Aker finally received his orders to move, but it was not until just before 8am that the 1st and 3rd Battalions and a machine-gun company of the 27th Regiment, which had been held in reserve near Maidos (present-day Eceabat), reached the remaining survivors of the 2nd Battalion at the southern end of Third Ridge near Anderson's Knoll. By that stage the Australians were already entrenching on Second Ridge and had established a tenuous beachhead at Anzac Cove.

Had the order been given to move forward the other reserve Battalions held back behind Third Ridge at either of these points in time, the Turks may have stopped the Australians from getting the crucial foothold on the first line of hills inland from the beach.

Similarly for the Anzacs, if they had of pressed on from 400 Plateau instead of digging in and supporting the small bands of Australians from the 3rd Brigade that had already reached the Third Ridge and secured it prior to the Turks arriving en masse, they may also have been able to change the course of the campaign. By having the high ground on the Third Ridge they would have delayed the flow of Turkish reinforcements making their way towards the Third Ridge by holding the dominant high ground, and possibly allowed for more of the 2nd Brigade to have pressed up to help secure the left flank and support the stretched 11th and 12th Battalions early in the battle. Could the Anzacs have secured the heights of the northern end of the Third Ridge and achieved its objectives of taking and holding Chunuk Bair and Hill 971 before Colonel Mustafa Kemal and his men from the 57th Regiment arrived?

In terms of achievements over the first few days, the men themselves felt a collective pride in having held their own in a battle that would have tested the mettle of seasoned soldiers. They knew that the 25th April, 1915 would be a watershed in their country's history.[168] Private Edward Richards of the 11th Battalion noted:

The reckless courage and strong determination of Australia's sons will keep that Sabbath morning so clearly distinct in Australian hearts that it will appear but of yesterday[169].

For the first time, allegiance to Imperial traditions became irrelevant and being Australian was something to be treasured. Those at home felt the same way when the first detailed report, glowingly written by British war correspondent Ellis Ashmead–Bartlett, appeared in their newspapers on 8th May, 1915. Although they were unaware that the landings had failed to achieve the objectives set, the news that the AIF had not been found wanting came as a huge relief to those back in Australia. As Carlyon indicates, the "six–bob–a–day–tourist" tag lost its derisory sting.[170]

General Birdwood, who was the Officer Commanding the Australian and New Zealand Army Corps, had the following to say about the deeds done by the men of the 3rd Brigade on the 25th April, 1915:

The GOC Australia and New Zealand Army Corps wishes to place on record his appreciation of the gallantry and dash with which the 3rd Australian Brigade carried out the difficult operation entrusted to it of landing in the face of opposition on an enemy beach. In spite of the enemy being ready, and of heavy casualties inflicted at short range, the Brigade pressed on carrying successive positions in the face of enemy fire, and completing a hazardous operation in the manner reflecting the highest credit on the commanders and on the troops engaged. During their advance the Brigade captured three Krupp guns.

Chapter 6

Hardship and Suffering at Gallipoli

Back home in Australia, Sunday, 25th April, 1915, Brisbane life continued as it always had for most families, albeit that many had their men folk serving in the armed forces. The families of the 9th Battalion men knew from letters that they had been in Egypt at Mena Camp and often letters from the men were published in the papers, giving accounts of the things and events that the men had witnessed. The weather was generally fine, except for some scattered showers in Brisbane late in the afternoon and some thunderstorms that had hit the Burnett region over the past few days, which had brought much needed rain. There were no major sporting events in Brisbane on the Sunday, but in Melbourne the opening rounds of the Australian Rules Football occurred on the Saturday, 24th April and Collingwood, 32, beat Essendon, 26. The papers indicated that for those young men who missed joining last week, recruiting for the Expeditionary Force in the Brisbane enrolment office would be open only on Sunday morning for men wishing to enlist in the great adventure – the European Picnic! The Australian population remained oblivious to the task that its soldiers were enduring on the Gallipoli Peninsula as they ate breakfast on that fateful Sunday morning in April 1915.

The *Courier Mail* on Saturday, 24th April, 1915, provided the weekend reading on current events, as there were no papers produced on a Sunday. While news concerning the war was focused on the events unfolding on the Western Front. The *Courier Mail* also indicated to its readership based predominately in South East Queensland, that the Allied fleet was bombarding the Gallipoli Peninsula where the Turks were erecting fortifications. No more details about the action were provided.

On Monday 26th and Tuesday 27th, April, the news across Australian newspapers was focused on the war on the Western Front. There was no news of Australians being involved in any attack in the Dardanelles. The *Courier Mail* on Monday, 26th April did report in a short paragraph buried among news from the Western Front, via an unofficial Greek report, that a decisive action at the Dardanelles had begun. The Allied squadrons had bombed the straits at various points west of Gallipoli and a landing had been affected at several points – Cape Suvla and Bulair, the Gallipoli Peninsula and Enos.

In terms of communication of world events, almost all news reached the masses through the newspaper media, and one of the major Australian metropolitan newspapers of the time was the *Argus*, which was published in Melbourne from 1846 to 1957.

On Friday, 30th April, however, the press via the *Argus* newspaper, for the first time linked Australian troops to the Dardanelles, but did not have much more information available to produce any details of substance without being caught out by later-breaking facts. Given that the war for the Australians soldiers was not expected to be anywhere other than the Western Front and this had been their focus, fighting in Turkey caught them by surprise. The paper indicated that Allied troops were advancing steadily up the Gallipoli Peninsula, adding with some poetic licence and drama, that the Turks had prepared deep pits with spiked bottoms. There was no mention of Anzac Cove or the specific landings of the Australian troops.

On Saturday, 1st May, the *Argus* ran the first casualty list from Gallipoli, outlining that there were 22 wounded officers and they indicated that no information was available as to whether any Australians had been killed in the fighting. New Zealand, however, not to be outdone by her friends across the Tasman, declared a public holiday to celebrate the landings. On Sunday, a week following the landings at Anzac Cove, the *Argus* produced a special war edition of its paper and indicated in a four-column story that 18 Australians were dead and 15 wounded during fighting on the Gallipoli Peninsula. On Monday, more than a week after the landing, came the first mention of Australian and New Zealand soldiers landing at a definitive location i.e. near Gaba Tepe. A few days later the *Melbourne Age* released a report that had been taken by a correspondent in Cairo who had interviewed returning wounded which stated:

Our big lads lifted some of the Turks on the end of their bayonets and other Turks ran screaming and howling in fear... our casualties were heavy, but very many of the wounds are slight...

With the news of the Gallipoli invasion and the natural assumption that the 9th Battalion would no doubt have been involved, although not clearly acknowledged by the papers at that stage, would have further amplified the desire of the remaining two Keid brothers still at home to be involved in the fight alongside their brothers. Leonard was also distressed by the receipt of an anonymous white feather, which signified that he was considered to be a coward and should be doing his duty.[171] This no doubt helped seal a decision for the last of the Keid boys to enlist. Both Leonard and Walter enlisted as reinforcements for the 9th Battalion. Leonard was sworn in on the 5th May and Walter the very next day and went into camp at Enogerra. This meant that all six of the Keid brothers were now enlisted in the AIF, a significant contribution by the Keid family to the war effort, and the real potential for significant sacrifice from a single family, with all sons exposed to the dangers of war.

On the 8th May, the first report came through from someone who was actually there on site. The report from Ashmead–Bartlett, which in grandiose wording and containing many inaccuracies and exaggerations, set the tone for reporting of the Australian troops fighting on the Gallipoli Peninsula for some weeks. Its lavish praise of the exploits of the Australian soldier and the mighty deeds being done in Turkey had the desired effect of ensuring that the recruitment offices remained full of young men eager to get involved in the great adventure. Hopefully there was still time for them to be part of it!

The Australian public was captivated by the report that, while mostly true, left out larger truths that Ashmead–Bartlett would not have been able to have included in his report due to censorship, even if he had wanted to. Gallipoli sounded like a romantic place, but it was actually far from it. The casualties were far greater than reported, and rather than giving up at the first sight of the Anzacs storming ashore as had been expected, the Turks were fighting well. The Anzacs were not making progress inland and had not done so for some days, but were clinging to 400 acre rough terrain no further than a kilometre or two from the landing beach. It was the start of a stalemate of men in trenches much like the Western Front.[172] For the war correspondents such as Charles Bean, journalists who wanted to convey to the Australian public back home the truth about the war on the Gallipoli Peninsula and the ordinary soldier in the field and what they were enduring, the stringent censorship regime frustrated their efforts. Press reports and letters had their text reduced to highly sanitised paragraphs, devoid of the writer's original account or message, and were often completely rewritten by the Chief Censor before leaving Gallipoli.[173]

Charles Bean stated in his diary on the 26th September, 1915:

This is the point to which censorship has reduced us – that the German official accounts are far truer than our own.

In many cases, standard worded postcards were available for the troops, which provided a choice of phrases to convey what had happened to the soldier i.e. I am wounded or sick, or convey that they had received letters or had not received any letters. Each senior officer was personally responsible for censoring letters written by the men under their command and removing sensitive references, especially those that exposed the horrific conditions or high death toll and may lead to public unrest or discourage men from joining the war effort. The censorship provisions outlined in the Commonwealth Governments War Precautions Act of 1914 (with amendments occurring in 1915) were strictly implemented. Their main purpose, like those of the Official Secrets Act in place today, was to prevent sensitive military information passing over to the enemy.[174]

The Australian newspaper editors were happy to report these uptempo but sterilised accounts, until the Australian Government started to release casualty figures from 2nd May, 1915, which were grossly lower than the true toll, a mere 18 Australian soldiers dead and 37 wounded. Later, however, when the reality of the true extent of dead and wounded men was released and started to flow into newspaper offices, taking up column after column of paper space, the upbeat mood of the journalists and the Australian people started to change.

Another young Queenslander that would have been reading with interest accounts of the war was Fred Williams, a 22 year old drayman who lived in Spring Hill, Brisbane. With some military service with the Queensland Moreton Militia Regiment prior to the outbreak of the war, he had a strong sense of military drill, discipline, mateship and certainly the importance of serving your country. He would have cheered on the 9th Battalion as they paraded through the Brisbane city streets, spoke to friends and men from work that had enlisted and then read with wide-eyed anticipation any news of what the Queenslanders who served as part of the 9th Battalion were doing. In fact, he probably scanned the pages looking for mention of men that he knew on overseas active service. As the year rolled on and casualties rose significantly from the bloody Gallipoli campaign, it would have become clear to most that this war would not end quickly. Reality was different and indeed many young men would not return from the great adventure. The cries of grieving parents and the number of wounded soldiers returning home were showing a darker side to the war. However, like most young men at that time, captivated by the stories of heroic soldiers and tales of overcoming great hardship with their mates, all lavishly written to encourage men to serve their country, Fred my great-great-uncle also succumbed and enlisted in January 1916. He was drafted into the 13th reinforcements for the Queensland raised 25th Battalion. Possibly as part of a New Years Eve resolution to serve his country.

Awaiting news from Gallipoli, a crowd waits outside the *Argus* newspaper in Melbourne late in 1915. (AWM H11613)

Back at Gallipoli, the remainder of the Gallipoli campaign for the 9th Battalion following the traumatic first few days after landing was less significant, although they had a crucial role to play in holding the line. Their heroics and indeed their campaign objective was to be completed in the first few days of the fighting. This objective was to land and press inland as quickly as possible, securing the landing site for other Anzac units landing later that day and then move inland to secure the southern end of the Third Ridge and Gaba Tepe.

Following the landing, there is not a lot written about the Battalion on the peninsula, mainly because they were not involved in any further major operations during the campaign. Given that their main task had been completed, although not achieved, the Battalion strength in officers and men was so weakened after the landing and first few days of fighting that their key role for the remainder of the campaign was primarily to man and defend the front-line trenches. As Harvey puts it, "stationary trench warfare, varied by a few engagements and raids." [175] Holding the line was in itself, however, not ever going to be an easy task.

Soldiers of the 9th Battalion in a trench on the Gallipoli Peninsula. (AWM C01445)

The main remnants of the 9th Battalion at the end of the first day were situated to the inland right of 400 Plateau, just above Victoria Gully (right southern front) somewhere around Brown's Dip, after having reached advanced positions spread between the 400 Plateau on the Second Ridge and the Third Ridge earlier in the day. These small pockets of 9th Battalion men had retreated back via the Cup, Johnson's Jolly and Owen's Gully where they had courageously held their positions for some time under duress from advancing Turkish Battalions from mid-morning through to early afternoon. By the end of the day they were mixed in with the 2nd Brigade from the main body of men to have landed later that morning. The 2nd Brigade Battalions had been coming up to support the troops of the covering force of the 3rd Brigade, which were holding the precarious front-line to the right around 400 Plateau.

By early May 1915, the 9th Battalion, having returned back to the front-line from rest in the reserve areas, was occupying the southernmost trenches of the Anzac line on the forward slope of Bolton's Ridge and resting in the support trenches slightly at the rear of the crest. Patrols were sent out every night along the seaward spur of Bolton's Ridge, sometimes as far as the barbed wire defending the Turkish positions at Gaba Tepe, or through the valleys south of Lone Pine. On the 7th May, a batch of 120 reinforcements for the Battalion arrived. They were most welcome on account of the heavy casualties that the Battalion had sustained, and brought its strength up to 630 men.

At about this time, Private Nelson Scrivener, having recovered from his wounds, returned to the front-line on the peninsula with his Battalion. The official records state he was away for six weeks but in a letter he later wrote, he indicated he was back within three weeks. After returning from hospital to Gallipoli, Nelson, in a article published in 1970, describes how he kept clean and what he ate when he first returned to his Battalion:

> *Although a lot of our men were down with dysentery, I was never sick and I think one reason was that I was never satisfied with slimy bully beef out of the tin and plum and apple jam more like dirty water ... I do not remember seeing any bread all the time I was there and I was there until we evacuated. We never had a bath except when we took the risk and went down to the sea – but that did not kill the chats [lice] – we were all lousy.*[176]

The 9th Battalion was next engaged in an offensive action on 27th May when Lieutenant Wilder–Neligen, with men of the 9th Battalion, attacked a

Turkish trench near the beach at Gaba Tepe. Then on 28th June, 1915, men of the 9th Battalion attacked the Turkish trenches at Sniper's Ridge and Knife Edge from Holly Ridge. There is an account of both actions below, along with a general account of the other significant events occurring on the peninsula in an informal, chronological order. Of note is that a number of the 9th Battalion men killed in these two actions are now buried at the picturesque Shell Green Cemetery overlooking the Aegean Sea, just below the southernmost end of Bolton's Ridge as it runs down to the beach.

The 9th Battalion became engaged in one of its most challenging actions since the landing, and possibly during the whole of its long service on the peninsula, when on the 19th May the Turks launched a large-scale attack along the whole front of the Anzac line with the objective of throwing the invaders into the sea. The Australian and New Zealand soldiers had been forewarned by the arrival of Turkish transports with troops on the far side of the peninsula, and thus the Brigades were standing to ready for the attack. On the 18th May, the Turkish rifle fire started to wane, puzzling the Anzacs, who had also wondered about the bombardment that had also taken place, which had been the heaviest yet, that had begun at 5pm and had continued until dusk. It all seemed to confirm that a Turkish attack was imminent. The heaviest fusillade experienced by the Australians in the war up to that point broke out from Quinn's and Courtney's posts and Baby 700. These positions seemed to have a greater allocation of Turkish soldiers, possibly due to the fact that if a break was made through Quinn's or Courtney's Post then the Turks could rush straight on down through Monash Valley. The valley was akin to a highway for the Turks, a direct route that would enable them to quickly get down to the beaches and Anzac Cove and get in behind the Australian lines. The imminent Turkish attack was launched at 3am on the 19th May by the Turkish 77th Arab Regiment, which advanced towards the Anzac trenches in two lines in close order. Thousands of bayonets could be seen glinting in the moonlight. Then came the familiar cry of "Allah! Allah!" set off by bugles and a band as the Turks commenced their human, wave assaults on the Australian trenches. "Our orders were to allow them to come quite close before opening fire," said Private James Murray Aitken of the 11th Battalion, an accountant from Kalgoorlie (later killed on the 10th August, 1918 in the battle of Villers-Bretonneux). "They were simply mowed down and yet, in spite of the terrible slaughter, they still kept coming."[177]

The support soldiers in the Australian trenches begged for a place on the firing steps. Private William Tope of the 12th Battalion fought for one:

When they filled the trench, I found I didn't have room because there were still men filing in, so I pushed this chap to the end and made him make some room ... I'd felt that I'd be buried there behind if I didn't have a go.[178]

Wave after wave of Turks crumpled under the withering fire. Many Australians sat up on the parapet itself to get a better shot. Subjected to five assaults, the garrison at Quinn's, which was mostly manned by the 15th and 16th Battalions (the 15th being the other Queensland Battalion on the peninsula who landed at 4pm on 25th April, part of the 4th Brigade), rose and opened fire as one to obliterate each wave of Turkish soldiers. Those skulking back to their own lines were easily picked off. "Play you again next Saturday", yelled one Australian.

Lieutenant Stan Milligan, a 27 year old draughtsman from Chatswood in Sydney in the 4th Battalion, was opposite German Officers' Trench, where the Turks were trying to file out of a trench under fire. "One out – got him," he counted. "Two out – got him; three out – got him; four, five out – get that man somebody." [179]

Only at Courtney's Post was the Australian line breached, and then only by nine Turks. While his mates distracted them, Private Albert Jacka of the 14th Battalion leapt into the group of Turks, shooting five and bayoneting two. The other two fled. With an unlit cigarette hanging from his mouth, Jacka told his officer: "I managed to get the beggars, Sir." He became World War I's first Australian recipient of the Victoria Cross.

The 9th Battalion was on the extreme right of the Anzac line by the 19th May, with its four companies A, B, C and D in that order, left to right, D being posted on the end of Bolton's Ridge and down the slope to the beach. The sector of the Battalion's line from the end of the ridge down to the beach was held by a series of posts only, each garrisoned by an officer and 25 men. This method of defence was adopted as there were not enough men to form a continuous line from within the Battalion. The attack on the 9th Battalion line was pressed almost without pause from midnight until just before daylight. Major Salisbury, who was in charge of the Battalion at that time, writes:

In the 9th Battalion the fire was so rapid and continuous that the hot rifle bolts began to jam and had to be well oiled. Sometimes the man on the fire step would borrow the rifle of a support man standing behind him and hand his own rifle down for it to cool, but this did not always suit the support man, for in a number of cases he said to his mate, "no, you get down and let me have a go."[180]

Each one weaker than the last, the assaults continued until late morning, when the air reeked of smoke, dust and the acrid smell of burnt cordite from the 950,000 rounds the Anzacs had blasted off. The Turks were in a state of shock. By their own account the Turks had lost over 10,000 men, of whom 3000 lay dead. On the Anzac's side, they had lost 160 killed and 468 wounded. The Anzacs, however, were unable to capitalise on the victory because they had not prepared any plans for counterattack.

The 9th Battalion lost 16 killed and 25 wounded, mostly from the initial shellfire just prior to the attack, while 200 Turkish dead were counted in front of the 9th trenches and about 600 dead lay in front of the entire 3rd Brigade lines. One of the surviving members of the Battalion in later years described that it was like firing into a paling fence.

The battle itself ended the Australians' hatred of the Turks. Before it they had showed no mercy on the battlefield, even firing on the Turkish burial parties.[181] Lance Corporal Mitchell of the 10th Battalion marvelled at their bravery:

Oh you poor devils, was all I could say, thinking only of the unfortunates if they got right up to us. It was a massacre.

In view of the smell from the piles of putrefying corpses in the summer heat and the rapid spread of disease that they represented, both sides were anxious to bury the dead. A Turkish envoy was sent from Gaba Tepe on 21st May and a nine-hour cease fire from 7.30am until 4.30pm took place three days later. Each side buried the dead in its own half of no-man's-land. Private Parker of the 5th Battalion noted that, "I don't suppose you will see a more gruesome and sickening sight". A Turkish Captain, part of the burial detail, said, "At this spectacle even the most gentle must feel savage, and the most savage must weep". Nearly all the bodies were Turkish, although the Australians did bring back some of their own that they found, mostly men killed on the day of the landing or in the days shortly afterwards.

Fifty men of the 9th Battalion were sent out as a demarcation party, to keep the Turks from approaching too close to the Australian parapet, while 200 men from the 3rd Brigade either buried the bodies on the spot or handed them over to the enemy for burial behind their lines.

The two armies mingled freely and cordially, exchanging names and cigarettes, shaking hands and making the most of the break from hostilities. As the armistice drew to an end at 4.30pm, both sides exchanged souvenirs and shook hands. "Goodbye, old chap; good luck!" the Australians called out. "Smiling may you go and smiling come again," their opponents called back. The Turks became "Jacko" or "Abdul" or "Johnnie Turk". The Australian and Turkish trenches at both Quinn's and Courtney's posts were very close, in some cases only metres apart. The Australians could hear the Turks talking and digging very clearly. From then on tins of bully beef and condensed milk were sometimes thrown into the Turkish trenches in return for boiled onions and smokes. Badges and photos were also swapped, with fire suspended to allow retrieval of items that fell short.

One interesting incident occurred to a 9th Battalion soldier (name was not noted), who was the man in the most extreme right-hand section of the demarcation line i.e. down on the beach. During the afternoon, as he was in a quiet sector and there was no burying being done near him, he lay down and went to sleep. On waking, he found a Turk standing next to him who had put two sticks in the sand beside his head and had arranged his own coat over them to keep the sun off his face. Abdul (general term used by the Australians for the Turkish soldier) now rolled a cigarette for him as soon as he saw the soldier was waking. In return, the Australian gave him some jam, which the Turk enjoyed. [182]

Of course, both sides made good use of the amnesty to reconnoiter each other's positions and retrieve weapons, and instead of burying their dead, the Turks merely threw the bodies down ravines, there being too many to dispose of otherwise. There were to be no more armistices and thereafter the dead remained where they fell, hosts to maggots and flies that tormented the men and laid them low in their thousands with dysentery, typhoid and gastric illnesses. The troops complained that the flies were worse than the Turks and, in fact, probably caused many more casualties.

The defeat of this counterattack was followed a week later by the following enterprising event of the 9th Battalion. General Birdwood wanted the Turks to believe that they were to be attacked on the southern flank of Anzac positions, which was held by the men of the 3rd Brigade. He ordered the

1st Division to keep up active patrolling and to undertake small actions with the objective of making the Turks apprehensive about the stability of the southern front. Accordingly, on the night of the 27th May, a party of 63 men of the 9th Battalion, mostly from D company and all who had volunteered to take part, under Lieutenant Wilder went out near the southern shore towards a trench that was occupied by the enemy on a ridge that overlooked the beach and was three-quarters of a mile beyond the flank. By prior arrangement, the destroyer *Rattlesnake,* which was laying off the coast, turned her searchlight on to the coastal spur and moved it slowly southward. Aboard the ship was Lieutenant Plant of the 9th Battalion, who pointed out the Turkish trench that was to be taken. As soon as the beam hit it, the destroyer fired 20 rounds of high explosive and shrapnel. Wilder kept his party closely following the beam of light. After shelling the trench the destroyer moved its searchlight and the destroyer's guns were directed at firing on a long communication sap leading to the Turkish trench from the direction of Gaba Tepe. At the same moment Wilder led his party up the hill to the trench. They found in it about 20 Turks dazed by the shelling. Wilder's men using only bayonets, in order to avoid noise so that the action would not draw any enemy artillery fire on the party, successfully captured the trench and returned to the lines without a casualty. One of the first to enter the trench was Sergeant "Darkie" Kenyon, a man who could see unusually well in the dark, who took hold of one of the Turks who was cowering in a covered section of the trench and slung him back to those who were following him saying, "Here, look after this one". Someone, however, misunderstanding the position, thought that it was one of the enemy attacking out of the darkness and bayoneted the prisoner. In the meantime, Kenyon had bayoneted six others and captured a seventh while the remainder took flight.[183] The attack subsequently caused the enemy to expect activity upon this flank. It is interesting to note that when a similar raid was made by the 9th Battalion three weeks later, the enemy fled upon the first indication of an impending attack.

John Edward Kenyon was 34 years old when he enlisted on the 24th August, 1914 with the 9th Battalion and was given the rank of Lance Corporal, probably due to his prior military experience with the British Army in India before the war. His service records indicate that he was born in England and decided to migrate to Australia where he worked as a "bush worker", living in Kyogle, NSW. He landed with the 9th on the 25th April at Anzac Cove and was promoted in the field on the 28th April, 1915 to Sergeant and was placed on the list of men that had been brought to the attention of the Army Corps

Commander for performing acts of conspicuous gallantry or valuable service during the first few days following the landing. In his case, Kenyon received a Distinguished Conduct Medal (DCM), one of the first of 35 issued to men of the 9th Battalion during the World War I. His citation read as follows:

On the 24th April, 1915, during operations near Gaba Tepe, for conspicuous courage and initiative in returning from the firing line under heavy fire, collecting reinforcements and assisting to lead a successful bayonet charge to the top of a hill, which was eventually held against great odds.

As will be outlined later, Sergeant Kenyon was again recognised for his bravery on the battlefields of the Western Front.

Anzac Cove at this stage of the campaign looked like a mining boom town. Hastily prepared shelters were perched on the hillsides facing the sea and lined the gullies behind and below the front-line, all of which were scarred by streaks of orange clay excavated from the dugouts that pockmarked the landscape. The beach, which was about 20 metres wide, behind Corps and Divisional Headquarters that were wedged among field ambulances and logistics depots, almost disappeared under piles of supplies and ammunitions. There was a constant flow of men and equipment, wide-eyed reinforcements moving upto the front-line, stretcher bearers bringing down the wounded and the general buzz of activity from an army that was establishing itself for a long campaign. Boats of all shapes and sizes docking at the jetty that reached out into sea at Anzac Cove, beyond which the larger navy battleships stood guard, from time to time firing their massive shells, which screamed overhead at targets inland. In most cases though, supplies were brought in and unloaded at night due to the piers being under constant exposure to Turkish shelling during the day.

The sea itself teemed with men trying to get clean and rid themselves of the lice and flies that infested their clothing.

Lieutenant Colonel John Corbin observed:

When the Turkish guns on Gaba Tepe opened up, the whole beach is quiet, not a man to be seen, no bathers no movement … then quiet from the enemy and in five minutes all are back at their jobs bathing, working and laughing as if the war were a million miles away.[184]

The odd swim at the beach was a welcome relief for the soldiers, but the risks of being killed or wounded by shrapnel from the Turkish artillery was reasonably high. One Turkish gun placement in particular, was named "Beachy Bill" by the Australian soldiers. One soldier wrote that one day he had seen a shell explode among a group of soldiers swimming at Anzac Cove and there were 17 casualties.

Peak hour on Anzac Cove beach. Soldiers and stores crowded the shoreline, boats bringing in supplies and men swimming. (AWM H03500)

For the most part, the Anzac troops were holding the line with minimal activity, relentless orders to stand to and then stand down, a constant search for water and the desire to maintain some cleanliness amid lice, fleas and decaying bodies that brought not only a foul smell, but millions of flies, which in turn carried diseases into the ranks. One Australian soldier so fed up with the flies famously stated:

> *Immediately I opened ... [my tin of jam] the flies rushed [it] ... all fighting among themselves. I wrapped my coat over the tin and gouged out the flies, then spread the biscuit, held my hand over it, and drew the biscuit out of the coat. But a lot of flies flew into my mouth and beat about inside ... I nearly howled with rage ... Of all the bastards of places this is the greatest bastard in the world.*[185]

Dysentery and other diseases were therefore rife among the men and there was a constant turnover of sick men between the front-line trenches and the casualty clearing stations. Those too sick to return to the front-line were taken off the peninsula to hospitals on Lemnos or back to Egypt for recuperation. Apart from the odd swim in the sea at Anzac Cove or time in the reserve trenches for a break from the fighting, the men occupied the trenches and made do with the little rations in their possession in their very cramped confines.

The foul stench of the dead, which were often lying only metres away from their trenches, would remain with the men for months and their food was blanketed by swarms of black flies. Fresh food was scarce and had to be carried up from the beach by hand or often by donkey. The bread was stale and mouldy, the biscuits were rumoured to have been left over from the Boer War 15 years before, or even the Crimean War and were so hard that it was often necessary to soak them in water before they could be eaten. The men would toss them into the air for target practice.

Macabre humour was also commonplace. In one case, a dead Turkish soldier was sitting in an upright position almost as if he were alive. The Australian soldiers garrisoned about this area called him "Jacko" and would often include him in their conversations as if he could answer back. The Australians found humour in many situations and played practical jokes on themselves and the enemy. A favourite pastime was to place a hat on a stick and raise it cautiously above the trench, which would invariably draw a hail of fire from the Turkish trenches to the great delight and noisy derision of the Anzacs. Sometimes they would lob a tin of jam close to the Turkish trenches, and when a Turk reached out to retrieve it, they would open fire on him. Another story is told that on one particular day a shell landed on the Anzac dentist's dugout and showered the hillside with porcelain and vulcanite false teeth. Suddenly everyone was sporting wide grins and even the enemy were thrown a few sets, much to their confusion. The Turks became even more convinced that the Anzac devils were quite mad.[186]

Another story retold was that of an older Turkish soldier that was affectionately known as "Ernst" to the Australians manning the trench opposite his line. Ernst would venture out every morning to collect firewood in no-man's-land between the opposing trenches. He would wave and the Australians would yell out to him and throw him cigarettes and he would thank them. This went on for a few days until another Anzac unit moved into the position. The relieving soldiers had no knowledge of the old Turk's routine and, unfortunately, Ernst was shot dead the next morning.

Shelling of each other's positions was common and many men were lost through artillery barrages. In addition, there were numerous small raids and frontal assaults that normally resulted in very little ground or advantage gained, but a heavy loss of life for the attackers. Attack and counterattack was the normal routine in the first few weeks, but over time as both combatant defences were strengthened, they realised the futility of such isolated attacks, which as a consequence helped to impose the stalemate for both sides.

Sniping by the professional riflemen, and for that matter, the ordinary soldier in the trenches continued to be rife on both sides due to both the hilly and scrub-covered terrain. Sniping was especially more effective for the Allied troops having as a tool of trade the periscope rifle, which was designed specifically for this purpose. The perfect terrain of the Anzac area for dedicated snipers on both sides enabled them to pick off men at will and then move to other positions before retaliation could be made against them. Many Australian officers were picked off by Turkish snipers mainly through their relative inexperience of dangerous section, of the line. The unfortunate officers were by no means limited to the more junior of officers, but also many senior officers did not take enough care, often trying to show by example to the men their courage and bravado when they were killed. One example of this was the death of General Bridges, who had been warned on several occasions about taking unnecessary risks in known spots where snipers diligently covered progress. He continued on. However, pretending he was bulletproof until the 15th May, on a visit to Steele's Post to see the commander of the 1st Light Horse. On this occasion he darted out across a gap in the trenches and was shot in the thigh, severing his femoral vein and artery. With heavy blood loss, no transfusions available and gangrene setting in, he had visits from both Hamilton and Birdwood on a hospital ship before dying at sea on the 18th May, 1915.

On the following day 19th May, John Simpson Kirkpatrick, the stretcher bearer with the donkey was killed in Shrapnel Gully from the bullet of a Turkish sniper on his way to the front-line. The man with the donkey, who was in fact English born, was a medic of the 3rd Field Ambulance and had over the first few weeks of fighting often risked his life under sniper fire while ferrying wounded men down from the high ground to the beaches via the myriad of Gullies that defined the battlefield in the Anzac sector. He was destined to become an icon in Australian folklore.

Sydney Loch indicated in one of his diary entries while at Anzac Cove, that around breakfast time:

A man gathering firewood climbed too high up the opposite hill. We watched him, realising he took a great risk. And indeed, a sniper's bullet hit him through the chest. He rolled down the hill and screamed like a wounded hare – never had I heard a man scream like that before. After rolling a short distance he became tangled up in a tree root. Then stretcher–bearers arrived and took charge. I don't know what became of him but my appetite for breakfast was ruined.[187]

During the latter part of May 1915, a lot of sapping i.e. digging tunnels and trenches, was being done forward from the front-line. In fact throughout June and July 1915, life for the men of the 9th Battalion as for many other troops at Gallipoli, consisted of trench digging, tunnelling, mining and patrolling. In addition, there were also a number of demonstrations that had the aim of keeping the enemy in the Anzac area rather than having them sent south, especially during the battles at Cape Helles. Most digging was done at night, as more often than not, the work was done under enemy observation. The digging itself took some nerve. Often their Turkish counterparts could be heard digging very close to the walls of the tunnel being dug by the Australians. One Australian soldier indicated that if the Turks stopped digging then we would also stop, as there was always the fear that they were about to blow up the mine just dug right next to where we were digging, which did happen from time to time. Private Tom Usher of the 9th Battalion was one of the men seconded for digging tunnels:

We started tunneling and they started tunnelling too. You could hear them digging. That's where most of our fella's got the fever from living in that underground place. We'd be tunnelling all night. It was awful, you'd see the boots and bits of bloke's trousers – dead ones, they weren't put very far down, you know ... Well eventually I got typhoid and was taken off.[188]

On the 19th June, the 9th Battalion positions were taken over by the 2nd Light Horse Brigade, and the men were withdrawn into the reserve area that had been made on the ledges adjoining Shell Green, the ridge between Victoria and Clarke Valleys. While in reserve, the 9th dug a sunken road from Shell Green to Shrapnel Gulley and by using the road movement between the 3rd Brigade's sector and the beach became possible with little risk of casualties.

The rest ended when as Lieutenant Ross in his diary[189] noted on 27 June, 1915, the 9th Battalion were roused out of bed owing to the enemy starting a bombardment of their position. Fifty men and two officers were casualties of this event. On the following day he writes that they were told at midday to make a demonstration in return against the Turks. From Holly Ridge they were ordered to advance on Turkish positions at Sniper's Ridge and the Knife Edge to prevent the Turks reinforcing the southern units who were fighting against the Tommies (British). Two companies of the 9th Battalion B and C, took part and lost over 100 men in the space of half an hour. Lieutenant Jordan was listed among the missing. The job was rather hurried, no–one seemed certain of what to do, and when met by cross-fire of shrapnel and machine-guns, they were forced to retire, leaving many men behind. Six Australians from the 9th Battalion were made prisoners of war by the Turks after this failed action. One of those was Private Daniel Creedon, a 21 year old from Maryborough, Queensland, who would later die in a Turkish prisoner of war camp on 27th February, 1917.

During this action, on reaching the First Ridge at Tasman's Post, a group of five soldiers including a Private by the name of W.J. Sullivan, was ordered to continue into the next valley. Private Sullivan was a 21 year old stockman from Kalgoorlie in Western Australia and had enlisted in the 9th Battalion and sailed with the first contingent of the Battalion on the *Omrah*. After reaching the base of the Valley of Despair, which formed part of no-man's- land, this group became separated from the rest of the Battalion and Private Sullivan was killed. There had been some talk among the survivors that he had been taken as a prisoner, but this was later dispelled via witness accounts and contacts from those men who had been taken prisoner.[190]

Although the attack on the Knife Edge had failed, the simultaneous attack against Sniper's Ridge did have some success. B Company was fired on as soon as they left the trenches, but the troops ran across the open bed of Cooee Gully and began to climb towards Sniper's Ridge. They managed to reach the Turkish trench, which was covered, and although they had been ordered not to enter the trench they lobbed bombs in to it forcing the Turks to retreat. The 9th Battalion held the ground taken for a few hours until word was received that the Turks were going to mount a counterattack and B Company had to be withdrawn. While most of the men knew the purpose of the attack, it evidently confused some. As Major Walsh led his B company back into their own trenches, with the Brigadier watching them, one of the soldiers growled,

"What sort of business is this sending us out there and bringing us back again?" Sinclair-MacLagan intervened, "I'll tell you why they sent you out there my lad. It was to help your mates down south". "Just as well there was some reason", said the soldier as he passed. The man following him explained to Sinclair-MacLagan that the growler had had three bullets through him and had refused to go to the medical officer to have his wounds dressed.[191]

The Battalion War Diary entry on the 28th June indicates that there were heavy casualties from this demonstration:

	Killed	*Wounded*	*Missing*
B Company	*12*	*46*	*7*
C Company	9	16	15

> *The missing in Company B were almost certain to be killed and it is possible that of the 15 missing in Company C, the party under Lieutenant Jordan, may be prisoners. [It was later confirmed that six men were taken prisoner] ... Arrangements made for parties for recovering dead upset owing to a demonstration against enemy. Secured five bodies early this morning [29th June, 1915], (they were) stripped of boots and clothing. General Birdwood visited the lines and congratulated our Battalion on yesterday's attack.*

As outlined in the Battalion diary above, much of the 29th June was spent trying to recover the bodies of the men who fell in the action on the previous day and burial services were held in the moonlight that night for those that could be recovered. Some of the men listed as killed by Lieutenant Ross were White from Gayndah, Warnes from Gympie, Preston from the Northern Rivers, NSW, along with Fox, Petersen, Warner, Glennie, Hanley and Jackson. Many of the 9th Battalion dead from this action are now buried in the cemetery at Shell Green.

Private Sullivan's body, however, was not recovered during the rest of the campaign, but was located by the Graves Registration Unit in 1922 and buried at Lone Pine Cemetery.

Also in June, Private Bill Keid of the 2nd Light Horse Regiment was killed at Quinn's Post, a particularly dangerous part of the Anzac front-line at Gallipoli. He was killed while throwing himself on a Turkish bomb that had been thrown into his trench, thereby saving many others in his regiment from becoming casualties. He was posthumously recommended for his bravery and awarded the Medaille Militaire. The first of the pink telegrams delivering the terrible news of his death would find its way to the Keids' family home at Graceville.

On the 1st July, the 9th Battalion moved back into the firing line from their reserve positions, taking over this time a segment that was occupied by the 10th Battalion. This section of the line was to the left of the section previously held by the 9th, still on Bolton's Ridge, just north of Tasmania Post and south of Allah Gully.

By mid July, conditions at the front were not good. Many of the young officers were discouraged by the blatant mismanagement, orders and counter orders, and the fact that in three months no worthwhile gains had been made. Ammunition was in short supply, illness rates were high and the morale of the men started to wane. Nerves frayed from the lack of sleep and the constant exposure to danger. The men bore little resemblance to the fit, confident and eager soldiers who landed on the beaches of Anzac Cove just under three months earlier. Bean noticed that the men were sacrificed needlessly by conflicting orders and poor management by the officers. Ashmead–Bartlett was so sickened by the unnecessary carnage, especially that of the British troops in the Cape Helles battlefield. He sent strongly worded letters to the British Prime Minister about the true state of affairs on the peninsula.

The 9th Battalion War Diary supports the fact that July 1915 was a trying time for the men in the trenches. The rate of sickness was on the increase and officers and men were constantly being evacuated and many would then return to the front-line following periods of hospitalisation. Command of the Battalion and Companies in the Battalion were in a constant state of change and the number of men available for active duties was dwindling at a rapid and alarming rate. On top of this, the Turkish artillery were regularly bombing the front-line trenches at all hours of the day or night and casualties were being incurred on a daily basis. On the 5th July, the Commanding Officer at that time writes in the Battalion diary that 250 Turkish shells had been fired over the trenches between 3am and 7am and the parapets had been "knocked about".

In addition, the Battalion War Diary entry on the 23rd July refers to a disturbing trend of self-inflicted wounding by men in order to leave the front-line and the Battalion officers had to start taking tough stands in an effort to discourage this practice.

Three cases lately of men cutting off or shooting off fingers the intention being to get sent to hospital. Case occurred today and arranged with the field ambulance to keep the man at Anzac instead of sending him away.

A new post called Tasmania Post had been established on Holly Ridge from successive mining and raids and an attack was ordered on the enemy trenches in front of it on the night of the 31st July. The attack was predominately conducted by the 11th Battalion and the 9th manned some new trenches to the left of Tasmania Post to stop any counterattacks that may have occurred from the Turks. The attack was successful and the new trench captured was later called Leane's Trench, on account of Captain Leane from the 11th Battalion, who had led the attack.

The 6th August marked the start of the Allies' August offensive, which would ensure their break–out from the stalemate that had taken hold over the past few months. The objective was for the Australian and New Zealand Division commanded by Major General Sir Alexander Godley, which comprised the Australian 4th Brigade and New Zealand Infantry Battalions, along with two newly arrived British Army Battalions and 29th Indian Brigade, to break out from the existing Anzac perimeter and to take the high ground of the Sari Bair Range, in particular Chunuk Bair and Hill 971. Diversions at Helles and Lone Pine, in particular, would help to take the focus off the main attack. After taking the Sari Bair Range, the 4th Brigade would then link up with the British IX Corps, that had landed further to the north at Suvla Bay and push across the Gallipoli Peninsula achieving what they had hoped to achieve soon after the April landings.

At 5.30pm on the 6th August, units of the Australian 1st Division AIF attacked the Turkish trenches at Lone Pine and by 6pm the Turkish front-line had fallen to the Australians and fierce Turkish counterattacks had began. (Refer also appendix 3). The role of the 9th Battalion during this action was to lay down heavy fire on the opposing trenches while Lone Pine was being attacked by the 1st Infantry Brigade i.e. 1st through to the 4th Battalions, all New South Wales based. It was noted that the men of the 9th Battalion were well aware of the fighting that was taking place, and during the battle some of the men sat on the parapet (along with some of the Turkish soldiers on the other side) and watched the battle rage.[192]

Within three days of fighting at the defence of Lone Pine, seven Victoria Crosses (VCs) had been awarded to Australian soldiers.

As a coincidence, Lance Corporal Neal in his diary refers to a mate of his named Gardiner when they were on Lemnos Island. On researching this name there was only one Gardiner listed with the 9th Battalion, an Alfred John Gardiner who embarked on the SS *Omrah*. In a recent documentary made for the ABC (Australian Broadcasting Commission), narrated by Andrew Denton,[193] he recounts the story of an "Alf" Gardiner who enlisted with the 9th Battalion while his brother Dick enlisted with the 7th Battalion in Victoria. Alf is listed on the 9th Battalion embarkation roll as being a labourer with an address at the time of enlistment as the *Criterion Hotel* in Mackay, Queensland and his next of kin living in West Footscray. All of the facts seem to indicate that this was the same Alf that the documentary refers too. For the two Gardiner brothers the plan was for them to get together, and this happened just before both went into action at Lone Pine on 6th August with the 7th Battalion. Dick Gardiner recounted in a letter back home to his family that:

> *We piled the trenches four or five high with dead and the stench was simply awful. They told us that the position was safe but we soon found out it was decidedly unsafe. Abdul started to bomb us and all the cry was for bombs. More bombs than stretcher bearers. Then, I don't know what happened. I'd been talking to Alf and the next minute he was down there, lying dead in the bottom of the trench.*[194]

Alf was listed as killed in action on the 8th or 9th of August at Lone Pine. Dick returned to Australia in 1918 having survived the war.

Portrait of Private A.J. Gardiner, 9th Battalion (late of the 7th Battalion), killed in action at Gallipoli. (AWM H05873)

On the 7th August, between 4.30am–4.45am, four waves of men from the 3rd Australian Lighthorse Brigade attacked Turkish trenches at the Nek. Each of the waves was a disaster and the Australians were annihilated. Charles Bean wrote that "the flower of youth of Victoria and Western Australia fell in that attempt." (Refer also appendix 6) At 4.30pm there were also other unsuccessful diversionary attacks being made from Quinn's Post, whereby 54 troopers of the 2nd Light Horse Regiment attacked Turkish trenches opposite their line and all but one man lost their lives. At Pope's Post, the 1st Light Horse Regiment with 200 men successfully occupied the Turkish trenches on Dead Man's Ridge, but were driven out again with 154 casualties. In addition, from Courtney's Post, 300 men of the 6th Battalion attacked, the German Officers Trench, losing 146 men without success. These were all extremely gallant attacks, where the Australians were greatly outnumbered by the Turks, but achieved almost nothing save forcing Turkish troops to man the line opposite the Australian positions rather than defend other areas where other designated key objectives were being fought for.

On the 8th August, soldiers of the New Zealand Infantry Brigade, along with British units in support, captured Chunuk Bair and held it despite strong Turkish counterattacks. (Refer also appendix 12)

On the 9th August, the New Zealand Wellington Battalion under Lieutenant Colonel William Malone courageously held on to Chunuk Bair and in the evening were relieved by British units.

On the 10th August, Turkish troops drove the British from Chunuk Bair, but were unable to push the British, Indian and NZ troops back down the valleys to the beach. The Allies' August offensive was now in tatters.

Back home in Australia, the wounded men from the fighting on Gallipoli were filtering back into the country bearing all the scars both physically and mentally of war. The Australian public, however, fuelled by the newspaper media, were primarily interested in hearing first hand accounts of the war and how the men were faring in battle. The demand was so great that public presentations were being organised in order to tell the story of the Anzac landing and lay the foundations for national patriotism for many years to come. One such event was a presentation in the Sydney Town Hall on 24th August, 1915. Chaplain-Colonel Rowe, who had just returned from Egypt and a recently returned soldier from the 9th Battalion, Private Frank Downes, addressed the public forum and described the Anzac area in some detail and the great deeds being achieved. Of interest, Private Frank Downes had been blinded by a bullet while serving in Gallipoli and had not been back in the country long before accepting a speaking engagement to talk specifically about his wartime experiences, which for many men would have been a very difficult and emotional task.

Captain Reg Bowman, Australian Army Medical Corps, visiting some of the 9th Battalion officers in a support trench. Left to right, Captain J.M. Dougall, Lt. M. Wilder–Neligan, Captain Bowman and Captain E.C.P Plant. (AWM P02194.008)

Back at Anzac Cove, life for the common soldier was becoming more and more challenging.

Lieutenant Ross writes in his diary on 11th August that he has not been well the past few days:

Things are quieter today although the artillery and naval guns are very busy. Late night the wind blew from the direction of the newly taken trenches and the stench of the dead bodies was frightful. Reports today are very favourable and Abdul seems to be getting a bad time all round, his losses are said to be 5 or 6 times ours and ours are pretty heavy. Vermin are getting to be a great nuisance.[195]

On the 19th August, the first units of the Australian 2nd Division, the 17th and 18th Battalion (NSW recruits), arrived at Anzac Cove. On the 21st August, in conjunction with the hapless British attack from Suvla Bay against Scimitar Hill, which was the last major action undertaken in the Suvla area, the Australian troops of the newly arrived 18th Battalion were given the task of taking Hill 60. Hill 60 lies midway between the Anzac and the Suvla sectors of the peninsula. However, by the 22nd August after some intensive fighting, the newly arrived 18th Battalion captured some of the trenches on the forward slope of the hill, but failed to break into the main Turkish positions. The Battalion in the process lost 200 men killed and many more were wounded. Their Battalion strength had been reduced to less than half within two days of their landing.

The Hill 60 attacks were the last major operations of the August offensive. With the failure of the offensive went the last real chance of success on the Gallipoli Peninsula.

From the end of August until mid November 1915, there was a period of relative quite on Gallipoli. The war had effectively returned to stalemate conditions. The front-lines were straightened out, tunnels dug and many more bombs thrown. Sickness among the Allied troops became worse and evacuations for sickness in October 1915 from the three battlefields, Anzac, Suvla Bay and Helles was approximately 600 per day. Most units were therefore undermanned. On October 10th there were 114,000 men at or near the battlefields; had all formations been up to strength, there would have been 200,000.

In August, Sergeant Frederic Scrivener was struck down with gastritis and evacuated from Gallipoli for one month. Even the most senior officers were not immune to becoming sick. Lieutenant Colonel Robertson, who had command of the 9th Battalion at the time, needed to be replaced also due to illness.

In late September 1915, a survey of the men holding the front-lines indicated that three–quarters of the men were totally unfit for active service. Bryce Courtenay in the book, An Anzac's Story, suggests that in those times stoicism was expected of men. Such a high percentage of unfit indicates that, if judged by today's standards, they should all have long since been removed from active duty.[196] Of course, in reality the War Cabinet could not afford to have Commanders remove all of the sick from the field, there simply were not enough men to replace them, and the capacity to move troops quickly was not comparable to today's standards. Therefore only the severe cases were taken from the field. The lack of fresh food, water and the constant stress and lack of sleep just made the rate of sickness worse and limited the capacity for men to recover. The rotation of units in and out of the line was essential to help in their recovery, and men looked forward to their chance away from the firing line when it came.

The previously fit and healthy Australians who had landed on the 25th April and had been likened by English observers while overseeing training exercises in Egypt to bronzed gods were now gaunt, thin shadows of their former selves, with lined faces and hollow cheeks. It hurt the men even to move. [197]

The standard of the Turkish soldiers in most cases was much worse. Most of the men lived in squalor, food was limited and their standard of dress was often very poor. Some fought without shoes, wrapping strips of material around their feet. They had not been paid for several months and their officers were very callous masters. Yet for all of this, they still maintained amazingly good levels of morale. The literacy rate among Turkish soldiers was about 5 per cent and pre–printed letters were used by soldiers signed with a thumbprint and sent home, but for those who could write, mainly the officers, they wrote home often. The major advantage that the Turkish Army did have was that they could access food and water and other supplies far easier than the Anzacs. There are many stories noted about families of Turkish soldiers that lived in the vicinity of the Gallipoli battlefields visiting troops and providing supplies.

By October 1915, the early signs that winter was coming were occurring and the first of the severe seasonal autumn storms hit the peninsula. Orders were sent out for as much galvanised iron and timber that could be sourced in Egypt and England, including trench pumps and horse rugs to be rushed to the peninsula.

Back on the home front, with the war having been going for more than a year, the Australian public ceased to predict optimistically that it would be over in a short time. Following the reports of dreadful massacres on Gallipoli, recruitment had fallen dramatically. Women veiled in deepest mourning, men wearing black armbands and wounded men in hospital-blue clothing were a common sight on the streets in Brisbane and elsewhere in Australian cities. No longer were the military promoters able to portray life as a soldier as a career fit for heroes, exciting and adventure filled when the newspapers and the casualty lists told another story.

Also in mid October, reports revealing the reality of what was occurring on the Gallipoli Peninsula were now starting to filter back into London, having managed to avoid the military censorship. In particular, a report by Ashmead–Bartlett and a scathing report back to the Australian Prime Minister by a young Australian journalist, Keith Murdoch. Each of these reports strongly criticised the Allied leadership, outlining examples of incompetence and failures of the senior officers in charge of the Gallipoli campaign. The British War Cabinet in parallel was also receiving continuous bad news through the military communication channels from the Gallipoli front and losses being sustained by the Allied Armies. They had finally had enough of General Hamilton and he was relieved from command of the campaign on the 15th October, 1915. Sir Charles Monro was appointed as his replacement. The new Commander's main task was now to understand the current situation and decide whether to leave or fight on. It did not take long, however, for him to recommend evacuation to Kitchener and he suggested that there could be as high as 40 per cent casualties during the withdrawal operation. [198]

On the 3rd November, the 9th Battalion again moved positions, this time replacing the men of the 1st Brigade who had survived the August offensive at Lone Pine and were being relieved back to the reserve area. These trenches had previously been held by the 12th Battalion and were immediately to the right and south of the 9th Battalion's previous position and directly behind Tasmania Post, which became their new home.

The next significant event was the visit of Field Marshal Lord Kitchener to the Anzac positions on the 13th November, 1915. Following his visit and discussions with General Monro and his staff, he recommended the withdrawal of all British and Dominion troops from Gallipoli.

The 9th Battalion, having been on the peninsula for nearly seven months, on the nights of the 16th and 17th November finally had its turn along with the other Battalions of the 3rd Brigade to have a rest period on Island of Lemnos. Both the 9th and the 10th Battalions left on the ship *Albassa.* At that time they did not know that they would not return to the peninsula and that a complete evacuation of the battlefield would occur in a month's time. The other Battalions of the 3rd Brigade were to follow and by the 26th November 1915, headquarters of the 3rd Brigade were set–up on the Island of Lemnos. The 7th and 8th reinforcements of the 9th Battalion were at Lemnos awaiting the war-weary Battalion's arrival and were absorbed into the Battalion when it was reorganised the next day. As noted earlier, the first two reinforcements for the 9th Battalion were taken to the front in line with Army procedure, which therefore meant that the Battalion had the 3rd through to the 6th reinforcements arrive to strengthen the Battalion while on active duty on Gallipoli. Without the knowledge of the full evacuation that would take place, the Battalion was told that in an effort to counteract the severe winter weather on the peninsula, before they were to return the men of the 9th Battalion (all ranks) were told to cease shaving and grow beards. After a week of this order, the Battalion became known as the 'Hairy 9th' or the 'Bearded 9th', which was soon corrupted to the 'Beery 9th'. The order was later cancelled on news of the impending evacuation.[199]

On the 22nd November, a preliminary plan was drawn up for the evacuation of all British held areas on the Gallipoli Peninsula; Helles, Anzac and Suvla. The plan was devised by Lieutenant Colonel Charles White, Chief of Staff, Anzac Corps. and the withdrawal of the men would take place in stages. Half the men would be off by December 18th, leaving a garrison of about 20,000 men at each beachhead. These garrisons would come off on the nights of the 18th and 19th December. The Turks had to be convinced that things were normal, even though they were not. Between the 24th and 27th November, silent stunts were ordered along the front-line which required troops not to fire unless they were attacked or threatened. The objective was to start deceiving the enemy to think that silence did not mean troop withdrawal.

The Turks concluded from the silent stunts that the Anzacs wanted quiet while they prepared their winter quarters.

On the 27th November there was heavy snowfall on Gallipoli followed by two days and nights of freezing winds and a bad storm. From the north to the south of the peninsula, both combatants were ravaged by storms and blizzards associated with the early onset of winter. In many places, open fighting ceased and soldiers from each side attempted to make their conditions bearable, often in full view of each other. The seas were so wild no vessel could approach the battlefield. First came hail and then pelting rain for 24 hours. It was the worst blizzard on the peninsula for 40 years. The men were issued with waterproof clothing and a ration of rum was issued to the troops in the front-line.

This pictures shows four men of the "BEARDED" 9th Battalion preparing for a winter return to the Gallipoli peninsula . (Wrench)

Only one man died of exposure at Anzac, although there were hundreds of cases of frostbite treated. It was the first snow that many Australians had seen. In some instances, the men were noted to have thrown snowballs to keep themselves warm. The situation was much worse, however, at Suvla among the British units, and there were a number of cases of men freezing to death. Had the campaign extended much more into the winter months there would have been far more deaths and a much greater tragedy would have unfolded, especially at Anzac where the front-line trenches would have become untenable.

The other problem facing the Allies was that the Turks started receiving Austrian howitzers (Skoda super heavy siege howitzers) via Bulgaria, in mid November 1915, and had started to use them with devastating effect. The narrow, shallow and crumbly soil of the Australian trenches had stood up well against the Turkish batteries' shrapnel fire. The howitzers though, with their lobbing angle of fire and explosive warhead, wrecked trenches and the men in them. The Australians were also used to Turkish shells failing to go off one in three times, however, with these new howitzers, their shells went off every time. On the 29th November, the front-line at Lone Pine was heavily shelled and there were 264 casualties recorded. The modern bombardment had now come to Gallipoli. If there was to be an evacuation, a decision would have to be made very soon.

Sergeant Cliff Pinnock, of the 8th Light Horse, wrote home concerning the new howitzers:

> *My God, I cannot imagine how those poor unfortunates in France ever stuck it. Where they dropped and exploded a hole was left as big as your drawing room, the explosion was simply fearful.*[200]

Cliff Pinnock was probably killed by one of these bombs not more than eight months later on the battlefields in France that he had written home about. On the 18th August, 1916, Cliff, then a Lieutenant, was killed in action as part of the 57th Battalion.

On the 8th December, General Birdwood was informed that the War Cabinet had decided to evacuate the troops, but only those at Suvla Bay and Anzac. The Cape Helles positions would stay for the time being.

The weather held and the Turks stayed quiescent. By the morning of the 18th December half the men had been taken off both fronts as planned.

Trench floors were broken up with picks and men's boots were wrapped in empty sandbags (for the first time footwear was referred to as sneakers) so that footfalls would not be heard. Self–firing rifles were set–up in the trenches throughout the Anzac positions, and combined with the use of the periscope rifle, they undoubtedly saved many lives at Gallipoli.

Twenty one year old Lance Corporal Scurry, a new arrival on Gallipoli, with a schoolmate from Monee Ponds in Melbourne invented what was to become known as the Scurry "pop off" rifle, or referred to more officially as the self-firing rifle.[201] It was a reasonably simple invention that relied on the slow release of water from a container that was placed above the rifle, into another container directly beneath it. This bottom container was attached to a small box of stones that would be pulled off when the bottom container was full of water. After about 20 minutes, the lower container would be full of water and overbalance the box of stones, which were attached by string to the trigger of the rifle, and effectively pull the trigger with its weight from the fall. Each of these rifles were positioned on sandbags facing the enemy trenches. Men were told to stand about smoking and talking within sight of the Turkish observers at Gaba Tepe, and that day some Light Horsemen played cricket on Shell Green in another display of "normalcy". While the game was being played shells were passing overhead.

Brigadier General Granville "Bull" Ryrie, Commanding Officer of the 2nd Light Horse Brigade, outlined in a letter to his wife:

> *We had a game of cricket on Shell Green. And when shells whistled by we pretended to field them. The men were wonderfully cheerful and seemed to take the whole thing as a huge joke .... They left all sorts of messages for the Turks generally beginning with My Dear Abdul and My Dear Jacko. It is I think the most extraordinary performance in the history of the world to think that two huge armies were only 20, 30, 40 and 50 yards apart in a lot of places and that one could slip away without the other knowing.* [202]

After 11pm on the 19th December, there were less than 2000 men holding the entire Anzac line. Trails of salt and flour had been laid to mark the way to the beach and shaded candles spluttered in biscuit boxes. The last units to leave lit fuses that would set off charges strategically laid that would destroy Turkish trenches, tunnels and saps mainly around the Nek. The 24th Battalion, one of the last to leave, was at Lone Pine and were ordered out at 2.40am. According to their Battalion history, the officers took one last look along the line. A Lieutenant saw a figure crouching over the parapet. He pointed his revolver and challenged him quietly. It was one of his own men having just one more shot at the Turks. Shortly after, the officer heard sounds of bombs exploding. He found a lone Australian trying out the new Mills bomb grenades, which had only just arrived and were rationed out due to cost. "It's a pity not to use them, they're great", stated the lone bomber.

A game of cricket played at Shell Green, on 17th December, 1915 to distract the Turks from the evacuation preparations of Allied soldiers. Shells were passing overhead while the game was in progress. Major George Macarthur Onslow of the Light Horse was batting at the time. (AWM G01289)

Australians playing two-up at Brown's Dip, behind Lone Pine, as a Turkish shell bursts nearby. Four minutes after this photo was taken, four of the men were killed by another Turkish shell. (AWM H03557)

The troops left the peninsula with heavy hearts. One was noted to have remarked to Birdwood while he marched down to the beach and gestured to the dead buried in a makeshift cemetery "I hope they don't hear us marching away". Generally the mood among the soldiers was sober, and many thought that they were letting their mates who had been killed down by leaving without having achieved a victory. One soldier remarked that he would rather have stuck it out rather than slink away.

A huge explosion was set off on the beach by engineers as the last of the Australian troops boarded ships, and as mentioned above, many explosives had been planted in tunnels under the Turkish front-line trenches at the Nek. About 70 Turks were killed in the explosion and probably hundreds more were wounded. The Turks opened fire with rifles and machine-guns towards the now vacant Anzac positions, thinking that this was the start of an attack.

At 4.10am on the 20th December, 1915, the evacuation from the Anzac positions was complete. An hour later the Turks were still shooting and defending the front-line against empty Anzac trenches. There had only been two casualties during the evacuation: one man wounded early in the evening and another hit in the arm by a spent bullet as he left the beach. The war at Helles, however, continued on until 8th January, 1916 when the last of the British units finally left.

Wrench indicates that no doubt many of the old 9th Battalion wished they had been there for the distinction it would give them of being able to say that they had been at the landing and at the evacuation.[203] In all, there were only 63 officers and men of the 9th Battalion who could say that they had been on Gallipoli from the first day to the last day before the Battalion left. One of these 9th Battalion men was newly promoted Corporal Ted Keid. His younger brother, Guy, who was part of the 3rd Field Ambulance supporting the 9th Battalion, also went right through the campaign.

The eight-and-a- half-month-long Gallipoli campaign involved a total of about one million men from both sides, of whom between one–third and one–half became casualties. About 500,000 Turkish soldiers are believed to have served on Gallipoli and their casualties are estimated at between 250,000 and 300,000, of whom (according to Turkish official sources) almost 87,000 died.

Between 50,000 and 60,000 Australians served on Gallipoli and a total of 8709 were killed in action or died of wounds or disease. In addition, a total of 19,441 Australians were wounded (including those wounded more than once) and 70 Australians were captured. There were 63,969 Australian cases of sickness that were reported during the campaign.

Of the 8556 New Zealanders who served in the campaign, 2721 died and 4752 were wounded.

Harvey indicates a contrary view to most of the teaching about Gallipoli that Australians are taught and passed on as folklore from each successive generation i.e. that the Gallipoli campaign was a disaster and a significant defeat for the Australian Army. Instead he indicates that as time goes on and people realise what was actually done on the peninsula and throughout the period of time in that region, it becomes increasingly plain that the fighting was a brilliant success.[204] While I would not agree with this glowing praise given the stalemate that occurred, the lack of achievement of the campaign's stated objectives, the callous loss of life and the incompetence of senior officers, particularly British officers, I do agree that a lot was achieved, and it was far from a defeat, especially for the Australians. The enemy did not throw them off the peninsula. They had hung on tenaciously and withstood many offensives from the Turks. In fact, there were some notable successes on the peninsula, in particular the attack on Lone Pine during the August offensive. The men who left Gallipoli in December 1915 were not defeated men, nor did their diaries indicate they felt as such. Rather, many wanted to stay on and finish what they had started, mainly for their mates that they were leaving behind. It is also interesting to note that among the military leadership there was a strong argument put forward to stick it out for the winter and mount another large-scale offensive with new divisions being brought to the front.

Fortunately another offensive aimed at breaking out of the stalemate did not get the support of the War Cabinet, and instead a calculated and well-planned withdrawal took place. The Allies chose the time that was right for them to withdraw, although a timely departure was required due to the coming winter that the soldiers were not prepared for and the deadly new weaponry specifically designed for trench warfare that the German Command was bringing to bear on the Allied trench systems.

The campaign is likely to have been much more successful if there were more troops provided at the beginning and if there was more artillery available to support the infantry throughout the operations.[205] The official British historian, Aspinall-Oglander stated:

> *At the expense of a casualty list which was less than double that which was incurred on the first day of the battle of the Somme, 1916, the Mediterranean Expeditionary Force in Gallipoli destroyed the flower of the Turkish Army, safeguarded the Suez Canal and laid the foundation of Turkey's final defeat.*[206]

In regard to Hamilton, the man with ultimate responsibility for the campaign, he was probably not the best man for the job. Unfortunately, Hamilton had been sent forth at a time when Britain hadn't learnt how to fight a world war, or indeed successfully mount an offensive campaign against machine-guns and defended positions. His biggest mistake was in not telling Kitchener in the fortnight after the landings had taken place and when it was becoming clear to most observers that he did not have enough men and guns needed to win the campaign. But that was not his way. He was an optimist, he saw hope in most scenarios and certainly did not want confrontation, even with his subordinates for whom he allowed too much latitude and bumbling and least of all with Kitchener himself.[207]

Sir Charles Monro was the man appointed to replace Hamilton by Kitchener towards the end of the campaign. He was the one who decided within 24 hours after a tour of the battlefields on the peninsula and discussions with each of the senior officers on the ground that evacuation was necessary. This conclusion was very clear for him. Certainly the other option of staying through the harsh winter and attempting a spring offensive, which was what Kitchener would have wanted, which would have required 400,000 men and support from the fleet, which had provided limited assistance during the campaign to date. Munro was shrewd, pragmatic and difficult to rattle once he had made up his mind. In Hamilton's own words, "He was born with another sort of mind from me."[208]

The most critical of the objectives for the campaign in both the Helles and Anzac sectors was undoubtedly the securing of the heights. The key high ground being the 700 feet-high hill the English referred to as "Achi Baba" in the Helles sector, which had a commanding view over the areas of the British landing site right up to the foot of the hill itself, and the Sari Bair ranges which rise to 1000 feet in the Anzac sector. The Sari Bair range, which includes the Second and Third Ridges, overlooked the coast, valleys and slopes to the west and north-west from Ari Burnu to Suvla Bay. Unfortunately these heights were held for the majority of the campaign by the Turkish Army and exposed the Allied forces significantly to observation, sniper fire (especially early in the campaign) and artillery firepower.

As Ekins notes,[209] without attaining those heights the Allied forces were unable to observe the enemy's positions, any movements of both guns and reinforcements or to accurately direct fire on to the enemy positions ... possession of the Sari Bair heights was held as the key to the entire campaign. But due to the nature of the terrain [which flattens quite considerably moving inland after the Third Ridge, across the narrow Maidos plain towards Maidos (present-day Eceabat) and the Dardanelles] the Turks could always reach, reinforce and supply the heights quicker from their side than the Allies. They had the topographical advantages of freshwater supplies, ready access to villages and rear areas. By the end of the Gallipoli campaign, the terrain of the peninsula was truly the "master of the battlefield", not the Allied attackers nor the Turkish defenders.

Rather than being the defining point of our nationhood, or in fact as some authors have suggested the birth of our nation, the campaign was most importantly the catalyst for the eventual severance of the umbilical cord that linked Australia to England. The fighting was the first time that Australian soldiers had proved themselves fully in the battlefield, and provided future Australian generations with the story that helps us to prove our character and resilience. The Australians had arrived as British colonials, but they left proudly as Anzac Diggers. The Australian nation had forged its own identity on the bloody slopes of Gallipoli and had come of age.[210]

> *Well! We're gone. We're out of it all! We've somewhere else to fight. And we strain our eyes from the transport deck, but ANZAC is out of sight! Valley and shore have vanished; vanished are cliff and hill; and we'll never go back to ANZAC ... But I think that some of us will!*
>
> From ANZAC, Major Oliver Hogue, 6th Light Horse Regiment, AIF.[211]

At the landing and here ever since.

The image above was initially drawn at Gallipoli. After eight months on the beach, some of the Diggers had become real characters, with the most celebrated being those who had been there from day one. (King)

Chapter 7

Now On to the Western Front

The evacuation of the Dardanelles had brought all three Anzac Divisions together on Lemnos Island. The climate, however, on Lemnos was not considered suitable for resting, refitting and reorganising these divisions and it was decided to transfer them immediately back to Egypt. A new site for the First Division was chosen at Tel el Kebir on the edge of the desert at the eastern entrance to Egypt, and the 9th Battalion subsequently departed on the SS *Grampian* on the 1st January, 1916, bound for Alexandria. On the 3rd January, they arrived at Alexandria Harbour and entrained in two parties for Tel el Kebir. The 9th was the first unit to occupy the camp. At this time, Leonard Keid joined the Battalion after his basic training had been completed and Walter joined the Battalion later in February 1916 as reinforcements.

What was to follow was three weeks of training, which included a component of elementary training that "riled" the whole of the Battalion.[212] As was expressed by one unknown historian, 'After the hard fighting on the peninsula the men felt humiliated at having to commence all over again the work they had completed in the early days of Enoggera. What irritated the men more was the apparent uselessness of this work for fighting purposes."

Back in Australia at about the same time that the 9th Battalion was holding the trenches at Bolton's Ridge back on the front-line at Anzac, Desmond Pitty, aged 32, a tailor who lived in Kingaroy in Queensland enlisted, and was assigned as a reinforcement of the 25th Battalion[213] (a Queensland Battalion raised at Enoggera comprising mainly of Queenslanders and a few men from Darwin). Presumably not happy using his real name, he enlisted under a pseudonym of David John Richards, and following his basic training left Brisbane on 21st October, 1915 aboard HMAT *Seang Bee*. In his diary[214] while on board the HMAT *Seang Bee*, he notes that by the time they reached Sydney Harbour there were already 11 cases of measles among the men. Describing briefly life on board the ship, he mentions the fact that on the 2nd November, 1915 a Melbourne Cup sweep was run, but he was not told the result of the race until the 14th November, and outlines that a Private Campbell died of pneumonia on the 17th and was buried at sea on the 18th November. He makes special mention of two hospital ships that his ship passed, en route to the Suez Canal from the fighting that had taken place on the Gallipoli Peninsula. Like all the other soldiers with him on the transport ship, they would have been keenly aware of the toll the Gallipoli campaign was having on his fellow countrymen. I am sure he would have been looking to identify whether they were Australian wounded or not on board.

The link that Private Pitty (aka Richards) has with the 9th Battalion is that as his ship reached the Suez Canal, he was reallocated to the 9th Battalion and joined them while they were camped at Gebel Habeita at the end of February 1916. He does not mention this in his diary, in fact there is a large gap in time until he writes again, which is when he is en route to France.

The defence of Egypt had been of great concern for the British military authorities for some time, and there appeared to be sufficient evidence to suggest that Turkey and Germany were contemplating another invasion of Egypt. Therefore, they were anxious for work on the Suez Canal defences to get under way. Following three weeks of training, the Australian Divisions eventually began their movement to the Suez Canal zone. The 9th arrived at Gebel Habeita (eight miles from Serapeum) on the 27th January, 1916 and began to construct entrenchments and strongposts for garrisoning in case of an attack by the Turks on the Canal. The practice was for half of each of the companies to be involved with the digging and the other half paraded for military training and vice versa.

At the same time also, about 1000 Australian officers and men were sent to various training courses in England. Many of the veterans of the Gallipoli campaign were to become sergeants and officers during this time. There were a considerable number of complaints made by the Australian troops, who were keen to see some action and were very frustrated with the endless regimentation of drills and constant digging. During the whole time that they were defending Egypt, the front-line of the defences never sighted the enemy nor actively engaged them.

On 15th February, 1916, information was received that half of the 9th Battalion was to be drafted into a newly formed Battalion. It had been decided to increase the size of the AIF by creating two new Infantry Divisions, and as there were only two spare infantry Battalions, General Birdwood decided that the original 16 Battalions would be halved and each brought up to full strength with reinforcements, thus forming 32 Battalions. The 9th's daughter Battalion, the 49th, was born and formed part of the 13th Brigade of the 4th Division AIF. Little more than 400 men of the old Battalion remained and they were quite depressed about the split, although the men did not make a fuss. For them their mates that had given them the strength to continue on and the strong friendships that had been formed in the perilous conditions and fighting on the peninsula were now being broken apart and the men split up. This would certainly have been a hard time for them. The Keid brothers were impacted in particular. No sooner had the four brothers meet up together Leonard and Walter were then reassigned from the 9th Battalion to the 49th Battalion. Harry and Ted would remain with the 9th Battalion. This would have been a bitter pill for the brothers to swallow.

The effect of the Gallipoli campaign on the nationalism of the Australian soldier and moreover his bond with his specific Battalion was very strong. Bean outlines that the AIF 1st and 2nd Divisions and the 4th Brigade, which were part of the Australian and New Zealand Division that had served on the Gallipoli Peninsula and were recuperating in Egypt after the evacuation, were a military force with strongly established, definitive traditions.

> *Not for anything, if he could avoid it, would an Australian now change his loose, faded tunic or battered hat for the smartest cloth or headgear of any other army. Men clung to their Australian uniforms till they were tattered to the limit of decency. Each of the regimental numbers which eight months before had been merely numbers, now carried a poignant meaning for every*

man serving with the AIF, and to some extent for the nation far away in Australia.

The 1st,2nd, 3rd and 4th Infantry Battalions – they had rushed Lone Pine; the 5th, 6th, 7th and 8th had made that swift advance at Helles; the 9th, 10th, 11th and 12th had stormed the Anzac heights; the 13th, 14th, 15th and 16th had first held Quinn's, Courtney's and Pope's; the Battalion numbers of the 2nd Division were becoming equally famous.[215]

During their stay at Serapeum, there were at first persistent rumours that the Australians would be sent to France. It must be remembered that for many of the Australian troops, this is where they should have been sent rather than Gallipoli. The rumours gradually crystallised and on or about the 19th March, 1916, an announcement was made that they would indeed be heading to France and consequently into a living hell that none of the men would ever have been able to contemplate. In fact, around camp at that time, the Australians cheered when they heard they were going to the Western Front. Finally they were going on to the real battle that they believed they should have been called to much earlier if not for the Gallipoli campaign. It is surprising to note that even after the horror and hardship at Gallipoli, a general disillusionment with war was not present, rather the opposite sentiment was in place. The men who left the trenches in Gallipoli still believed in the righteousness of England's war against Germany.[216]

On March 26th, the 9th Battalion embarked shortly after dawn on the *Saxonia* headed for Marseilles, France. This is about the time when Private Pitty decides to make some further entries in his diary again. They entered Marseilles harbour on the 2nd April, 1916, and disembarked, marching directly to the station to board a train.

After travelling by train for two and a half days, the train arrived at the little Flemish village of Godewaersvelde, not far from Ypres, on the 5th April, 1916. For the men of the 9th Battalion, who had been in the desert for so long, the beautiful countryside that they viewed from the train, which was in a full bloom of flowers, farmhouses with bright red roofs, the tracks running alongside the River Rhone and the majestic view of the Alps on the horizon, made them think they were in a fairyland.[217] As news of the approaching troop train spread, women, boys and old men waved to them as they passed. At each of the regular stops on the line, tea and coffee were supplied by the local French authorities, or in some cases, by the French ladies, much to the joy of the troops. Local men and women pressed upon the men presents of fruit and wine.

After a couple of hours marching, Private Pitty outlines in his diary that the Battalion was billeted in farmhouses near the village of Strazeele. The men could hear the sound of guns pounding the front-line in the distance and it was cold and wet. For the 9th Battalion, their campaigning in France had just begun, but for Private Pitty is was about to end. The 18th of April, 1916 was his last diary entry.

A full year at that time, to within a few days, had passed since the Battalion had received its baptism of fire at the landing at Anzac Cove. Each one who had been through that ordeal would have remembered the tense feeling that gripped him as his boat approached the shore and the sudden impulse of excitement as he rushed up the beach through the withering fire of the unseen Turk. With the second occasion approaching, each would now be contemplating, perhaps uneasily, how soon it would be before a German bombardment fell upon them.[218] They had been told that the shelling on Gallipoli had not been nearly so heavy or sustained as that on the Western Front. They had now reached the forward area, but everything was so quiet and different from expectations, and at that stage, without incident. However, the heavy shelling would soon catch up with them.

On 20th April, 1916, Bean indicates that the Anzac troops first experienced the power of the German artillery. Unfortunately it came at the 9th Battalion's expense, whereby they were billeted at Rouge de Bout, which was supposed to be a quiet part of the line. The men of C company were inside a farmhouse when at 1.15pm per the Battalion War Diary entry that day, they were surprised by a burst of a shell on the road nearby. Others followed soon after. The fourth shell fell at the entrance to a house and wounded several men. Others ran to help them and another shell burst among them. Lieutenant Fothergrill was calling men to shelter, and many men were clustering beneath a wall of a house when the wall was struck and brought down by a shell, killing or injuring nearly 50 men. If the men had been ordered to disperse there would have been minimal loss of life. The fire was coming from a German battery of 5.9-inch howitzers and continued for an hour before ceasing. Fothergrill and 24 men had been killed, and the medical officer (Captain McKillop) and 48 others were wounded. The Battalion Dairy entry for that day indicated that between 50-60 high-explosive shells had landed in the area of the billet around the time of the incident and that all of those killed were buried in a local English cemetery.

One of the 24 men killed was Private Pitty. His diary was among his personal effects that were sent home to his family after his death. Of interest is that his wallet was pierced by a bullet and the hole was approximately 10mm in diameter. The bullet had also marked a postcard from his stay in Egypt for training and a small mirror in a canvas cover had also been smashed by the bullet's impact. Given Private Pitty did not see action on the front-line before his death, it is expected that the damage to the wallet occurred sometime after his death. On the photocopied version of his diary, the damage is clearly evident on each of the pages.[219]

The devastated C company of the 9th Battalion, suffering from its severe casualties, almost one in three, was relieved by a company of the 3rd Battalion and departed with the other three companies of the 9th Battalion from the forward area.

What a way for the 9th to start its campaigning on the Western Front!

An amusing story that came out of this tragedy for the 9th Battalion was recounted by Private Jack (James) Quinlan:

> *The next morning following the shelling, when a burial party returned it noticed that one body remained, covered with a blanket on a stretcher. The Sergeant was notified that they had missed one poor beggar and all of the men gathered around. When the blanket was lifted the "corpse" arose with a yell. When we recovered from shock, we found it was Alf Tickle who had slept the night on the stretcher, had heard himself referred to as the poor beggar we forgot to bury and remained motionless until the blanket was lifted. We got a fright but had to laugh. He was a natural humorist and gave us many laughs.*[220]

Interestingly, on 5th May, 1916, steel helmets were issued to all ranks. This headgear which was now worn by all troops in the forward zone, was a very valuable piece of equipment and resulted in many men's lives being saved. It also had a considerable effect on the morale of the troops, as a man wearing a steel helmet knew that one of his vital spots was protected from shell splinters and shrapnel pellets and he was able to endure shell–fire with much more confidence. Potentially, the casualties at Rouge de Bout may have been less if they had of been issued two weeks earlier to the men of the 9th Battalion.

Around this time, on the 4th May, 1916, Private Fred Williams of A company, 25th Battalion – 7th Brigade, had set sail from Brisbane on the HMAT *Seang Choon*, bound for the fighting on the Western Front. With him serving as part of the 25th Battalion on the troopship was Private Harry Tealby, a 21 year old coppersmith who lists his home address as Hawthorne Street, New Farm in Brisbane. Harry had enlisted 14 days after Freddie and was part of the Battalion's B company.

Much has been written about the 9th Battalion's exploits over the next three years, from 1916 through to 1918, in great detail, especially in the historical accounts of the Battalion's history as documented by both Wrench and Harvey (refer bibliography). Both books take the reader into significant detail regarding their battles, the soldiers, hardships and rest periods. To do this justice would mean significant time rewriting their good work. While I have taken the time to read through both books, my original intention was not to spend a lot of time outlining the activities of the 9th Battalion after they entered their next theatre of war, being the Western Front. Rather the focus was on the Gallipoli campaign. However, as I read and researched about the Western Front and the role of the Australians, particularly the 9th Battalion, the more it became clear that some time needed to be devoted to this period of the Battalion's war experiences. This is important in order to further understand the men and what they went through following Gallipoli, and thereby enable a more balanced account of the war from the 9th Battalion's perspective. I have focused on providing a summary of the key battles that the 9th Battalion were involved in and a brief outline of their role and impact the battle had on the Battalion in terms of casualties and morale. In many cases, however, the battles of the 9th Battalion formed a vital part of the main battles in which the Australian Divisions were engaged, having varying levels of involvement.

From the middle of May until the end of June 1916, the 9th Battalion was in the Petillon sector of the front, which was about 3.5 kilometres south of Fleurbaix. This was the first time that it was garrisoned on the French front-line. It also was a fairly quiet area.

During June and early July 1916, the first Anzac Corps carried out a number of raids on the German lines. One such raid was carried out on the nights of the 1st and 2nd July, by Battalions within the 3rd Brigade. The raid required of the 9th Battalion was led by Captain Wilder–Neligan on the night of the 2nd July. As with most raids, volunteers were called and approximately

150 men stepped forward to take part in the attack, which was planned to take place near Rue du Bois, north-east of the "Sugar–loaf Salient". The attack, which began at about 2 in the morning was a success. Sergeant John "Darkie" Kenyon was once again recognised for gallantry and courage and awarded the Military Medal for his actions that night. The story is told that Kenyon during the few minutes that were spare before it was time for the Australian raiders to return to their lines, was heard singing on the parados of the German trench, singing not in English or German but Hindustani, no doubt learnt during his time in India.[221]

Following the disastrous opening battles of the Somme offensive, Sir Douglas Haig (Commander and Chief of the Allied Armies) decided to send in the 1st Australian Division to spearhead a fresh assault at a place called Pozieres, a tiny village situated on rising ground in the otherwise flat Somme Valley. It was held by the Germans, who regarded their position as virtually unassailable. On no less than four occasions the British had attacked the enemy positions and had been repulsed at great loss. Haig was convinced that the heavily fortified ridge known as Hill 160 held the key to the domination of the Somme.

Haig had a dislike for the Australian troops, whom he referred to as the colonials and claimed they were insolent, arrogant and undisciplined, which was probably true in many respects. However, recognising the Australians' initiative and daring, Haig was quick to assign them the worst and most difficult, even hopeless areas of conflict throughout the war, and frequently used them as a vanguard to sever the barbed-wire defences before the British went into action.

By mid July 1916, the 1st and 2nd Australian Divisions, which included the 9th Battalion, were ordered to move from the Messines area 60 miles south to the Amiens sector for the assault at a place called Pozieres as part of the Somme offensive.

For two days the Australian artillery blasted Hill 160 to cut the maze of wire and to destroy the five-feet-thick fortifications. Then, the moment the guns ceased, just after midnight on the 23rd July, 1916, the troops of the 1st Australian Division leapt from their trenches and charged into no-man's-land, advancing swiftly to take Pozieres and killing and capturing Germans as they went. This was the only advance made on the entire front at that time.

At Pozieres, the men of the 9th Battalion were attacking on the extreme right of the line. As soon as the barrage lifted, A and B companies attacked. The men of B company had been lying out in the jumping-off position beyond the front–line trench. Each man had during the barrage rolled up both sleeves to the elbow as an aid to identification until daylight. Creeping forward they rushed the enemy trenches the moment the barrage lifted and secured the first trench almost immediately. Lieutenant Monteath's platoon advanced, but were held up by two machine-guns not far ahead that forced them to take cover. The Germans with their egg bombs, which they could throw further, were again outthrowing the Australian bombs and many casualties were being suffered. Then as noted by Bean:

> *Before means could be devised of ending the deadlock, a man of the 9th, Private John Leak a teamster from Rockhampton, jumped out of the trench without orders, and ran forward, threw three bombs into the German position, and then jumped into it. There Monteath presently found him, wiping blood off his bayonet with his felt hat.*[222]

Three bayoneted Germans were lying nearby. For his actions that day, Private Leak was awarded the Victoria Cross, the only one awarded to a man of the 9th Battalion. (Refer appendix 15.)

After the first objective had been taken, C and D companies passed over the captured trenches and waited in front of them for the barrage to lift. In these two companies following their advance, all the officers except two became casualties. These companies were then, understandably, not as effective for the remaining part of the battle. The Battalion fought in this area for four days, from 23rd to 26th July, 1916. In that time, all ranks had little or no sleep. When not engaged in fighting, they were occupied with digging trenches. All the time, both day and night, they were under heavy enemy bombardment which continued on with hardly any pause.

Sergeant John Kenyon of the 9th Battalion, the hero of Gallipoli and Fleurbaix, was one of the many 9th men killed in action on the 29th July, 1916, on the Pozieres battlefield. Wrench in his writing about the 9th Battalion World War I history refers to Kenyon as one of the 9th's most daring and dynamic soldiers. Sergeant George Jamieson, who was part of the 9th Battalion's machine-gun company, recounted that while he moved across no-man's-land following the attacking troops in front, he came across "Darkie" Kenyon lying in the mud with a ghastly stomach wound – beyond help. In possibly his last words before dying, he told George in blasphemous language to get on with the fight and leave him alone. Wrench indicates that he died as he had lived.[223]

The 9th Battalion historians indicate that the whole Brigade had been through a horrible ordeal at Pozieres, the result of which can best be described in an account written by a Sergeant E.J. Rule of the 14th Battalion, which passed the 3rd Brigade column on its march out from Albert (where it had stayed overnight), as the 4th Brigade was making its way up to the front-line:

Although we knew it was stiff fighting, we had our eyes opened when we saw these men march by. Those who saw them will never forget it as long as they live. They looked like men who had been in Hell. Almost without exception each man looked drawn and haggard, and so dazed that they appeared to be walking in a dream, and their eyes looked glassy and starey. What they must have looked like before they had a nights sleep and clean up must have been twice as bad as what we saw. We could see they had lost a lot of men – some companies seemed to have been nearly wiped out – and others seemed as if they had not fared quite so bad. In all my experience I have never seen men quite so shaken up as these.[224]

Sergeant Rule survived the war.

At one point during the battle for Pozieres, the howitzer shells were landing at one every three seconds. Sergeant Archie Barwick, 1st Battalion, who survived the war wrote:

All day long the ground swayed and rocked, backwards and forwards... men were driven stark staring mad and more than one of them rushed out of the trench over towards the Germans. Any amount of them could be seen crying and sobbing like children their nerves completely gone... We were nearly all in a state of silliness and half dazed... Men were buried by the dozen, but were frantically dug out again some dead, some alive.[225]

Shortly after this battle, Nelson Scrivener of the 9th Battalion was promoted to Second Lieutenant.

The Germans, determined to regain Pozieres, were quick to counterattack with a furious bombardment that rained ceaselessly down on the Australians for three days. So concentrated was the shelling that the thunder was heard clearly in the southern counties of England. Now this for the Anzacs had been their true baptism of fire, a holocaust the likes of which had never before been seen on the battlefield. One veteran was later to remark that Gallipoli had been a pleasant Sunday picnic compared to the fiery bloodbath of Pozieres.

Corporal Arthur Thomas, 6th Battalion, a tailor from Toorak in Melbourne, writes in his diary through the day:

> *[early morning] Would someone write a book on the life of an infantryman and by so doing will quietly prevent these shocking tragedies… I have seen things here that will make the bloody Military aristocrats' name stink forever. [11am] hundreds of shells from big 12 inch howitzers are being fired at us. God! It is cruel. What humans will stand is astonishing. [1.30pm] I turned my head sharply right and saw a man decapitated, one of ours. It is bloody gruesome – ah well it will end soon – this awful game. Plenty of lives just gun fodder. Our casualties are very heavy, this truly is the Valley of the Shadows – God help us.*[226]

Corporal Thomas later wrote in his diary in March 1918, after seeing so much death he noted, "I have had a damned long run and should be out of it by now, but men are wanted… so I will stick it to the end." He was killed three months later during the battle of Villers-Bretonneux.

Carlyon[227] indicates that after Pozieres, a change in the men is clear. The soldiers had never seen an artillery barrage like it. One of the soldiers indicated that it took six weeks for him to stop shaking and be able to write again.

The shelling at Pozieres did not merely probe the character and nerve of each soldier, it laid them stark naked as no other experience of the AIF ever did.[228] In a single tour of this battle, the Australian Divisions were subjected to greater stress than in the whole of the Gallipoli campaign.

Observers recorded that when the Anzacs were relieved by Canadian units, they strode off, proudly erect, in full view and contemptuous of the German guns, as though they were strolling down Pitt Street. Unlike the British conscripts, who scurried, crouching from the field.[229]

The 9th Battalion suffered the following casualties at Pozieres:

Killed	**3 Officers**	**54 other ranks**
Wounded	**8 Officers**	**263 other ranks**
Missing	**2 Officers**	**63 other ranks**
Total 393		

More Australians lie in the ground at Pozieres than in any other battlefield. Three Australian Divisions suffered 23,000 casualties in less than seven weeks, the equivalent of one complete Division. When compared to the British losses this even seems insignificant considering that on one day during the Battle of the Somme, the casualties were assessed as 57,470, of whom 19,240 were dead. Most of these came in the first few hours of the battle and most to machine- gun fire rather than artillery.

Carthew outlines that Field Marshal Haig, as usual, in his triumphant communiqués to the newspapers, had ascribed the significant victory at Pozieres to the British troops. It was clear he did not wish the colonials to be credited with the victories they were entitled to.[230]

At about the same time that the 9th Battalion was fighting at Pozieres, in another part of the flat plains of French Flanders the Australians of the 5th Division were about to take part in what many military historians agree was the most tragic military event in Australian history – The Battle of Fromelles.

The battle was planned as a feint attack to hold German reserves in this sector and away from moving south to the Somme where the main thrust of the Allied offensive had already started on 1st July, 1916. The battle of Fromelles had been poorly planned right from the start and was executed in a reckless manner. The 12 Battalions of the 5th Australian Division commanded by Major General James M'Cay were still considered raw and untried. They had only just arrived in France from training in Egypt and were sent to attack the heavily fortified German front-line in front of Aubers Ridge. They would be joined by the British 61st Division in the attack that would start at 6pm on the 19th July, 1916, following a seven-hour bombardment of the German defensive line.

The 40-metre-high Aubers Ridge was the highest piece of ground in the area and held a commanding view of both the British and Australian preparations and the open ground of no-man's-land that the Australians would need to cross. The German defences were very strong and included concrete blockhouses and a strong redoubt.

Even before the Australian soldiers had left the trench, standing shoulder-to-shoulder they suffered many casualties from German artillery fire and from "drop shorts" fired by their own Allied artillery. At 6pm, with still two hours of broad daylight remaining, the Australian 5th Division went over the top, and heavily laden with scaling ladders, picks, shovels and bags of grenades they moved forward over the open ground approximately 400 metres at its widest part under direct observation from the German lines. Almost immediately they came under withering machine-gun fire, and as recalled by Sergeant "Jimmy" Downing of the 57th Battalion:

Hundreds were mown down in the flicker of an eyelid, like great rows of teeth knocked from a comb ... Men were cut in two by streams of bullets ... it was all over in five minutes.[231]

The Allied bombardment had been ineffective and had failed to destroy the German machine- gun posts. A message was not sent to indicate that the Brigade of the British 61st Division was not advancing and hence a flank of the Australian 15th Brigade was left exposed. The carnage was extreme for the newly arrived Australian soldiers. More than 5500 Australians became casualties in that single night, almost 2000 were killed in action or died of wounds and 470 were captured. The 15th (Victorian) Brigade was destroyed within 15 minutes, entire companies being virtually annihilated. Their commander, Brigadier General Harold "Pompey" Elliott was speechless after the attack. The tears were streaming down his face as he shook hands with the returning survivors. "I felt almost as if I were in the presence of a man who had just lost his wife," wrote Charles Bean.

By dawn on the 20th July, the Australian trenches were filled with wounded and dying men. For the next three days, many Australians risked their lives to go out under fire and bring back wounded men from no-man's-land. The Germans constantly opened fire on any movement. For several days after the battle a blinded and dazed Australian officer staggered about near German lines and a number of men were killed trying to rescue him. Eventually, the Germans shot the man.

The 9th Battalion had only been in Berteaucourt, just out from Albert, on recuperation for a short time when news went round that the 1st Division would be shortly going back into the line. This of course gave rise to some unrest among the men for no–one looked forward to a repetition of recent experiences at Pozieres. The 3rd Brigade therefore relieved the 1st Brigade on the 19th August, 1916 at Mouquet Farm, which was to be the location of their next battle. During this battle, the 3rd Brigade once again took terrible losses, some 840 men being lost in front of Mouquet Farm. The 9th Battalion suffered 164 casualties, 64 killed. Unfortunately this action could only be described as a partial success. Just prior to the commencement of the attack, the 10th Battalion suffered the loss of 120 officers and men within an hour. The slightest movement by one side or the other brought down a furious artillery onslaught and machine-gun fire, which made consolidation by the Australians in the loosened ground impossible. Also, the narrowness of each individual local assault added to the Australians' difficulty by inviting a terrific concentration of enemy artillery fire on a small area.

The 49th Battalion suffered terribly in the fighting around Moquet Farm. Among the casualties were both Lieutenant Leonard Keid of A company and Sergeant Walter Keid of D company. Australian Red Cross records indicate they were both casualties from the action on Sunday, 3rd September, 1916 as part of the same advance on the first line of German trenches. Witnesses indicated that Walter had been killed by a shell during the advance not far from the top of the parapet and was buried in a shell hole close to where he was killed. Leonard led the charge of his men in A company across no-man's-land at about 5.30am towards the German trenches. He was seen entering the German trench system just prior to a shell exploding in the same location. He was badly wounded in the back by shrapnel and had broken his thigh and lay in no-man's-land for almost 24 hours whereby he succumbed to his injuries. Private William Power of the 49th Battalion later described Leonard as a man who always displayed the greatest coolness and courage, and was well liked by all his men.

Now there were only three Keid brothers alive and still in the war zone. It was not long though before Guy, profoundly affected by the death of his brothers, was discharged from the Army and sent home, arriving in Sydney on the 8th March, 1917.

From Mouquet Farm, the 9th Battalion fought in the following battles between August 1916 and September 1918:

- The Maze (Le Barque)
- Lagnicourt
- Bullecourt II
- Menin Road (Polygon Wood)
- Broodseinde Ridge
- Meteren

- Lihons (Crepy Wood)
- Froissy Beacon (Chuignes)
- Villeret

This photo was entitled "up the line to death". These men of the 2nd Division AIF were heading up to the front-lines during the winter of 1916–17. Considering where they are heading they still wave and smile for the camera. (AWM EZ0120)

In September, the Battalion moved back to the Ypres area and the Hill 60 sector where they relieved the Canadians.

The Battalion rejoined the line on the 9th November, 1916 at Flers, taking over from the 2nd Battalion. What they found were trenches filled with mud and in very bad condition. The mud at the bottom of the trenches was about 12 inches deep, with occasional patches going down to a depth of two feet deep, and most was thick and sticky. There was no shelter from the rain and the men in the circumstances had to stand there exposed to the rain or sit on a ledge scooped out of the side of the trench. Just as the battles of Pozieres and Mouquet Farm were noted for the heavy enemy bombardments, so Flers was remembered by the troops on account of the mud. One man grimly described it as, "the defunct village that lends its name to the sector of mud and corpses that we guarded for the winter".[232]

The weather was also very cold, many men were sick and a number suffered from trench foot, best described as a form of frostbite, and had to be evacuated. Measures were taken to improve the conditions of the trenches and working parties were organised to scoop out the mud and slush and throw it over the sides of the trenches. In addition, all officers were required to make frequent foot inspections of the troops with the objective of reducing unnecessary evacuations of men from the front-line. By the 12th November, much of the trenches were clear of mud. The troops' stay in Flers was one of the rare occasions when the 9th was not required to take any offensive action and very little occurred.

During the second Battle of Bullecourt, the 9th Battalion attacked a number of German trench positions and fought within the enemy trenches with fierce bomb-throwing battles along the narrow passageways and advances between trenches under heavy fire. The action eventually ended in the capture by the Battalion of some 650 yards of trenches, with the Battalion's casualties being 25 other ranks killed and one officer and 135 other ranks wounded.

Following the battle, the 9th Battalion had considerable rest from the front-line and training for the men was carried out over a four month period from the end of December 1916. By the end of this time the Battalion was well over strength, and Harvey indicates that it was by far the strongest in the 3rd Brigade. On 31st August, 1917 it numbered 53 officers and 1204 other ranks.[233]

Lieutenant–Colonel Ross of the 9th Battalion wrote afterwards in regard to this period;

> *The battalion was now at its peak in numbers, training and spirit. It was a fine Battalion before the landing and again before the blood bath of the Somme, but on neither of these occasions was it the splendid fighting instrument which it now was, nor did it rise to the same heights afterwards… It had been given time to recover from the terrible battering at Pozieres and Mouquet Farm and the chamber of horrors at Flers. The minor actions at the Maze and Lagnicourt had given the men a good opinion of their prowess as fighters, and the heavy and successful fighting at the 2nd Bullecourt had served to confirm that opinion.*[234]

Private Fred Williams, as a reinforcement for the 25th Battalion, reached the fighting in France in early October 1916. His Battalion had just fought its first battle on the Western Front at Pozieres in late July through to the 7th

August and suffered 785 casualties. No doubt the reinforcements were sorely needed to replace the fallen. Private Williams entered the fray of battle for the first time with the Battalion fighting in the Somme mud to the east of Flers, as part of the major British offensive in October and November 1916. The mud and conditions in the trenches were almost unbearable for the men and Fred indicates that they could only do 48 hours at a time, as the men could not stand it any longer in the trenches than this. Many men suffered from trench foot and bad colds during this time. After being in France for only six weeks Fred was shot in the shoulder in mid November 1916 and hospitalised in France and then transferred to England. In a letter to his mother, Private Williams writes:

> *Monday 13th November, in the trenches it is still muddy and under fire about 5am in the morning. My pal got wounded through the face … … Tuesday the 14th November we had a big hop over, we captured two of the German lines and I got a wound in the shoulder … we were cut about abit, but they copped it too, we had no mercy on them … They are alright about 15 yards but when you get near them they threw up their hands. Wednesday 15th November I was in the field hospital ready to be taken away, we left that evening for Rouen Hospital arriving there on Thursday morning.*[235]

In the months leading up to the action by the 9th Battalion at Lagnicourt, February through to March 1917, the German Army secretly began their withdrawal to Bapaume and the Hindenburg Line beyond. The Australian Divisions were involved in activity aimed at seeking out any unoccupied front-line trenches and ground that had been vacated by the enemy. The Australian Brigades operating along the front-line sent out strong patrols forward to determine where the enemy was and to report back on German withdrawals. Often these patrols were sent out at night and it was quite difficult to keep track of where the patrol was among a misty landscape of shell craters and deep mud. Hidden from cover were German machine-gun crews and snipers who were tasked with slowing up the Allied advance. It was difficult and dangerous work and put a strain on the men in each of the patrols. For the 9th Battalion alone, four officers were killed and many others were wounded, and there were 74 casualties from other ranks recorded in these actions. At this time Nelson Scrivener, now with the rank of Lieutenant, was involved in a number of these patrols and was recommended for, and subsequently received, the Military Cross during a successful patrol on the outskirts of the village of La Barque.

The next phase of battle for the 9th Battalion was at Menin Road (Polygon Wood), to be followed by that of Broodseinde Ridge, in which the 3rd Brigade only had a limited role and entered the front-line for short periods of time, before proceeding on to Passchendaele.

The Battle of Polygon Wood was greeted with satisfaction in that it would be the first time two Australian Divisions would be taking part in an attack side-by-side. This battle formed part of the 2nd stage of the great offensive known as the 3rd Battle of Ypres. Both the 9th and 10th Battalions were just arriving through Chateau Wood at 4.20am (just to the left of Polygon Wood area) on their way to the 3rd Brigade staging area when a coloured German flare was seen to go up from the corner of nearby woodlands. This was subsequently followed in a few minutes by an enemy bombardment that fell on the incoming troops and lasted for 20 minutes. The men of the 9th Battalion among other AIF Battalions, were right in the firing line.[236] The men were packed very closely together so that they would not lose touch in the dark, so it was therefore surprising that the casualties were not more numerous.[237] The 20 minute bombardment seemed to the troops to last more like an hour. After 20 minutes of recovery, at 5am the German bombardment recommenced and casualties were again heavy. The men of B company found that gas shells were falling on them and had to put on their respirators. In these two bombardments at Chateau Wood, the 9th Battalion lost all its company commanders and half its junior officers.

Bean[238] noted that the ensuing battle was probably the best example of the creeping barrage that had been employed up until this date. At zero hour 5.40am, on the 20th September, 1917, just after first light of dawn had appeared, a barrage from over 3000 guns suddenly crashed out and the line immediately began to move forward. Almost every man as he rose from the ground lit a cigarette. Three companies of the 9th Battalion advanced behind the troops detailed to take the first and second objectives. The barrage advanced across the ground at a rate of 100 yards in six minutes, so this also had to be the rate of progress of the troops. The Germans were mostly located in concrete strongposts or "pill–boxes" and in most cases, surrendered as soon as they were reached. The only fighting occurred when the occasional post refused to surrender. The operation might be described as an artillerymen's battle, as the infantry had only to walk behind it and occupy each objective. The barrage was so perfect like a wall in front of the men so that they could walk close behind it.

The 9th Battalion lost 10 officers and 228 other ranks killed or wounded during this battle. The Battalion was relieved on the night of the 21st September, 1917 and moved back together with other Battalions of the 1st Division to billets in the Dickebusch area.

Australian soldiers in craters on the edge of Polygon Wood. The Wood itself has been destroyed by artillery fire. (AWM E00971)

Passchendaele is now a word renowned for the monstrous futility of war. It was Australia's costliest campaign of Australia's bloodiest year ever, 1917. Like Gallipoli, it was marked by great courage, but ultimately achieved nothing. The four-month stint cost 36,000 Australian lives. Four months later, the Germans won back every inch of ground taken in just three days.[239]

The battle of Passchendaele was notorious for several reasons. It was the first time that Germany used mustard gas, which apart from being extremely painful, caused skin blistering, lung damage, eye irritation and even blindness. In addition, the battle was also fought in terrible battlefield conditions, caused by the incessant rain that fell on average one day in every two, which in the end proved a major opponent for the men involved. The troops fought on a battlefield that was reclaimed marshland that was swampy, even without the rain. Adding to the swampy terrain, a continuous volley of shells rendered the landscape a bog that proved virtually impassable. Troops had little alternative but to walk to the front over wooden duckboards laid across the mud. Those carrying heavy equipment that slipped off the wooden path would sometimes drown in the liquid mud on either side before they could be rescued. The newly developed tanks, which were beginning to play a greater role on the battlefield, quickly became bogged down having little further impact on the battle. The landscape became littered with the bodies of thousands of men.[240]

The German General Erich Ludendorff stated:

> *It was no longer life at all, it was mere unspeakable suffering. Through this world of mud the attackers dragged themselves, slowly, but steadily, and in dense masses.*[241]

Australian soldiers walking along duckboards over thick mud during the Battle of Passchendaele. (AWM E01220)

The extent of the destruction can scarcely be imagined, but aerial photographs taken prior to and after the bombardment indicate that the original pre-war village of Passchendaele was bombed out of existence. More than one million artillery shell holes were created within an area of just one square mile. The British alone fired more than four million shells during the battle.

The Allies objective was to drive a hole in the German lines and advance to the Belgian coast. However, the Germans were well entrenched and unfortunately the advancing Allied troops became little more than cannon fodder. The taking of Passchendaele developed into a much more drawn-out and costly operation than either Polygon Wood or Broodseinde, and was more strenuously contested by what appeared to be a more resolute German Army as combatant.

The first attack was on the 9th October, 1917, the Australian Second Division (5th and 6th Brigades, supported by two British Divisions, would take a lead role in the attack. The battle itself took the name of Poelcappelle after the name of a small village in the area leading to Passchendaele. The battlefield was a deep quagmire following heavy rain earlier in the week. The guns found no firm foundation and artillery barrages to support the advancing troops were wild and feeble and offered the men little protection after the first round was fired.

Consequently, both Brigades lumbering through the dense mud, without fire support, advancing slowly under heavy machine-gun and shelling were quickly decimated and had to retreat.

The second attack on the 12th October would unfortunately go ahead, even though Haig was advised that there was no chance of success. Haig would have none of such talk stating that, "It was simply the mud which defeated us … the men did splendidly to get through as they did." The 3rd Australian Division and the New Zealanders took the lead in this attack. The second attack as predicted did not fare much better, in fact probably worse than the first attack for the Australians. They had to cover more ground with German machine-gunners and snipers sweeping the lines of men and then the artillery began pounding them as well.

Many stretcher bearers were required to struggle through the sticky mud in order to carry a single wounded soldier out for treatment, early October 1917 – Battle of Poelcappelle. (AWM P05380.002)

"After we had gone about 100 yards we were all being bogged," wrote Sergeant Thomas Dial of the 34th Battalion. The German machine-guns ripped into the men of the 10th Brigade as it struggled along through gluey mud, generally up to knee deep, but in some places up to the waist.

"Our dead lay everywhere, it was the worst slaughter I have ever seen," said one Australian doctor. He sobbed at the sight of so many casualties. Such was the horror of the scenario that the Germans mercifully left the stretcher-bearers alone. Many even pointed to where wounded were lying and German snipers pointed to where their victims were.[242]

For Lieutenant Russell Harris of the 27th Battalion, an accountant from Adelaide, being unable to recover the wounded due to the sheer weight of numbers and the difficulty through all the mud was almost unbearable:

The feeling of frustration of having been unable at times to go to the help of men in those mud holes is still a painful memory. It was impossible to shut

> *one's ears to their cries, and when silence came it was almost like a physical blow, engendering a feeling bordering on guilt.*[243]

The Canadians were then detailed to make the third attempt, which took place on 26th October, followed by subsequent attacks that resulted in the capture of the Passchendaele Ridge by the Canadians and ending the third battle of Ypres.

On the 26th October, 1917, Fred Williams, now a Lance Corporal, proceeded with the 25th Battalion to the firing line around Ypres. He writes:

> *We travelled in cars as far as Ypres, got there about 3 o'clock, then moved out to our huts outside of Ypres for the night and I can tell you it was the most beautiful sight I've seen ... the next morning we moved upto the front-line for a week just on the right of the well known ridge [Passchendaele Ridge], which we were after. Well everything went lovely for the first four days till he (hun) started to send over some "gas". He starts about 11 o'clock of a night time and keeps it up till about 6 in the morning, then of course he is getting plenty from our lads. Well I got my mouth full about 2 o'clock on the 1st November 1917 in the morning ... it puts you out of the line for four months.*[244]

Fortunately for the 3rd Brigade, hence the 9th Battalion, they did not take part in these attacks. On the initial suggestion that the 1st Division might participate, Birdwood told Plumer that the objectives were "far beyond the capacity of my troops in their exhausted conditions". The 1st Division would do no more than safeguard the flanks. The 1st Division had taken the brunt of the losses in the previous battle at Broodseinde on 4th October, 1917; the Division's total losses were 2448 men compared to 2174 and 1810 for the 2nd and 3rd Divisions respectively.

Fortunately for the 9th Battalion, they also did not play a significant part in the battle of Broodseinde Ridge and only entered the front-line for short periods of time, in the days following the main attack.

The 9th Battalion, however, while not involved directly, was still taking casualties from shellfire and smaller engagements. A counterattack was made by elements of both the A and C Companies to capture a strong and stubbornly held trench, which earlier bomb attacks had failed to do on the 3rd November, 1917 at Tyne Cot, just south of Passchendaele. Total casualties for the Battalion in this battle were seven officers and 102 other ranks.

Unfortunately, around this time on the 1st November, 1917, Sergeant Ted Keid became a 9th Battalion casualty and was wounded by shellfire. He was taken from the battlefield with wounds to his head, which he succumbed to while in a casualty clearing station, dying from his wounds on the following day. There was now only Private Harry Keid alive on active duty, although he was at that stage in a War Hospital in Bath, England with severe pleurisy after suffering from an earlier bout of pneumonia. In what could be termed a "Saving Private Ryan" event, after the Steven Speilberg movie of that name, the Australian Government on realising the significant sacrifice that the Keid family had already made, put a request into General Birdwood to bring Harry home as soon as possible. The suffering of the Keid family back home in Brisbane would have been almost unbearable at that point as further deaths would surely have brought the scorn of the nation on to the Army! Harry was returned to Australia on the 23rd March, 1918, discharged for "family reasons".

The Australian 3rd Division had lost 3000 men, a little over 35 men per yard. Going up afterwards, official Australian war photographer Frank Hurley saw how the battle had affected the Australians. He stated that under a questionably sheltered bank lay a group of dead men. Sitting by them in little scooped-out recesses sat a few living; but so emaciated by fatigue and shellshock that it was hard to differentiate the living from the dead. He managed to take a photo of these men at that point in time. The photo conveys clearly the sight he describes along with a gruesome image of a dismembered body in the foreground. Given the conditions of the fighting and the frightful condition of the men involved, it was therefore understandable how important it was to get these men out of the firing line and taken for rest. What is even more astonishing is that after a period of recuperation behind lines in the reserve areas, these same men in most cases were then able to gather together their resolve and return to the front-line after what they had been through.

Roy Kyle, who was one of the last surviving Anzacs, writes in his book that:

If you are lucky you come out of such a hell physically untouched but mentally dead. Such is the resilience of the human mind that, physically removed to softer conditions, you soon recover your normal powers of thought and behaviour, but you don't lose the belief that you will go once too often to the front-line, and each time you go, you wonder whether it will be the last.[245]

Monash fumed after the Passchendaele battle that:

Our men are being put into the hottest fighting and are being sacrificed in hare brained schemes like Bullecourt and Passchendaele, and there is no one in the War Cabinet to lift a voice in protest.

While it could only be said in whispers, Australia began to see England following the disasters of the Somme battlefields, the once cherished mother country, for what she had become – a mother essentially preoccupied with herself, careless to a fault with the lives of her native sons, and even less caring of the fate of those from her colonies. As the wounded began to return and the daily published lists of dead grew even longer, the euphoria was over and some level of doubt about the war's objectives and how it was been managed by the British Command started taking place.[246]

At this stage of the war, it was fair to say that the British Army and its colonial armies had been severely stretched and were at breaking point.

For Lance Corporal Williams, his style of writing also changes and reflects the mood at the time in a letter to his mother back home in Brisbane:

I suppose you have heard by now that I was slightly gassed the other week at Ypres… it is now 12 months since I was last in hospital before, but it is nothing to speak of, it only means another gold bar on my arm, so that makes two I have now and I think it is quite enough… I have seen all I want to see over this part, no doubt it was a great eye opener especially to me.[247]

On the 13th November, 1917, soon after the 9th Battalion finished its involvement in fighting at Tyne Cot, it was withdrawn from the line for rest and did not move again into the forward areas until 13th December when it ventured into the Messines area. The entire 1st Division remained in this area through until April 1918. It was a reasonably quiet sector of the front and the Battalion was involved mainly with non-combat duties or fatigues, and a lot of training. Although it was in this sector on the afternoon of the 6th March that the Battalion suffered the greatest number of casualties than at any comparable time during the whole of the unit's active service.[248]

At 4pm a heavy bombardment of German gas shells, which ensued over a four-hour period around Battalion headquarters, fell directly on 9th Battalion D company's position in the reserve area. As the air was very still, the deadly fumes laid about in the low ground of the gully and when the men took off their respirators after the shelling had stopped, most of them were immediately gassed. The casualties were very heavy, with the Commanding Officer, Lieutenant Colonel Mullen, 11 other officers and 150 other ranks needing to be evacuated for treatment. Of the officers evacuated, two died from the effects of gas a few days later.

From July 1916 to November 1918, Australia fielded five Divisions on the Western Front in France and Belgium. In these campaigns, the Australians finally had the chance to face the foremost enemy, the Germans, in the primary theatre of war, and by 1918 they were achieving notable victories. However, the victories came at a terrible cost. By October 1918, as the war ground down to its final chapters, the Australian Divisions had also been ground down to about half their strength.

With a new year of renewed fighting ready to unfold in the European winter of 1918, the Allies were bracing themselves for the major offensive that must come soon, if the enemy hoped to snatch victory before the Americans, who had declared war on Germany in April 1917, could make any useful contribution to the action.

The German Army had its forces considerably strengthened in early 1918 by 35 Divisions, each of 4000 men and 2000 heavy guns, which had been redirected to the front-line trenches of the Western Front following the collapse of the Russian front. Although the Allied high command knew of the coming offensive and a buildup of troops, they had little knowledge of the scale of the forces that were being marshalled against them. Ranging along the whole of the Western Front were massed 206 German Divisions, comprising nearly one million men, which faced Allied forces of a mere 35 Divisions. The troops of the Allied nations were war weary and morale was low by winter's end. They had endured unspeakable conditions in very shallow, freezing mud-filled trenches. The men were stinking, filthy and lice ridden. The Germans, however, were in much better condition with well dug and fortified trenches. At dawn on 21st March, 1918, following the conclusion of a bitter winter, General Ludendorff unleashed his offensive with a shattering roar, deluging the British sector with lethal gas shells and detonating explosives in saps beneath the British lines. A dense fog that morning also favoured the enemy and the British were unable to see the massed approaching rows of the German troops moving through no-man's-land.

Soldiers from the 53rd Battalion enjoy a final cigarette together before going over the top at the Battle of Fromelles. Of the eight men shown in the picture, five would soon be killed and the other three wounded. (AWM A03042)

Many British and French units were soon overwhelmed by wave after wave of well-trained German troops. While the British rallied with a counterattack late in the afternoon it did not stop the onslaught. The Allies were forced to retreat again and again and within three weeks the British 5th Army was almost wiped out and General Gough's 3rd Army had been driven back nearly 40 miles. Most of the Allies involved had had no sleep or rest for days and performed like sleepwalkers, not caring whether they lived or died, some no longer taking shelter from snipers or shells. They lost more territory during those three weeks than they had gained in the previous three years, at a dreadful cost of millions of lives – an average of 7000 men dead each day.

The Germans too were tired, but flushed with triumph. They believed that victory was theirs if they could continue to drive the Allies into the sea and ultimate defeat. The Kaiser himself was jubilant at the headlong advance. By the 25th March, 1918, no Allied line stood between the Germans and the vital rail junction at Amiens. At this point the 3rd and 4th Australian Divisions under Monash were rushed to the front. They were stunned to find that Pozieres, Mouquet Farm, Baupaume, Hamel and many more villages and miles of bloodstained territory they had fought and died for had been reclaimed by the Germans, and that Villers–Bretonneux and Amiens looked certain to fall undefended. British General Congreve was heard to remark: "Thank heavens the Australians have arrived".

As the Australians marched towards the front-line, thousands of refugees who clogged the road fleeing the enemy advance halted and began to straggle back, overjoyed that "les Australiens" had arrived. Retreating British troops jeered tiredly at the Australians, shouting that they were going the wrong way. Many had already fled their units in blind panic in the confusion of the retreat, abandoning their weapons as they ran. Some heartened by the Australian reinforcements were recruited by Monash to join his Anzac Corps. On April 24th, in spite of little rest or food after their hasty, forced march, and greatly outnumbered, the two Australian Divisions stemmed the German juggernaut after several days of fierce fighting near Villers- Bretonneux, saving the town and nearby Amiens from total destruction. Apart from being a turning point in the war, this battle showed the Germans, the British and indeed the world that the Anzacs, when under their own command, were certainly a force to be reckoned with.

To this day, the citizens and school children of Villers-Bretonneux honour the memory of those Anzacs who died or were wounded while repelling the German advance and preserving the town in April 1918. The Mayor's chambers are proudly adorned with both the Australian and French flags.

While the 9th Battalion was not directly involved in the fighting at Villers-Bretonneux, the 49th Battalion, which was part of the 13th Brigade and was the Battalion formed with half the 9th Battalion's surviving Gallipoli veterans, was in the thick of the costly but successful counterattack. This attack led to the eventual capture of the town of Villers-Bretonneux, which the Brigade achieved with the help of the 15th Brigade. It is also interesting to note that involved with the 50th Battalion of the 13th Brigade as their Commanding Officer was Lieutenant Colonel A.G. Salisbury, who by default due to casualties of other more senior officers was the original Commanding Officer of the 9th Battalion for the day of the landing at Gallipoli and over the ensuing few weeks.

The Brigades of the 1st Australian Division by mid April 1918 were all located in the Hazebrouck area. They had just been rushed down from the north only six days earlier, and while they were not involved in the fighting, they filled a vital role as a Reserve Division in the defence of the critical railhead.

While the fighting around Villers-Bretonneux was considered the beginning of the end for the German Army, there were, however, several more battles that the 9th Battalion were involved in during the final year of the war. Following the defence of Hazebrouck and the capture of Le Waton, the Battalion went south to the Somme and participated in the last great series of victories for the AIF; fighting at Crepy Wood, capturing Froissy Beacon on the edge of the village of Cappy and finally capturing the town of Villeret and penetrating nearly to the Hindenburg Line.

While the 9th had many successes, one other battle that the 9th Battalion was involved in, but classified as a failure in achieving the stated objectives, was the attack by the 3rd Brigade at Meteren in mid June 1918. Brigadier General, H. Gordon Bennett noted in his diary after the advance that:

> *Evidently units of the 3rd Brigade are not ready to engage in open warfare after their long experience of the trenches and reliance on heavy artillery support.*

However, as Wrench strenuously points out in the Brigade's defence and speaking specifically about the 9th Battalion, this is really the General smarting over the failure of his operational order, using the troops as a scapegoat. Deprived of the necessary artillery support, misled by faulty intelligence estimates of the enemy's strength, low morale and determined to utilise the Battalion's recent training in open warfare, the Battalion was sent into an attack that was doomed for failure with heavy loss of life.[249] This, unfortunately, became an all too familiar theme for the AIF throughout the campaigns in France.

The attack on Meteren was in two phases. The first was a night advance on the village to encircle, and the second night, which was allocated to the 9th and 10th Battalions, was to attack from both flanks, but also via a frontal assault. Unfortunately for the 9th and 10th Battalions, the German garrison was already much stronger than anticipated and the enemy, observing the activities the night before, had prepared themselves for the inevitable attack the following morning. They increased the machine-gun defences in readiness for the attack that the Australians would need to make frontally across a couple of hundred yards of farming land with ditches, hedges and fencing without any artillery support before or during the attack, nor tanks, massed mortars and natural cover such as mist. The attacking Battalions were sitting shots for the massed and hidden German machine-guns, with the sad results shown in the long casualty list for the 9th and 10th Battalions.

An Australian platoon, now reduced to just 17 men, attends roll call during the Battle of Amiens. At this stage of the war, Australian fighting numbers were low and there were virtually no new recruits. The men who were left, however, were hardened and experienced. (AWM E02790)

An interesting story is noted by Harvey[250], which occurred just before the Battalion went into action at Lihons and provides a great account of how the Australian soldiers dealt with the hardships of war and losing mates on an all too frequent basis. One man had a run of good luck while playing a game of "two up" and he went into action carrying in his pocket French bank notes amounting to 10,000 francs – about £370 at that time. A 5.9 inch shell burst alongside him and he was blown to pieces, bank notes and all. After the battle, his mates were loud in their lamentations that so much good money had gone up into the air, but no word of regret was heard for "poor old blank"!

A reserve platoon from the 9th Battalion waits in a field to escape the shelling of the village in which it is billeted, before a German attack near Hazebrouck on 17th April, 1918. Two men were killed during the evacuation. The stakes of a newly erected wire entanglement are visible on the right, in front of the shell smoke. (AWM E02088)

Private Frederic Scrivener was also doing heroic deeds around this time and received a Military Medal for his actions while stretcher bearing on the 20th June, 1918, near the town of Strazeele. The fighting itself was described as a minor operation with the intention of advancing the front-line 200 yards forward. The action for the 9th Battalion continued until late afternoon, when a machine-gun post was finally captured. The Battalion lost six other ranks and two officers killed, and 16 other ranks were wounded. Frederic's part in the operation was described in the commendation as follows:

> *In the operation against the enemy position near Strazeele on the morning of the 20th June 1918, Private Scrivener as a stretcher bearer showed splendid devotion to duty and a disregard of personal danger. With Private Speight he cleared all our wounded from the forward position under very heavy machine-gun fire. By his gallantry and devotion to duty he set a splendid example to his comrades.*[251]

However, unlike his younger brother Nelson, who was climbing through the officer ranks, Frederic was demoted back to Private for a number of AWOL (absent without leave) indiscretions.

For Lance Corporal Williams, his luck certainly had not improved in 1918, and again he was admitted to hospital in late March 1918 with a case of trench fever, barely one month after returning to the line after recovering from gas wounding. Trench fever is normally a five-day fever and is transmitted by body lice, the onset of symptoms is sudden and the soldier would normally experience high fever, severe headache, pain on moving his eyes, soreness of muscles in the legs and back and sensitivity of the shins. One-third of all British troops that reported ill during the course of the war had trench fever. After a period of hospitalisation in England and recuperation time, Lance Corporal Williams again returned to the front-line in late July 1918.

By late August 1918, the ranks of the 9th Battalion had become so depleted that the number of those engaged in the attack at the battle of Chuignes, also known by the Battalion as Foissy Beacon or Cappy, was a little under 250. The casualties suffered were four officers and 76 other ranks. The number of German men and equipment captured and attributed to the work of the 9th Battalion amounted to 110 prisoners, three field guns, 10 machine-guns and a quantity of light railway material. Those captured by the whole 1st Division was 20 field guns, scores of machine-guns, and nearly 3000 prisoners. This was described as the greatest number of prisoners captured by any one Allied Division in 24 consecutive hours during the whole war.

The 9th Battalion's last operation, known officially as the Battle of Epehy, was a great success, with the Australian Corps penetrating the enemy lines to a greater depth than any other troops engaged, advancing almost three miles.

Just following this battle an incident occurred that Harvey[252] indicates illustrates the "fortune of war". About this time the first draft of men left the Battalion on what was termed "Anzac Leave". This was special long service leave of two clear months to return back to Australia, which was given to the men who had embarked during 1914, and of whom the vast majority had served at Gallipoli. For one of the original members of the Battalion, Private Peter Cloherty, he received news on the last night the Battalion was in the line before a rest period that he had been granted leave to Australia. While collecting his gear to go off, he was blown to pieces by a shell that burst in the entrance to his dugout. Given the late stage of the war at that time, I would think that he would have been one of the last few of the casualties suffered by the Battalion prior to the armistice.

The 9th Battalion enjoyed a rest period at Gorenflos during late September and October 1918 (seven weeks in all), a period that they thought would be an extended one, taking them through the winter months before they would need to go back to the front. This was not to be, and grudgingly the men had to pack up and be ready to move out as the enemy, who had been in retreat, was making a determined stand in the Mormal Forest sector, near the Belgian border.

Meanwhile, on the 2nd October, 1918, the 25th Battalion relieved the 20th Battalion in the front-line trenches at about 11pm and prepared for an attack the following day starting at 6.05am. Each of the Company Commanders had been briefed at 4pm that afternoon in regard to the objectives of the attack on the final systems of German trenches named the Beaurevoir Line, which lie behind the Hindenburg Line, and the eventual capture of the village of Beaurepair. By 1.15am on the 3rd October, the relief of the 20th Battalion was completed and the men slept tentatively awaiting the attack, which they would have all hoped would be their last as it was clear the German Army was in retreat and these were now mopping up operations. Hopefully there would be little resistance from the enemy and they would all return safely, including Lance Corporal Fred Williams.

At zero hour, three companies (A, C and D) of the 25th Battalion left the jumping-off line and went over the top, moving forward in a thin line behind the creeping barrage of shelling. The men met no enemy resistance at all over the first 500 yards, until they encountered machine-gun posts echeloned across the front up to the Beaurevoir line. The enemy laid down heavy machine-gun fire and the advance was halted for several minutes.

Unfortunately the Germans would not be giving up so easily. The Australians needed to move quickly and shut down the machine-guns, for men such as Lance Corporal Williams, a designated bomber, would be among the first to hop over into the hail of bullets to attack individual machine-gun placements and remove the danger. Private Harry Tealby of the 25th Battalion, a mate of Fred's, much later after the battle remembered seeing Fred clambering to his feet at about 7am, quite close to where he had been, and rush forward to bomb a machine-gun post when he was killed instantly by machine-gun fire, hitting him across his chest. He provided a good account of Fred in his letter for the Red Cross and noted that they were both from Brisbane and left together on the same ship for the war. After considerable German resistance and with the support of two tanks that had caught up with the advance, the enemy line was taken by 7.15am. Over 500 German prisoners and 45 machine-guns were captured. At one strongpost alone up to 50 prisoners and eight machine-guns were captured. It had been a successful attack, although it came at some cost; 18 other ranks killed (including Lance Corporal Williams) and 83 wounded. Private Olsen of A company, 25th Battalion, noted that he buried Fred just near where he had fallen.

The statement of service for Lance Corporal Fred Williams was stamped Killed in Action, 3rd October, 1918 and ruled off. The saddest thing of all was that the 25th Battalion remained as a fighting unit for only another nine days before it was disbanded, being absorbed into the 26th Battalion. This was the last battle for the 25th and 26th Battalions. Fred had been very unlucky.

The 9th Battalion, after some postponements, left Gorenflos on the 8th November, 1918 and was advancing to meet the enemy yet again. It was billeted at a town called Tincourt on the 10th November, 1918. Early in the morning there was heard the tooting of locomotive whistles in the distance, which indicated something out of the ordinary had happened. Then rumours reached the village that an armistice had been signed; the war was over. While most of the officers and men had an idea that something was about to happen, they did not expect that it would come so soon, especially as they were heading back to the front-line. Harvey indicates that all ranks took the news very quietly. There was no excitement whatever. The general feeling of the men seemed to be that they had left a good home at Gorenflos and they should now be allowed to march straight into Germany.

Carthew in his book[253] states that it would be impossible to describe the depths of misery suffered by those men in that hell on earth. No mere words could describe their courage, borne with dignity and humour, the quite heroism shown day after day in the face of appalling danger and privation. Nor would it be possible to portray the close mateship born of that peril; a new dimension of love that bonded men far closer than brothers.

After reading so much about the Western Front and the courageous deeds of the Anzacs and what they went through the title of this book once again seems to sum it all up. Truly these Australian soldiers were ordinary men doing extraordinary service for their country.

All this suffering, death and destruction of property and lives, both on the battlefield and at home, was presided over by Generals often very far away from the fighting and with seemingly little regard for the men under their control. It was essentially a battle of attrition, and it was callously assumed by these Generals after each of the battles that caused such appalling loss of life that there would always be other young men that would sign up and be willing to die for King and country. The men of that time had a very high sense of duty, honour and the courage to follow orders, even though it meant certain death and that it was clearly evident that their actions would not achieve any significant purpose.

This style of warfare could have only been tolerated in their time, not that Australian politicians and officers did not question decisions and the loss of life being suffered by Australian soldiers, especially during the later years of the war, but the British military leadership and War Cabinet was bloody minded, it was their way only. As Carlyon points out,[254] they were fighting a new age battle that required new approaches not yet used against new weapons that traditional fighting techniques and principles would not match. They did not know how to fight in this new age of war. The battles in which sheer weight of numbers, reputation, courage, daring and bravado would win the day with minimal loss of life were over, and now there was significant loss of life.

This is best illustrated by the carnage suffered in the first few battles in 1915 on the Western Front. Lieutenant-General Richard Haking, who as Carylon outlines was a Haig man, seemed to believe that a battle could be won through the force of character. Haking was in command at the battle of Loos and had control over two Divisions of volunteers who had never seen action before. They were required to advance on the Germans positions without any covering fire, as if they were carrying out a parade-ground drill. The German machine-gunners, less than a mile away, couldn't believe what they were seeing. They shot down Haking's two Divisions without risk, with casualties coming to about 8000 men, half the number of those involved. It is said that on the second day, the Germans after scything down row after row of British soldiers, decided to cease the practice out of sheer pity for them. In a book by Robert Graves, he tells of an officer who whistled for his platoon, which had gone 20 yards, to resume its advance. No-one moved. The officer jumped up and waved, still no movement. "You bloody cowards", the officer stated, "are you leaving me to go alone?". His sergeant answered, his shoulder broken, "not cowards, sir. Willing enough, but they are all dead!" A machine-gun had caught them as they rose to the first whistle.[255]

If the loss of British life for King and country through walking into machine-gun storms was not enough for the troops, then the decision in the autumn of 1915 during the battle of Loos in which the British used gas against the Germans for the first time must have caused further consternation. After releasing some 5000 poison-gas cylinders, the wind changed direction and it was blown back on their own troops with 2600 casualties.

Loos was a defeat, proof of the power of the machine-guns and the insanity of attackers parading in front of them as though they were at Waterloo. Haig was documented to have said five months before the battle of Loos that the machine-gun was a "much overrated weapon". In fact he had brought up cavalry in the hope of having them charge through the gap in the German lines. Unfortunately, Haig would never change his underrated opinion of the machine-gun for the remainder of the war. Carylon states that one criticism of Haig was that he lacked imagination. This needs qualification he suggests, as all through the war he dreamt of cavalrymen galloping through gaps in the German lines.[256]

The year 1915 was a disastrous year for the Allies in terms of losses. The French had up to 1.9 million casualties, including the loss of 50,000 officers. One million of these men were dead. British casualties (including those representing the dominions) were in the order of half a million. The most terrible thought arising from these statistics was that despite the general opinion on the outbreak of war that it would all be over within a few months, at that point in time there was no end in sight.

Fortunately, as the war progressed, more Australian officers were allowed to take greater command of the Anzac troops in the field. Leaders such as Birdwood and Brundell–White made significant differences to the treatment of the troops, and then later, the very popular and successful General John Monash, who replaced Birdwood. With John Monash the Australian Army now had, as Carlyon states, a "modern man" leading the army who ensured that the disregard for Australians and significant loss of life would be rectified through careful planning and better operational effectiveness. By 1918, the majority of opinion on how to conduct the war was closer to the theories of Monash, which were mainly supported by his emphatic victories. The true role of infantry, Monash was to write:

> *was not to expend itself on heroic physical effort, nor to wither away under merciless machine-gun fire, nor to impale itself on hostile bayonets, nor to tear itself to pieces in hostile entanglements .... but, on the contrary, to advance under the maximum possible protection of the maximum possible array of mechanical resources.*

Carlyon states that Monash came from another place and, when it came to war, he was no mystic.[257]

With the advancements of technology, live-feed media coverage of today's war zones, there is limited tolerance for the death of any of a nation's soldiers, especially if there the slightest chance that their deaths could have been avoided. This is particularly the case in Western democratic society, where media has seemingly unlimited capacity to question tactics and objectives, placing heavy scrutiny on generals and their decisions and tactics. Moreover, the media expect that an answer would be forthcoming. Field Marshal Douglas Haig and his officers would not have been able to get away with their actions and the resulting disasters today. Of the Allied High Command, Carthew is most scathing of Haig. He indicates that many historians have labelled Haig as a callous murderer, incompetent, arrogant, vain and pompous, achieving his high office by virtue of his birth and influence. He has few apologists for the wholesale massacres for which he was responsible, irrationally and against the advice of many of his military advisors. His plans were to virtually wipe out an entire generation of men during four years of war. There were some like Haig though, that still believe that the end justified the means.[258]

Throughout the war there were many examples of men being wounded several times and returning to the front-line after a period of convalescence. My great-great-uncle Lance Corporal Williams was one very good example. Such was their dedication to the Battalion and their mates many could not bear the wait and would repeatedly ask to be returned to ensure that they did their fair share of the hard work and did not let down their mates. This is particularly amazing given the terrible conditions and the high mortality rate of soldiers. They would all have known that each time they returned to the front it could be their last. Another amazing story is that of Company Sergeant Major Oswald Williams, no relation to Fred Williams, of the 9th Battalion, a clerk from Brisbane, who sailed on the SS *Omrah* as a Private with the first contingent of Queenslanders.

Private Williams was promoted to Lance Corporal on 18th April, 1915. He landed with the Battalion in the first wave on the 25th April at Anzac Cove and was wounded in the left foot that day. Although wounded, he stayed with the Battalion at Gallipoli until it was relieved a few days later. He was then hospitalised for a period of time before rejoining the Battalion back on the Gallipoli Peninsula in July 1915. After the 9th Battalion finally left the fight on the peninsula, he was promoted to Corporal on 12th December, 1915 and sailed to France for service on the Western Front with the 9th Battalion. He was promoted to Sergeant on 18th March, 1916. During the first few months of action on the Western Front in the Petillon sector, he received severe gunshot wounds to his chest and arm on 31st May, 1916, and after some time recuperating in England, he again rejoined the Battalion in France in October of that same year. He was subsequently promoted to Company Sergeant Major on 23rd February, 1917. On the 20th October that year he suffered gunshot wounds to his forehead and was again sent to England. Again after lengthy recuperation, he rejoined the Battalion in France in February 1918, but possibly due to trauma was then transferred to a Headquarters Unit in England in August not long before the end of the war.[259]

The Sergeant Major returned to Australia on 15th September, 1918, and worked as a clerk and then an inspector for the Brisbane City Council until he died on 8th June, 1938.

Portrait of Company Sergeant Major Oswald Williams of the 9th Battalion. (AWM 04892.001)

CHAPTER 8

The War is Over

The last action for the men of the AIF was an assault by the 6th Brigade at Montbrehain on 5th October, 1918. Then the men of the Australian Corps were retired for a well-earnt rest.

By October, Germany concluded that the war must be ended and began to retire. Germany soon after sued for unconditional peace. In spite of this, hostilities continued unabated during negotiations, and many hundreds of men on both sides were killed tragically and unnecessarily, even after the terms of the surrender had been accepted. One British general who tried to order his troops into action around this time was pelted with mud and stones by infuriated soldiers. They had seen too much death caused by callous commanders. There would be no more bloodshed so obviously close to the end of the war. The focus was now to get back home.

At precisely the 11th hour of the 11th day of the 11th month of 1918, the guns abruptly fell silent. After more than four long, terrible years of ruthless attrition of soldiers on all sides and massive loss of both the lives and property of civilians caught up in a war that encompassed almost the entire civilised world, the war, for most, was finally over. It would have been expected that the news would have been greeted by the Australian soldiers with great celebration and relief. In fact this was not generally the case, there were too many mates that would not be joining in the celebrations and too many bad memories to contend with to make rejoicing a priority. An AIF Brigadier noted:

> *There was no cheering or excitement among the men. They seemed too exhausted, and no-one seemed to be able to comprehend that it was all over.*[260]

However, back home in Australia, the end of the war was celebrated in every city and country town as the news filtered down to the people from media outlets and local newspapers. In Sydney, celebrations started three days early due to a cable report that was wrong. Then three days later, after the armistice was actually signed, the celebrations started in earnest again, complete with the re–burning of the effigy of the Kaiser. The Melbourne *Age* newspaper went so far as to ask the public to refrain from letting off fireworks in the interests of the returned soldiers, particularly those suffering from shell–shock.[261]

Between 1915 and 1919, the Australian soldiers were awarded 66 Victoria Crosses (this includes two awarded for service in North Russia in 1919), which was the highest award for wartime bravery among the Allied Armies. Nine Victoria Crosses were awarded for acts of bravery during the Gallipoli campaign. It could be contended that many more should have been awarded to other Australian soldiers whose deeds went unreported. In fact for many Australian soldiers, awards for bravery were received with some level of unease as they considered they were either just doing their job and helping their mates, or felt that those around them at the time were just as worthy but had not been noticed.

The test of a man's courage and capacity to overcome fear was constantly put squarely at the feet of all men on the front-line. Captain George Mitchell of the 48th Battalion, who won the Distinguished Conduct Medal at Bullecourt in 1917, and the Military Cross in March 1918 stated that:

> *In battle ... the soul of every participant is laid bare for all to see. Battle strips all masks and shams from every one, each having to stand naked to the gaze of his companions... Fear grips you everywhere; constricting your throat, squeezing your heart. It is like a lump of ice in your stomach. Then panic surges over you and you are ready to run – run anywhere.*[262]

Sergeant Archie Barwick of the 1st Battalion, a veteran of both Gallipoli and the Western Front, expressed his experience of fear and his struggle to contain it in battle:

> *I know myself that I never felt the slightest fear that first day or two, it was when we began to realize that bullets hurt when they hit you, that we knew what fear was. The first time that fear came to me was on the third day when we were in a perfect hail of bullets and men were being killed all around me that I felt frightened. I am not to ashamed to say that I had a terrible fight*

with myself that day, one part of me wanted to run away and leave the rest of my mates to face it and another part said no we will stop and see it out at any cost rather than show the white feather. This sort of thing went on for about an hour and a bayonet charge settled the argument for me, I was fairly right after that.[263]

Following the armistice, there were some 180,000 Australian soldiers that needed to be kept occupied until ships were arranged to take them back to Australia Many of the Australian soldiers expected that they would join the soldiers from the other Allied nations in forming part of the occupying force that entered Germany in December 1918. However, this was not the case and the Australian forces were not invited to have troops available for the occupation, unlike the other dominion nations such as New Zealand and Canada. No doubt their well-deserved reputation as fun loving, high spirited, and their lack of discipline particularly when away from the front-line, made them unsuitable candidates for the purpose of maintaining law and order among their former enemy.

Presenting the contrary view, the Canadians were not at all keen to go into Germany, in fact many considered the Australians had put one over them by getting out of it. Everybody was demanding to know why the Aussies were being favoured. One story was that all the available boats were to be used to take the Aussies home first as they had the furtherest to go. Another story was that Canada and Australia were to provide an army of occupation between them, Canada to do six months then Australia six months.[264]

General Monash was appointed Director-General of Repatriation and Demobilisation to plan and oversee the task of getting the AIF home and had started work on the planning in London by 21st November, 1918. Unlike the approach initially favoured by Prime Minister Hughes, which would have had the men return home unit by unit, Monash argued successfully for men to be returned according to their priority as dictated by the length of service. While the Australians were anxious to be getting home, the departure of the first drafts early in 1919 occasioned deep melancholy among the troops.[265] By making a man's mate his chief reason for being, the war had drawn men closer than brothers, a bond that was difficult to break and important to keep the men going during combat. Now the men started to realise that these friendships and Battalions were beginning to be broken down and men were being shipped out as individuals rather than with their mates and under their Battalion banner that they had fought and died for. The AIF was slowly dissolving, and by the 1st April, 1921, the AIF officially ceased to exist.

The first large quota of 1100 men for repatriation from the 3rd Brigade back to Australia occurred on 29th January, 1919, including many men from the 9th Battalion (one-fifth of the current strength) and the last commanding officer of the 9th Battalion, Lieutenant Colonel C.F. Ross. Due to the depletion of troop numbers by the draft for repatriation and non-military employment, the 9th and 10th Battalions were merged on the 5th February, 1919 into the 9/10th Australian Infantry Battalion. On 6th February the 11th and 12th Battalions merged, and then on 28th March, all four Battalions of the 3rd Brigade merged into what would be known as the 3rd Australian Infantry Brigade and the old Battalions became companies.

Most of the remaining men of the 9th Battalion, some 13 officers and 298 other ranks, sailed for Australia on the *Takada* on 19th July, 1919. The first sight of Australian landfall was the West Australian coast as they approached Fremantle on 29th August. At this point, another informal breaking up of the 3rd Brigade happened when the 11th Battalion men disembarked at Fremantle dock. The *Takada* continued its journey and arrived at Port Adelaide on 4th September where the men of the 10th disembarked. Next port was Port Melbourne, arriving early on 7th September and was the disembarkation point for all personnel for Queensland and New South Wales. The Queenslanders were then ushered on to special trains bound for Brisbane.

Private Frederic Scrivener returned to Australia on 19th June, 1919, having served for five years and 32 days. He spent his later years living in an aged home in Ipswich and died in the late 1970s.

Lieutenant Nelson Scrivener returned to Australia on 31st March, 1919, with a wife, a Military Cross and no work prospects. The former clerk was offered a labouring job in his home town crushing rocks for a war memorial, however, he did not last long in this role. The Depression years were not easy for his wife, Grace, and himself, but they managed and brought a house on the Gold Coast in Queensland. In 1970 his memoirs of Gallipoli were published and he died in 1977 aged 83. Grace died six weeks later.[266]

On arrival in Brisbane of the *Takada* on the 9th September, 1919, just over five years from the time when the Battalion had come into existence, the men were given a heroes' welcome by relatives and friends. There were also a few earlier returned 9th Battalion soldiers there to cheer them on and look for mates that had made it home.

Australia's losses in northern France and Belgium are worth contemplating. At Gallipoli, 8709 soldiers were killed, whereas 48,671 died in France and Belgium. Out of a population of 4.97 million, Australia lost 61,700 in the Great War, with another 155,000 wounded. The Australian Army suffered a 64.8 per cent casualty rate, by far the greatest percentage of any Allied army. This high rate could be explained partially by General Haig's predilection for sending the Anzacs into the worst, most difficult and dangerous areas of the front.[267]

In regard specifically to the 9th Battalion, the original complement comprised 32 officers and 1005 other ranks. There were 26 detachments of reinforcements for the 9th Battalion that left Australia between December 1914 and October 1917, numbering 4364 of all ranks. Although, it should be noted, that not all of the reinforcements made it into the 9th Battalion. After October 1917, all new recruits embarked as general reinforcements. The total number of men who belonged to the 9th at one time or other amounted to about 8000 men.[268]

The casualties of the Battalion were:

	Officers	**Other Ranks**	**Total**
Killed in action	32	746	778
Died of wounds	11	233	244
Wounded	79	2014	2093
Gassed	21	308	329
Prisoners of war	1	8	9
Total battle casualties	144	3309	3453

In the two theatres of war:

	Gallipoli	**France**
Killed in action, died of wounds or gassing	236	786
Wounded, gassed and prisoners	397	2034

From the 25th to 30th of April, 1915, the 9th sustained 515 casualties. These were the heaviest casualties of any battalion, except for the 7th Battalion, which received 541.[269]

A special medal was made up for those men who had been on the Gallipoli Peninsula for six months unbroken service with the 9th Battalion – the Butler Medal. The medal was sent to six officers and 88 other ranks. Lieutenant Nelson Scrivener was one of those to receive the medal, but Sergeant Frederic Scrivener was not awarded the medal due to the fact that he left the peninsula for a month with sickness. Interestingly, when the Battalion finally left the peninsula there were only 63 officers and men of the original Battalion of approximately 1000 who had remained with the unit without a break since 25th April, 1915.

These are the statistics that many observers of the war conclude on, but it is worth considering that many more men returned home severely impacted both physically and mentally from the terror of war and the horrific conditions they had to endure. They were never themselves again. While they had returned home in one piece, they were still never far from the horror and would continue to relive it every day. The war-weary soldiers often battled on in silence. The services offered as standard practice today for returned soldiers were not at the same or even comparable levels then, and most returned to suffer in silence and work through their issues alone.

Transcripts of interviews with relatives of returned soldiers often recount the torment that the men went through trying to adjust back to normal life. Many family and friends indicated that the veterans would never want to talk about their war experiences. This was certainly the case for Harry Keid, who refused to talk about the war and it seemed to some that he seemed to be somewhat ashamed to have taken any part in it. Anzac Day in Harry's house was kept silent and a sad day, no-one did any work and unnecessary conversation was forbidden. Harry never went to Anzac Day services, nor did he join any of the organisations supporting returned servicemen. Younger members of the family described him as being severe, even bitter,[270] but anyone who knew what he had endured would have understood that the memories were just too painful to reflect on. For some, especially those who had received severe shell-shock, even the starting of a mower or the hitting of a nail would give them a fright or could even send them cowering to the floor. The condition now referred to as Post Traumatic Stress Disorder was not recognised in those days and hence no treatment or counselling was available for the afflicted. Friends and family were not able to understand what they were going through and could not help them deal with their personal traumas. A great number of men withdrew from their families and friends and died younger than they should have. The scale of such deaths is unlikely to ever be known.

For the wounded, however, the suffering did not stop when the war ended. Of the 155,000 men of the AIF wounded, the number who later died as a direct result of wounds in the decade after the war doubled the official "killed in action" figures. The casualties were still being counted during the 1930s. By then another estimated 60,000 men had died from wounds or illnesses directly caused by the war. At least one generation and potentially many from the second generation, of women and children also suffered terribly from having loved ones not return or seeing loved ones return in body but not the same men mentally and emotionally as those that had left.[271]

My mind drifts back to the tragedy of the Keid family of Brisbane that sacrificed so much. Four sons killed in the war out of six that enlisted and the suffering back home. The waiting and then the agony of the receipt of the pink telegram bearing the painful news, followed by the parcel of personal belongings that could be recovered from the dead soldier received in the mail. Their loss was also noted within the community and the Sherwood Shire Council in a letter to the family indicates sympathy for the great loss endured and bestows honour on the Keid family on behalf of the Council. Hampson[272] goes on to note in his book that Mary Keid, the mother of the brothers, suffered a minor stroke caused by shock and worry. While Leonard's wife, Eliza, suffered terribly following news of his death and fell into a screaming fit and suffered from a deep depression and received electric shock treatment to help control the affliction. She continued to have high blood pressure and narrowly avoided a stroke.

While the 1st AIF officially ceased to exist on 1st April, 1921, its rehabilitation and the pensioning of its soldiers had still not been completed by the time World War II broke out in 1939. When that happened, there were still 2000 World War I veterans in Australian hospitals and another 50,000 attending as outpatients. The "wingies and stumpies" the amputees, were familiar sights in city streets, some on crutches, some pushing themselves along in self-propelled wheelchairs. [273]

Carthew[274] notes in his book that for some, following the end of the war, the anguish had just begun. A large number of men joyful to be home and looking forward to a reunion with their wives or sweethearts found that they had moved on to other men, many of whom had not served in the war. Other wives/girlfriends found they could not accept that the young handsome man that had left years before was now horribly disfigured or an amputee, and many veterans found themselves rejected, some taking their own lives after making it through years of a living hell. Some returned soldiers became invalid cases and a burden to be cared for seven days a week by their families, destroying harmony and reducing family members to nervous wrecks.

Many of the returned veterans could not erase the terrible things they had witnessed, death and killing, the images and the fear returning frequently. For others such as those who were the shell-shocked or head-injured for whom the war would never really end, each day unimaginable horrors of the war continued for them. Frightened of even their own shadows, loud noises and often sobbing and shaking uncontrollably, many of these men were destined for psychiatric care in state run institutions.

It was a common occurrence for Gallipoli veterans in military hospitals back home to be heard screaming out throughout the night, plagued by recurring nightmares, reliving the death of friends or waking up after imagining that shells were shrieking overhead and landing in the room around their bed.

However, the majority of men who returned were able to get on with their lives again, albeit with difficulty. They were expected to be the same men who had jauntily waved goodbye three of four years earlier, but they were as different from those naïve, happy-go-lucky, fun loving young men looking for mischief and adventure as night is to day. They were still young in years, but older than time itself in bitter experience.[275] The returned soldiers preferred to meet with the mates who had gone through the same things with them, comfortable only with them at the regimental reunions or Anzac Day ceremonies when they were held during the year. In the tough spirit and character of men of that time, they just got on with it and made the best of things.

As Roy Kyle, who was one of the last surviving original Anzacs writes:

War really changed a person. Soldiers who went over came back different men.[276]

The War Service Land Settlement Scheme was a Government initiative, administered by the respective State Governments, which was aimed at helping the returned soldiers get back on their feet by providing them with land as compensation for their war service to the country. Crown land was used where possible, but much of the land had to be acquired. Every discharged soldier was entitled to apply for land and financial assistance, and this also extended to war workers, munitions workers and the dependants of soldiers killed during the war.

The Australian Bureau of Statistic – 1925 noted that by 1924 just over 24 million acres had been acquired or allocated. Of this nearly 6.3 million acres was purchased with the balance Crown land that had been set aside and some 23,367 farms were established across Australia by returned soldiers. The Queensland scheme commenced in 1916 and some 2000 settlement farms were established, from as far north as the fertile plateau of the Atherton Tablelands (south-west of Cairns) down to south-east Queensland rural areas such as the fruit growing Granite Belt, where many of the settlements bore the names of World War I battlefields and some 400 soldiers in particular, located on settlements at Beerburrum to the north of Brisbane. While the settlements resulted in success for some, for many others it resulted in despair. The new farmers, unable to cope with the climatic changes, were given little skill or direction and with limited capital to invest into additional stock or equipment, simply chose to walk off the land and return to the towns and cities they lived in prior to the war to look for work. For those soldiers taking up settlements on the Granite Belt as orchardists, in particular, within a decade of working and managing their farms many were beaten by the scourge of the fruit fly and depressed fruit prices.

The outpouring of grief throughout every capital cities and in most towns across Australia was immense as families struggled to come to terms with the loss of loved ones who were buried overseas and could therefore not properly be laid to rest in their home towns. Instead, what occurred was a period when many memorials were built across Australia, both functional such as parks, honour drives and trees dedicated to fallen soldiers and commemorative monuments. The latter normally being a statue of a "Digger" with a list of the names of local boys that did not return. It was the responsibility of each family to ensure the name of their loved one was recorded and communities took the time to plan for the most appropriate site for their memorial statue to ensure access, and the area around the memorial was spacious enough to allow a crowd to gather on Anzac Day ceremonies. This practice helped not only the families who lost loved ones to mourn, but promoted a strong community spirit of support that still endures today. The prominence of these monuments in many suburbs of our capital cities and in most towns throughout Australia ensures that the memory of those killed during the war remains a focal point for each of these communities.

In a speech made in 1993 by the then Prime Minister of Australia, Paul Keating, he outlined in regard to the sacrifices of Australian soldiers during World War I:

> *It is a legend not of sweeping victories but of triumph against the odds, of courage and ingenuity in adversity. This is the very essence of the Anzac story, the Australian legend which emerged from the war ... They were the heroes, not the generals and the politicians, but the soldiers, sailors and nurses – those who taught us to endure hardship, to show courage, be bold as well as resilient, to believe in ourselves, to stick together.*

Chapter 9

Final Thoughts

Throughout my time researching and writing this book, I must say that for me personally reading the diaries and notes written by the Australian soldiers during and following the war, I began to develop an understanding of them as men and their character beneath the uniform. No more so than the letters of my great-great-uncle Lance Corporal Fred Williams. I admire their candid comments about how they dealt with the circumstances they were confronted with, their humanity amid horror and more often than not their disgust of the war in which they fought. They vividly reflected on the life they lived before the war and how precious they held on to the memories of home and loved ones.

What this does for the reader today tracing their course through the war is that a bond is built with them, you start to get to know them as people rather than just soldiers. Men with lives, loves, dreams, fears and concerns – they were ordinary men. More often than not, they were men with a strong sense of duty and incredible courage. Their mates were special and they displayed incredible optimism in the face of terrible adversity. It therefore comes as a sad realization when they are suddenly killed and do not return, one feels for them and their families. Their story ends on the battlefield far from home.

Carlyon indicated that throughout his research he drew close, intimately so, to a generation of Australians buried in France. He states,

I don't think you can avoid it. One of the things that struck me is when you read a lot of letters from one bloke, is that you see that he uses a different tone in how he writes to his mother, sister and father. He might write gently to his sister and respectfully to his father. In reading the letters you get a sense of the family but you also get a sense of the man. I found it possible to feel, particularly if he had a good sense of humour, that if I had known this bloke then I would have liked him. Then you turn over the last page and read, KIA – Killed in Action.[277]

For these fighting men their time writing in a diary or writing letters was a special task and the only real mode of communication home available to them. Their letters and entries clearly show the pride, great passion and emotion in which they were written. This was one of the tasks they ensured they found time for when away from the firing line. Even during the fighting they would still try to take whatever time was available to record thoughts and messages home, in some cases even stopping mid-sentence when they were required to go over the top or even when being shot at. Communicating with family and friends was of great importance, particularly given that death was always around them and never far away. Most men on the Western Front thought that they would not make it through the day, let alone the war, so each letter might be their last communication. They saw mates and relatives wounded and killed and knew first-hand the pain of loss and the desperate need to obtain information about the welfare of those close to them fighting at other parts of the front-line. They pined for letters from loved ones back home, expressing the joy when a package of gifts from home came through. It was not only uplifting to the morale of the soldier, but often also to those around him. The men would write on anything they could. Writing paper was often a premium at the front-line and there were accounts of men writing on leaves and any scrap paper they found that happened to float across their part of the battlefield.

One of the saddest stories for Carlyon was the story of Corporal Thomas, who enlisted from Melbourne at the age of 37, and he featured quite a lot in the materials that he had researched on Pozieres.

By the time he gets to 1918, you really get to know him. He senses the end of the war is coming and he writes with feeling that it is incredible that he has survived. Then he adds, what a pity, I'm childless. A month later he is dead. I felt as if I'd known him.[278]

For me, the stories about brothers who joined up together and tried to communicate with each other are the ones that struck a closer chord. An older brother trying desperately to communicate with the younger brother, for whom he has sworn to his mother that he would look after and bring home safely, only to find after months of writing with no response the hope ends with news that he has died a few months before. Or the story of an older brother sending letters back to his younger brothers imploring them not to enlist and how terrible it was compared with what they had initially expected.

One story that touched me was the story of the three Carthew brothers, Charles (the oldest), Fred and James from Victoria. The story has been compiled by James's son Noel[279] from the many letters written back home by each of the brothers, which provides a vivid account of their lives, thoughts and trials during the war. Each of the brothers grew up around horses and loved the bush and hence it was not surprising that they rushed to join the Light Horse regiments. Charles joining the 8th Light Horse in Victoria and Fred joined the 10th Light Horse in Western Australia, because he was in that State with a friend at the time. The youngest brother, James, had tried desperately to join his brothers, however, due to his asthma, he failed on the first attempt, but vowed to try again later.

Charles and Fred met up with each other in Egypt while training and then both went to the Gallipoli Peninsula at the same time, landing during mid to late May 1915. Around mid June 1915, Fred fell ill with influenza, and as was the practice, was removed from the peninsula and taken to an Egyptian hospital. On the 8th August, Fred writes to his family to say that he has not yet heard from Charles and that there are many men of the Light Horse flowing into the hospitals having been evacuated wounded from the peninsula. You can sense in his writing his anxiety about his brother, but he continues to hope that all is well. Some days later he reads that Charles is listed as missing following the fatal charges by the Light Horse regiments at the Nek on the 7th August. Two weeks later a Corporal from the 8th Light Horse, who was the sole survivor of Charles' troop, informs Fred that Charles is dead.

During late August and September 1915, continued assaults on the peninsula caused further large-scale casualties and as a result recruitment dropped sharply. To make good the losses, where possible convalescent troops in Egypt were rushed back to the front. For many this was what they wanted, to get back to their mates and the front-line as soon as possible. To

Fred's great satisfaction, this was what happened by the end of October 1915. Noel writes that as soon as his Uncle Fred was off duty from the front-lines, he made a pilgrimage to the Nek to see the place where his brother had charged to his death. As he stood on the fire steps of the Australian trench, surveying the rugged terrain, he must surely have tried to recognize his brother's remains among the pathetic mounds of the dead.[280]

The bodies of the Light Horse men were not recovered during the course of the campaign. Even following the war in 1919, when Australians returned to recover bodies and bury the remains, the bones of the Light Horse men killed several years before shone out in the sun.

Fred stayed on the peninsula for the remaining period of time until he left with the evacuation on the 20th December, 1915. Following his time at Gallipoli, he spent the rest of his war years in Egypt and Palestine fighting the Turks and returned home at the end of 1919 following the cessation of hostilities.

For the youngest brother, James, he was finally able to enlist in October 1915 in the Second Field Artillery Battery and arrived on the Western Front in May 1916, in time for the big push in the Somme. For James and his mates, it seemed impossible that any human could survive death, which principally came from a shell fired by a German howitzer or from machine-gun fire that never ceased for an instant throughout the day and night. No doubt from accounts of the Battle of the Somme and the way the war was being fought as outlined in Chapter 7, James saw many things that would have shaken him to the core; the worst display of humankind. In late July 1916, he was buried underground in a trench following shelling of his area and just managed to be pulled out in time, barely alive. He was sent to hospital in France, but like most of the wounded who recovered was back at the front in November 1916. Not long after, while working on the artillery battery, a shell exploded close by and he received wounds to his shoulder and was taken unconscious off the battlefield and back to hospital, this time in England. By August 1917, after a period of several months of convalescence, James had returned to the front-line again. However, his luck ran out after just four months in the line and James was severely gassed and blinded from mustard-gas burns to his eyes. He was again hospitalised in England. To my amazement, James in his letters still wrote that he expected to be returned to France to join the front-line again with his unit! In my mind this is the essence of extraordinary service after all that he had endured. I would imagine that there would be few men among us today who could go through this experience and still be prepared to put their life on the line again. In fact it would not be expected of men to do so in today's armies. However, this is the way it was in this time and this was their nature. Fortunately, James was not to return to the battlefield and was loaded on to a hospital ship bound for Fremantle on 23rd September, 1918 to his family's great relief.

As Noel Carthew writes about his father:

It must have been an emotional moment when James and the rest of his wounded mates first sighted the shores of Western Australia. They were well up before dawn, the blind guided and those unable to walk carried on deck by their cobbers and placed near the ship's railings, the others standing silently, straining their eyes to the horizon for the first glimpse of that low, sandy, unimpressive but beloved coastline. Then as the sky paled and the first vague outline of the coast was revealed, a low wordless murmur was heard. Somewhere on that packed foredeck someone had begun to play "Home Sweet Home" on his mouth organ and suddenly, every eye was blinded by the tears dammed up during the endless, terrible years of their long exile. They were home, they were home![281]

Like the resilience and strength of character of Company Sergeant Major Oswald Williams, outlined in Chapter 7, the story of the Carthew brothers is a true testament to the phrase ordinary men providing extraordinary service. Equally, I would expect that they are merely two of many thousands of stories of men that served during the Great War for their country and king that have a very similar story of great courage and loss.

Reflecting now on the Gallipoli campaign specifically, in 1919 a mission was sent to the Dardanelles with the objective of carrying out research on the battlefields, discuss plans for the war graves and obtain information from the Turkish soldiers present during the campaign about their understanding of the fighting that took place. The mission was lead by Charles Bean, the official war historian who spent so much time with the Anzacs during the Gallipoli campaign, and seven other Australians. They included George Lambert, the artist who painted the two famous images of the Anzac landing that depict Australian soldiers scaling the cliffs of Ari Burnu and of the Australians charging at the Nek, and Hubert Wilkins, an accomplished photographer who amassed over 200 plate-glass photos taken during his time at Gallipoli Peninsula. Most interestingly, they were also accompanied by a Turkish officer, Major Zeki Bey, who was the commander of the Turkish 1st Battalion of the 57th Regiment. He specifically provided his insight as a Turkish officer who was present during the battles and throughout the campaign. Bean would often subject him to nightly "interrogation" sessions.

It is interesting to reflect on how each must have felt upon returning to the battlefield. Reading through Bean's book entitled *Gallipoli Mission*[282], he outlines what was discovered during this mission back to the Gallipoli battlefields in 1919. Throughout his writings in this book you can see the emotion and the enthusiasm in which he moved about the battlefield for the first time without concern for his safety. For now the mysteries of what was on the Turkish side of the battlefield were being revealed, along with answers to his questions about terrain and the actions that took place that he had only observed from the Allies' side. Bean reflected on all the events he had witnessed, the courage he wrote about and the tragic sacrifice of the soldiers. It would have all flowed back to him in waves of emotion, and much of the battlefield would have been the same as when he had left it, just more densely covered by foliage. He writes:

> *Thus as we rode northwards along this road the trenches were never, except where a gully broke them, more than about 50 yards away on either hand ... It gave a strange thrill to ride along this space in front of Steele's, Courtney's and Quinn's where three years before men could not even crawl at night. The bones and tattered uniforms of men were scattered everywhere.*

Later Bean comments:

> *Saddest of all, our unburied dead – the faded red and purple emblems on the uniforms of the 6th Battalion lying where they had fallen at Lone Pine, the tragic skeletons half clad in rotting uniforms bearing the yellow and black of the 10th Light Horse and the yellow and green of the 8th (Charles Carthew's regiment), lying on an area less than three tennis courts on the Nek, where they died in one of the bravest charges ever made.*

When Carlyon was at Gallipoli pulling together his thoughts for his book entitled *Gallipoli*, he wrote in an article for *The Sydney Morning Herald* that while standing at the Nek battlefield:

> *... as it so often does, Gallipoli challenges the imagination. You have to let it sink in. Where you stand life ended for several accountants, a Perth architect, a bunch of farm kids from Victoria' s Western District, a schoolmaster from*

Geelong, a vigneron from Rutherglen, several barristers, an ironmonger, a grocer, a Rhodes Scholar, old boys from Scotch and Melbourne Grammar and four sets of brothers. Yes, a lost generation.[283]

Geoffrey Blainey stated:

... perhaps the most drastic effect of the war on Australia would never be enumerated: it was the loss of all those talented people ... (taking up roles within the community) and the fathers of another generation of Australians. It was a war in which those with the gift of leadership, the spark of courage, and the willingness to make sacrifices often took the highest risks.[284]

The Australian soldiers of the AIF were all volunteers, the best physically that the country had to offer. It was said that you could always tell throughout the war those AIF men that had enlisted in the first wave of men for the front as they where much broader and stood head and shoulders above the other men. We possibly lost on the battlefields of Gallipoli and France the most generous spirits of a generation.[285]

Carlyon writes:[286]

... tramping over the battlefield day after day, is like going back to the childhood farm: everything is smaller than it should be. Lone Pine is a little plateau, a few hectares. Shrapnel Valley is not so much a valley as a gap between two ridges. Nothing is big here, except the cemeteries. And it's so silent. Romantics who think they are going to hear voices are soon disappointed. The ghosts are shy. When you hear a bird call, it so breaks the silence it startles you. Mostly all you hear is the keening of the wind and the plop of the waves. Mostly you feel like an intruder. Sometimes you feel the dead are telling you to go away and leave them alone.

It does not seem to matter that those who landed here were different from us, and neither does it much matter that Gallipoli the place is obscure. Or that Gallipoli the battle was a defeat. Gallipoli the spirit – that is what these pilgrimages are about. Because what we can't be disavowed is that Australians did great things here, the sort of things that don't get much done these days. It wasn't just the heroics. The spirit of the place probably has more to do with the stoicism and dry humour. Early in the campaign, a kid crawled down Shrapnel Valley with one hand and half a leg shot off. A corporal went to help him. The boy said others needed help more than he did. "Anyway", he said, "I don't think I'll last more than an hour." Towards the end of the campaign, a private eventually went to see a doctor and said apologetically, that he was having a little trouble. He had dysentery, a compound fracture of the arm, two bullets in his thigh and bullet wounds to the liver and diaphragm.

Taking up on Carlyon's thoughts, for me the Gallipoli campaign is an awesome story, it has everything that a great story should have. It is a "page turner". It is no wonder that movies have been made about the campaign Australians are brought up with the story told from generation to generation, documentaries are made and many books have been written. It has captured the hearts and minds of Australians, especially those from more recent generations.

It was the first major battle that Australians fought as true "Australian" soldiers, a nation that desperately wanted to prove itself and show the mother country what it could do. The best men of their time who had volunteered for an adventure in mid 1914, which they thought would be over before Christmas that year and they would be fighting the Germans in France. Suddenly they were thrown into a war that was not what they had signed up for, nor could they have ever imagined. It was brutal, offered great hardship, torment and was deadly. The men were often poorly lead and the actions they were required to take part in were often futile and a tragedy for those involved, yet they got on with the business and relied on their mates. As Carlyon states:

Australians especially of the time, saw Gallipoli as a piece of nation building. Here was proof that the 14 year old Commonwealth was more than an appendage of Britain. The Australians had not won, but they had hung on when they had no right to. They had fought as well as any British troops. Innocence had been among the casualties at Gallipoli and if one was going to fight the Great War out to its finish, innocence was a good thing to be rid of. Gallipoli certainly gave Australia a sense of worth of its people.[287]

Bryce Courtenay notes in the book *An Anzac's Story*[288], that the battleground itself was another significant part of the grand story to come. No commander in his right mind would have chosen to fight on such terrain; one that was clearly always going to be to the ultimate advantage of a determined enemy who commanded the heights. While some reconnaissance of the battlefield from a ship sailing along the coast line was made by Hamilton and his senior staff, it was clear that they did not understand the difficulties of directing troops, planning battlefield manoeuvers and generally knowing where the men were among the series of ridges and gulleys that lie just over the first hills visible from the sea. The impact of the challenging terrain upon the capacity for officers to provide clear orders and leadership to the men due to limited line of sight of operations ahead, and the inability to locate men and for that matter, whole battalions, meant coordinated attacks were difficult and men had to operate in small units or with men from other Battalions. This was especially the case during the first few days of the fighting following the landings at Anzac Cove on the 25th April.

Colonel Sinclair-MacLagan, commander of the 3rd Brigade, who went ashore with the first wave of men, commented later that:

> *... the further the troops penetrated, the more hopeless any chance of reorganization became as it was impossible to see more than a few yards ... The lack of command caused by the disorganisation consequent on the "rush" through the scrub and over broken ground was the principal factor in causing subsequent delay and confusion.*

The late landing of the 2nd Brigade at Anzac Cove was unfortunate, because at the time they were due to land the 3rd Brigade had succeeded in establishing themselves on 400 Plateau and had advanced forward of this position. Although in small numbers, they had reached the objectives of the day and were extending out to the right towards Gaba Tepe. Had they been able to push on through the 3rd Brigade men, who were by this time exhausted and depleted in number, in line with the original timetable, they may have been able to hold these objectives. The 2nd Brigade were due to land at 5am, but did not arrive until 7am, and most of the men were not ashore until at least 8am due to ferrying problems, and in no small way, due to their commander, Colonel James McCay, not being in a fit state to command i.e. incapacitated through disorientation and a temporary nervous attack.

There was also a severe lack of Allied artillery support for the troops on the first day and throughout the campaign generally, which would have helped to suppress the devastating Turkish artillery batteries placed strategically on the high ground. One of the main reasons for this was due to the difficulty in moving heavy guns over the terrain and steep ridges behind Anzac Cove. In addition, the naval guns were unable to accurately identify targets over the horizon line, effectively over the tops of the First Ridge, of the Anzac battlefield. Their flat trajectory and firing at close range meant that it was very difficult even to clear the first line of ridges. Where set battle plans and coordinates could be provided to the mobile batteries and naval gun crews, along with some form of forward observation on the ground or in the air to confirm accuracy, this was less of an issue. However, this was rarely the case at Gallipoli. In most cases they relied on more basic techniques such as "shooting from the map" using aircraft and balloons, which again was difficult as there was no accurate ordnance survey, reliable aircraft or wireless communications available.

The difficult terrain, limited prior knowledge of the landscape of the battlefield, delays getting the 2nd Brigade landed and lack of artillery firepower ensured that during the first few hours, the Australians, while valiant and courageous in their attempts, were not able to secure and hold their objectives attained.

In addition, while the need to secure the high ground was clearly understood by the Allied planners of the campaign and became an objective for the first day, this was also very much understood by the Turks, who knew this part of their country very well. With the Allies announcing their intentions to land on the peninsula well in advance, it meant that right along the coast line at the strategic heights the Turks were well dug in, and if not, as was the case at the Anzac landing sites, they quickly moved to cut–off any advantage that the Australians on the first day might have been able to achieve on the high ground.

The difficult terrain over which the battles were fought and the acts of courage and the bravery of the men, the unfortunate events which led to the landing on the wrong beach, lack of proper medical facilities, limited food and water supplies, extreme weather, inept leadership that forced men to deal with duty and loyalty, poor planning and loss of life on a grand scale makes the Gallipoli campaign compelling reading. It is a sobering message about the truth surrounding war and the sacrifice made by the participants. It is not a story to celebrate but to contemplate and remember what was done by so few for so many.

Most of all it is a story we can be proud of, while not a victory, it is a great tale that proves an insight into the Australian character. The character, which is still demonstrated today and certainly intrinsic in the lives of those of that time, to be strong, resilient, courageous; the cheeky larrikin that makes fun of formality and themselves, but most importantly persists through hardship to get a job done. These are all the standard expressions that writers normally use to describe the character of Anzacs. We all want to feel an affinity with this character, to bond with these men and lay claim to this description of the

Australian and accept it as a critical part of our culture and history. For me it is all of these things, but specifically, it is a testament to the ordinary men, their spirit and character. Getting a greater understanding of what these men were like at the time and how this shaped them enables us to understand how they fought and survived the war in the way they did.

It is clear that they were, however, very different in their outlook and the expectations they had from life at that time, compared to myself and most other Australians today. The Australia they lived in following the turn of the century differs significantly from the Australia that we have today. Carlyon states that Gallipoli is the story of Australians from a nation that no longer exists. I doubt that many of us today would be willing to accept the same hardships and sacrifice with the same fortitude and stoicism that they did. They were different, bounded strongly to the British Empire, yet underneath this link to mother England they were starting to develop their own distinctively Australian disposition. These men also had families, jobs, loves and dreams, having many of the same character traits and values as we hold dear today. We are now, however, seemingly more self-centred and more cautious of the world around us. More informed about what we should have and more forthright about the way we should be treated and the opportunities we should have. Over time as our culture changes, having been influenced by new ideas, a greater knowledge about the world around us, increased multiculturalism coupled with new beliefs from abroad, technological changes and access to information, I think the Gallipoli legend will start to become less a definition of the Australian character. The way we define our culture will change because we will see less and less of ourselves in these men. It will, however, always remain a great story of courage and bravery in the face of adversity, and something all Australians will feel proud of and embrace for many generations to come.

It seems that in current times younger generations are bonding to the Gallipoli legend like no other generation before. The numbers of young Australians visiting the peninsula and being touched by the story are growing year on year. In recent times, dawn services at Anzac Cove have attracted 15,000 or more Australians and New Zealander pilgrims. Carlyon states that the end of the Cold War has brought a change in perceptions. Gallipoli is no longer linked, as it was for decades, to the military causes of the day. Finally it stands alone.[289]

The grandchildren and the great-grandchildren of those that landed at Gallipoli in April 1915 can see the campaign through "gentler" eyes as Carlyon puts it, looking at the war through the eyes of those that have known only peace and prosperity at home.[290] They did not have to bear the pressures of looking after loved ones who had returned but never really left the battlefield and lived with continual torment. Nor have they lost direct family members to a war and suffered the subsequent pain of loss. Reliving painful memories by attending Anzac Day memorials was probably not high on the agenda of those that lived through both world wars, but for the next generations of Australians can view it without baggage.

In the late 1950s, hardly anyone visited the Gallipoli cemeteries. In 1965, commemorating 50 years since the landing in 1915, some 200 ex–servicemen from Australia and New Zealand returned for Anzac Day services, complete with a mock landing in boats similar to those used on the day. It is also important to note that prior to the early '80s, a visit to the Gallipoli battlefields was not part of the Turkish tourist route and was a lot more difficult to arrange than more recent times. Fewster in his book[291] comments that Betty Roland, a Victorian, indicated that she was the only person in attendance at Lone Pine and at Gallipoli on Anzac Day 1961.

However, following the release in 1981 of the Peter Weir movie *Gallipoli* a significant impact on the Australian psyche occurred and the movie stirred a desire in the average Australian to understand more about what happened and to consider traveling to this isolated and remote corner of the globe. At the Anzac Day services in 1984 and 1985, there were only a few hundred in attendance at the dawn service at Ari Burnu, although the numbers were beginning to increase. Coupled with the rejuvenated interest in the campaign brought about in no small part by the movie, and the well-covered and attended 1990 Anzac Day dawn service, which was attended by 58 Anzac and eight Turkish veterans and approximately 4000 visitors, the start of a wave of interest had been set in motion.

Another practical reason why it has become more popular to attend the services at Anzac Cove is that travel to Turkey and the Gallipoli Peninsula for Australians, especially the younger generations, is simply easier than ever before. As I recently noted, to make travel arrangements to visit the Gallipoli battlegrounds is a reasonably easy task, and there is a myriad of tour operators, designated hotels, guides, package tours and facilities available to cater for travellers needs. Most accommodation in or around the Gallipoli

Peninsula is located within a half-day coach trip from the bustle of Istanbul, while the peak time for Australian tourists is during the latter part of April and early May, effectively around the Anzac Day service which is principally held at dawn at North Beach. The afternoon trip down to the peninsula from Istanbul, an overnight stay among the headstones, the early dawn Anzac Day service and the visit to the key landmarks in the Anzac area is a prerequisite of the young Australian and New Zealand traveller's itinerary during a visit to Turkey. If you are staying longer on the peninsula and happen to be in the town of Canakkale, the Hotel Anzac screens the Peter Weir movie *Gallipoli* throughout the day and night to get you in the mood. The young traveller can join other Australians and Kiwis for a beer in one of the many bars around the wharf area and share stories about the day's sightseeing. Then walk back to the Anzac House Youth Hostel and arrange a tour to the ancient ruins of Troy with the Anzac Travel Agency. When at Anzac Cove and travelling around the surrounding battlefields, you can park in the designated carparks and enjoy Anzac biscuits at one of a myriad of stalls located at Chunuk Bair, or ice creams while browsing the souvenir stalls under the gazing eye of the Turkish statue of the "Hero of the 57th Regiment", located just north of Quinn's Post Cemetery.

Fewster[292] outlines that Turkish media is certainly baffled by the motives of the youthful Anzac pilgrims. In recent years, Turkish papers have carried several stories in late April admitting an inability to understand why young backpackers spend thousands of dollars to be present at the Dawn Service, yet once there, they get very drunk and unruly on the eve of such a sombre ceremony.

This was not always the case though. From the 1920s when the first group of Australians returned to the battlefield up until the '60s and '70s, this was a very difficult and costly journey. Much of the Gallipoli Peninsula remained as it had been when the Allies left in 1915. There were few comforts or signposted trails. Under the terms of the armistice with Turkey, the British Army (Imperial War Graves Commission) re–entered the peninsula at the end of 1918 and cleared the battlefields of the bodies still unburied. With the exception of their visible efforts to bury remains and establish some of the present-day monuments such as the Lone Pine Memorial and establishing some modest tracks, visitors to the Gallipoli battlefields over a number of decades were left to their own devices. Fortunately, most travellers in those days were ex–servicemen returning to a familiar place or family members determined to find some solace, visiting the graves to make peace with those left behind. For one such traveller, Lieutenant General Hobbs, a former commander of an artillery unit at Anzac who made the trip back to the battlefields in March 1930, it was a three month voyage on a steamer to eventually reach the Dardanelles. The journey was expensive and involved a great deal of trouble, and once there he had to rely on the hospitality of the local War Graves Commission contact, old Anzac Major Tasman Millington, as there were almost no provisions for visitors. In the Lieutenant General's words, "I don't know where else I could have stayed in this half-ruined, poverty-stricken town [of Cannakale]."[293]

Major Millington and a group of local Turks, Greeks and some Russians were entrusted for a period of almost 30 years with the care of the war graves of the Empire and Commonwealth soldiers. The Major would act as the guide and facilitator of many of the small groups that would visit the site. Driving an old Ford, he would take visitors over some very rough roads to the key locations on the peninsula.

I was fortunate enough to travel to the Gallipoli Peninsula in October 2008 and spend four days trekking around the battlefields of both the Anzac and Cape Helles sectors. In particular, I spent two special days with Kenan Celik OAM, the well-renowned and probably the most knowledgeable local guide for the Gallipoli battlefields. He passionately led me around the battlefields providing a detailed commentary on the campaign, often placing a specific emphasis on the Turkish perspective of the war for which many Australian travellers often tend to overlook. Frequently I found myself writing furiously in my notebook when I had a chance, to ensure I remembered the gems of information he provided as we toured around the battlefield.

One story that Carlyon writes about Celik, of which I regret that I did not enquire about during our time together, was that Celik used to have tea with a white–whiskered old man at his house in Big Anafarta. This old man, who was in his 80s, was Adil Sahin, an old soldier and veteran of the Anzac landings in 1915. He remembered well the day that Adil recounted how he and his small group of men had seen the British warships off the coast and had witnessed the men landing on the beaches from his coastal sentry post. Realising that his men would be quickly overrun, he had retreated to Scrubby Knoll and was lucky to live and to grow tomatoes.

In 2008, our first stop on the tour was not any of the battlefields of the Anzac area, but a small Turkish village named "Bigali". This town has historical meaning for the Turkish people because in a house in one of the narrow streets on the 25th April, 1915, Colonel Mustafa Kemal was informed of the landing of the "English" at Ari Burnu. The 19th Ottoman Division under Kemal was stationed here and was the reserve Turkish Division. As I talked with Celik and drank tea at the little café off the main square in the village, under the watchful eyes of the statue of Mustafa Kemal, it was clear that he wanted me to understand and be aware that the Gallipoli Peninsula is also a place of sacrifice and significance for the Turkish people. I was grateful for this grounding and the need to understand the Turkish perspective of the battle in order for me to really appreciate what had occurred. The Turks, who had 10 times as many men killed within the eight-month campaign as the Anzac forces, were defending their homeland not only against the Anzacs, but also against the English, French and Indian troops. The Turkish soldiers, who were not volunteers in the same sense as the Australian and New Zealand soldiers were, they had to fight to defend their homeland and to uphold religious beliefs. For them this was a Jihad. In an Australian Intelligence Bulletin, notes were made from an interview with a captured Turkish soldier who had lain among the bodies of his comrades for two days following an attack that wiped out two Battalions of Turkish soldiers, until spotted by Australian soldiers who threw him a rope and pulled him in. "Thanks be to God that I am with you in safety. We have to fight, as it is a Jihad, but we long for peace."

Remarkably, the Turkish nation has allowed the building of cemeteries, the erection of structures, signage and regular remembrance ceremonies by her old enemies each year and they have accepted the renaming of the landing area as Anzac Cove on Turkish maps. In addition, the area has been set aside as a public reserve and the Australian Government in particular has input, provides some direction and is consulted on the usage and construction undertaken within the reserve. While we could be sceptical that the key reason for this lies with the flow of the tourist dollars into Turkey each year from thousands of Australian and New Zealand travellers, it should be recognised that this was a gesture that many other countries probably would not contemplate, yet the Turkish Government has consistently supported. Possibly this is due to the mutual respect of old enemies for each other and the reverence bestowed on the peninsula and the resting place of Turkey's enemies of the first President of the modern Republic of Turkey in 1923, Mustafa Kemal. I like to think that it is the continued respect of former combatants generated by soldiers in the trenches at Quinn's or Popes Posts, where the trenches were only a few metres apart and men of each side exchanged views and came to the realisation that the enemy were men just like themselves.

A letter written by a Queensland country doctor after the war, who was serving at Quinn's Post during the campaign, noted one unofficial truce that took place one day in November 1915 and lasted only 15 minutes. He writes:

The Turks put their heads about the parapets and began signaling to the Australians. Shortly after, there was the thud of something landing in the Australian trench. The Australians scattered, thinking it was a bomb. When the parcel didn't go off, I picked it up. It contained cigarettes. Written on one of the packets were two sentences in French: "Take pleasure, our heroic enemies. Send some milk." The Turks and the Australians then climbed out of their trenches and mingled for fifteen minutes. Afterwards they fired a few shots into the air, walked back to their trenches, and went on with the war.

Apart from the early days of the conflict when neither side was interested in taking prisoners, for the most part, the conflict came about as close as such things can to that curious phrase "war with honour"[294]. In years gone by, the old Anzacs and their former enemies the Turks at Anzac Day commemorations could sit down together and talk about the conflict as friends would without bitterness, guilt or shame, like the descendants of those men can also do today. Those men who fought each other fiercely for eight months during the campaign ended up respecting each other.

For me, the trip to the Gallipoli Peninsula was a realisation of a long-held dream to see the battlefield first-hand and piece together the rugged terrain, matching the names of the key landmarks and sites where certain events took place. Making the trip during the month of October, outside the months of high tourist traffic of April and May each year for the Anzac visitors, and in March specifically for the Turkish visitors who place special significance on the victory at the Dardanelles over the Allied fleet, ensured that I had the Anzac area almost to myself. I could wander through cemeteries, walk along the beaches, climb gullies and wander up valleys at my leisure in peace and tranquillity. October is almost the end of the tourist season, with most hotels in the area closing down or scaling down due to the onslaught of the winter months, which can be wet and very cold.

Travelling towards Anzac Cove in a cheap rental car, it took some time for me to collect myself when rounding the bend on the coast road, having just left the Hotel Kum not 10 minutes earlier I found myself passing a signpost indicating directions to Shell Green, Shrapnel Valley and Plugge's Plateau cemeteries. The ease of the drive and the close proximity of my accommodation had not really sunk in and I was taken by surprise. Each of these signs held great significance for anyone studying the endeavours of the Anzacs, particularly those men of the 9th Battalion. Then suddenly the car park for Beach Cemetery sprang into view and before I knew it I had passed Anzac Cove and was at Ari Burnu headland with a view of the unmistakable "Sphinx" landmark on the skyline. I was confused and elated all at the one time. Where to look first and where to stop! It was only the horn of an oncoming tractor driven by a local farmer that brought me back to earth and helped me register that I was (and had been for some time) driving on the wrong side of the road. My adventure could have finished as quickly as it had started!

Like many visitors to the Anzac area in the past, this experience also exemplified how small this area actually is. The Anzac enclave held by the Australian and New Zealand soldiers is less than three kilometres long and just over one kilometre deep, measured from the seashore to Quinn's Post. That first afternoon I wandered through Beach Cemetery at Hell Spit (on some maps also referred to as Queensland Point as boats from the HMS *Beagle* landed men of the 9th Battalion here first on the 25th April), which sits at the southern end of Anzac Cove. Beach Cemetery was first used as a place of burial on the day of the landings and continued to be used for this purpose throughout the entire length of the campaign. It contains the graves of 285 Australian and 21 New Zealand soldiers who were identified, and there are also many British soldiers, particularly sailors and marines, buried here also. With only the soft monotonous chugging sound of a few small trawlers making their way up and down the coastline and the barking of a few stray dogs, I noted row upon row of whitewashed headstones, in particular stopping at those of the few 9th Battalion men buried there. These men were not officers but simple men, privates most of them, many much younger than myself. I thought of what their home lives must have been like, where they lived and then what their parents had gone through when told, possibly many days, if not weeks after their death, that they would not be returning home. They were not just names, but real people who had paid the ultimate price for their country.

- Private George Scoones, age 19, a wood turner, listed with the same address as his parents at Red Hill, Brisbane, died 28th June, 1915.
- Private Volney McInnes, age 22, a farmer from Casino, NSW, listed as residing at the same address as his parents. His father's name was Donald. Died 24th June, 1915.
- Private William Turton, age 24, a whip maker, living in Stanley Street, South Brisbane, listed as residing at the same address as his mother, Ellen Turton. Died 20th May, 1915.
- Private John Farrell, age 21, a labourer, listed as residing in the Criterion Hotel in Mackay. Died 22nd May, 1915.
- Private Andrew Bell, age 20, a collar maker, listed as residing with his parents at Wyandra Street, Bulimba, Brisbane. Died 8th May, 1915.
- Private George Lillie, age 19, a labourer from Killarney. Died 5th May, 1915.

These were all men of the 9th Battalion who had sailed on the SS *Omrah* out of Pinkenba Wharf in Brisbane on the morning of the 24th September, 1914. Never to see home again.

Taking in the scene, I looked up at the heights directly in front of Plugge's Plateau with its flat top and then to MacLagan's Ridge, which joins Plugge's and runs down to the beach and forms one side of Shrapnel Gully. Then over to the north and the clearly distinguishable "Sphinx" feature with its harsh, bare and heavily eroded ridges running down to the beaches. Then back over to the southern sector of the Anzac battlefield, towards the Gaba Tepe headland, which was the site for a number of Turkish guns throughout the campaign and was a key objective for the 9th Battalion. All these landmarks of the campaign were now bathed with a yellow-orange hue, cast by the setting sun. These were the battlefield landmarks that I had read about many times, this was where the men of D Company 9th Battalion had landed and made their way frantically inland. My trip was now a reality. The ridges and slopes around the Anzac landing area are certainly foreboding and harsh. The words steep and treacherous are almost an understatement in describing some areas of the battlefield. How they managed to scale these slopes, in the early morning dawn light, wet, ripped and cut by the thorn and thicket bushes, disorientated by the neverending ridges and valleys and under constant fire, was an incredible feat for these ordinary men.

Over the years the battlefield has become covered with dense scrub in many areas, much thicker in some places than in 1915. It is true that with so much shelling, digging and men and equipment moving around, certainly after the first few weeks post-landing, as is confirmed by photos, the valleys winding through the steep ridges were clear of vegetation. Not so today, however. As I pushed up through an eerie Shrapnel Gully along a moist, sandy, creek bed, it became very difficult to move forward and I had to give up after a few hundred metres as the scrub became too thick. At one stage while on my hands and knees climbing a steep embankment in Shrapnel Gully, I came face-to-face with the native Gallipoli tortoise, locally named the "Kaplumbaga". It was small and well camouflaged to blend with the thick scrub in which it makes its home. Shrapnel Gully, which was given its name soon after the landing due the fact that as it was becoming the major highway for the Anzacs to move from the landing beaches to the front-line positions up along the ridge, was constantly targeted by the Turks with shrapnel shells.

There are many tracks that are frequently used that have easy to moderate access, however, for many of the areas the scrub and thorny weeds have taken hold. Certainly you do not have to venture far off the beaten track to find the going tough. Seeing ahead in many cases when down in the gullies and valleys is almost impossible. If trying to move through at night the chances of getting lost and disoriented would be very high. What is amazing are the number of ridges and the complexity of the terrain. It is hard to determine which ridge you are viewing, let alone where it starts and ends. Witnessing this first-hand confirms the difficulties that officers had directing and leading men on those first few days.

This battlefield is made for defence and it is not hard to understand how the sniper, especially the Turkish sniper, came to rule the battleground over the first few days. Wherever you are on the slopes, ridges and valleys leading up to the higher ground along Bolton's Ridge, right up to the Nek, the soldiers were exposed to shelling and enemy fire. The range of the Turkish Mauser rifles would mean that even weeks into the fighting after the Anzac soldiers had established their trenches, Australian soldiers on the beaches swimming could be hit by Turkish fire, given the proximity of the front-line trenches and the exposure these lower areas had to the enemy.

Like most visitors, I walked along the beach on Anzac Cove passing the fallen concrete pillboxes, that are relics from the World War II and imagined the scenes of men, equipment, animals and stores piled high along the beach.

The beach today is quite narrow, although it was in some places another 30 metres wider in 1915. The beach still harbors the rounded, slippery rocks just offshore that the Anzacs slipped on when scrambling out of their boats on the day of the landing. There were no waves to speak of and the Aegean Sea off the beach at Anzac Cove was flat, calm and a beautiful blue in the sunlight. Small lapping waves push up on to the beach and among the seaweed are many small shells. The heights immediately up off the beach that the Australians clambered up are much more eroded than in 1915, and the roadwork that has enabled car and bus access for tourists has left its marks permanently on the cliff face.

The whole area is a picturesque place. The harsh ridges that fall away to the beach and the turquoise water of the Aegean that glistens in the sun and spreads out towards the misty island of Imbros is pure magic. The island of Imbros witnessed the passing of the landing flotilla packed with men bound for Anzac Cove on the morning of the 25th April, 1915, and was where Hamilton set up his headquarters in June 1915. During the campaign the island also was a place for rest and recreation for the troops on Gallipoli during their rotation off the battlefield. It had a number of large tented camps, casualty clearing stations, field bakeries, airfields and supply depots. Its harbour area always bristled with action.

The scenery in many places and the vistas stretching over many miles from the high ground is breathtaking. The scarred and potholed cliff faces where the men dug out their rough dwellings to shelter from the bullets and shells, the well-beaten paths up most of the valleys up to the heights of the front-line that the men streamed and the piles and piles of provisions and equipment are now long gone. Nature has had its way. Bean wrote of sitting up on Plugge's Plateau, 150 metres up, having an evening meal and watching the beauty of the setting sun over the Aegean Sea and the distant mountains on the islands offshore. Hospital ships anchored in Anzac Cove below them, "like a beautiful memory of peace", while behind him the devastation and destruction of war took place and the odd stray bullet whizzed overhead.

Venturing up to the heights, I visited each of the Anzac cemeteries along the bitumen roadway that takes the visitor up Second Ridge (also called Pine Ridge) and then on to the top end of Bolton's ridge, where today the roadway separates what was once no-man's-land between both the Anzac and Turkish trenches, leading up eventually to Chunuk Bair. When Charles Bean walked this way in 1919, he came across the tattered uniforms and bones of men scattered everywhere.

Like most Australians on their pilgrimage, I stopped at the Lone Pine Cemetery where the battle was so intense that seven Victoria Crosses were awarded to Australian soldiers (see also appendix 3), then wandered across 400 Plateau noting the old trenches that still remain, where the 3rd Brigade endured heavy shelling and machine-gun fire on the first day of the campaign, taking in also the areas known as the Daisy Patch, Brown's Dip and Johnston's Jolly. Then up to one of the most dangerous places on the Anzac front, where the trenches were only separated by a few metres. Quinn's Post, which was named after Major Hugh Quinn, 15th Battalion (a Queensland unit), was the site of some of the most intense fighting, with bomb-throwing one of the main pastimes. The Turks, in fact, referred to this position as Bomba Sirt (Bomb Ridge). This position represented the heart of the Anzac defensive line, and as Charles Bean wrote, had such a reputation that men passing the fork in Monash Valley used to glance up at this place as a man looks at a haunted house. Standing on a vantage point on the white wall at the back of the cemetery, I looked down the sheer drop immediately behind where the old Australian trenches would have been towards the beach and sea beyond. The breathtaking view laid wide the much fought over access from the heights down to the beaches. This was the point in the line where the Turks were so desperate to break through the Anzac defences. Their aim was to sever the Anzac forces via moving down Monash's Highway, which runs down Monash Valley on to Shrapnel Gully and then to the beach. The strong defence of this post in particular, had kept the Turkish attacks in the north early on in the campaign in check, but had been at great cost to the Anzac soldiers. Signaller Ellis Silas from the 16th Battalion commented in relation to Quinn's Post:

> *Yards and yards of trench were at times empty of all save the dead and wounded men, and in some cases the Turks effected a footing in them; they were always driven out again. Our fellows were simply magnificent; budge they would not ... to make room for the living we had to throw the bodies out over the back.*[295]

Given that the trench line as I mentioned above is so precariously placed right on the very edge of the crest of the ridge, the bodies Ellis refers to would roll down to the foot of the hill. He further comments that it was not the most encouraging sight for new reinforcements making their way up to the front-line to take the place of these often long-dead men.

The next stop was Pope's Post, following the spur onwards out to the narrow area of the Nek, where I stood trying to imagine where both the Australian and Turkish trenches were located on a seemingly impossible small battleground. Baby 700 and Battleship Hill are the next places of interest and mark the point where Captain Tulloch and his men from the 11th Battalion were stopped by the Turkish counterattack on the first day. This was also the area where Major Sydney B. Robertson of the 9th Battalion was killed, as mentioned in Chapter 5. I visited his grave along with those of 12 other Australians at the Walker's Ridge Cemetery, which lies south-west along the dirt road from the Nek Cemetery and is situated perched up on the ridge line, with commanding views down Mule Gully, the Sphinx and over to North Beach and further south to Ari Burnu headland. This was the furtherest the Australians were to advance up this ridge during the entire campaign and remained in Turkish hands for the rest of the fighting. When Bean returned to the battlefields in 1919, he found an Australian soldier's water bottle with a bullet hole in it at Battleship Hill, evidence that the Australians had been there, albeit for a brief time. At various places along this path up the ridge towards Chunuk Bair, the traveller can see clearly views of the Dardanelles and the Maidos plain, the ultimate objective of the Allies campaign.

There were many other moments to reflect on some of the events I have researched and covered in this book. Such as standing at the place called the "Cup", which during the campaign had no English name and was only named as such when Charles Bean returned in 1919. The Cup, which is situated at the inland side of the Lone Pine Plateau and looking out towards the Third Ridge, is where Lieutenant Costin was killed and many others in the Machine-gun section of the 9th Battalion. Wandering on I walked through the now shallow remains of trenches around Brown's Dip where the 3rd Brigade had dug in on the first day. Then marching down Artillery Road, which follows the path of the original track that was built soon after landing to enable guns to be hauled up from the beach to the ridges above. Scrambling up the steep embankment from the road to stand in the trenches located in the area around Allah Gulley and Tasmania Post that was the site where the 9th Battalion spent time in the front-line. Following the road further on to Shell Green and standing on the ground where the 9th Battalion had the sombre roll call a few days after landing and the first confirmation for the survivors of the terrible toll of dead and wounded that had been exacted on the Battalion. Here at Shell Green in the afternoon with its scenic backdrop, the wind whistling up from the Aegean Sea, which is spread out in the backdrop, and the cold chill indicating the first signs of the coming winter season, I was brought back to the stark reality that many men had died here in this area. A line of 9th Battalion graves in a neat white line stood to attention in front of me, the names of men that I had read about and the action they were killed in springing to mind. The names of men such as Fox, Petersen, Warner and Preston, which were listed in Lieutenant Ross's diary entry as having been killed in the "demonstration" against the Turks positioned at Sniper's Ridge and Knife Edge on the 28th June, 1915. Their bodies were recovered on the 29th June and a moonlight burial had taken place that night. This is a place of reflection, contemplation and reverence.

A final part of my visit to Gallipoli was a dawn sea trip aboard the small Turkish fishing boat the *Olsun*, which chugged along the darkened shores of the Anzac battlefield where 93 years earlier other young Australians approached these same beaches in very different circumstances. Along with two friends we travelled under the command of Captain Mesfit, a local Turkish fisherman who was well prepared for tourists and no doubt had completed this journey for other Australian pilgrims on many prior occasions. We anchored off Ari Burnu headland and waited in the darkness until the light of dawn lit up the sky and the first rays appeared over the line of ridges behind Anzac Cove. It was a special time for us, with only the sound of lapping waves, a slight breeze, the sea with very little current and the chugging of the boat's engine the only noise that could be heard, helping us to cast our minds back to that fateful morning of the landing. Slowly the features of the battlefield became evident and the outlines of the key landmarks such as the Sphinx and Plugge's Plateau became clear. One key thing that was confirmed for me was how difficult it was to determine landmarks in the dark before the dawn light. Even when the sun had risen the broken terrain, ridges, headlands and coves made it very difficult to identify exactly what we were looking at, even with the aid of a very accurate map. How much more so for the navy men charged with bringing the Australians of the 3rd Brigade to shore in 1915. Landing off course was seemingly "par for the course".

The modern-day Turkish State is very much aware of how important the tourist dollar is for the economy and how much a drawcard the battlefields are for the foreign tourist. The hunger to entice more and more visitors to the area is starting to takes its toll on the battlefields. The place is being loved to death! Wider roads to take bigger buses, souvenir shops, car parks, sound and light spectaculars, rubbish buildup just off the roads and an ever-increasing number of monuments, most of which have recently been Turkish, are beginning to take away some of the solemnity and special character of the battlefields. I sincerely hope that the local authorities can strike a balance between making the area accessible to visitors and maintaining the true character of the place, and respecting the final resting place for so many soldiers of both sides that fought and died there.

The Turkish Government is also very focused on drawing the Turkish people to the peninsula and increasing awareness of the sacrifice and successes achieved by the Turkish forces of 1915. Turkish monuments seem to be going up at such a rate at present that you would be inclined to think they were trying to even up the number of Anzac and Turkish monuments. In some cases, the speed to erect monuments comes at the cost of factual accuracy, and in a number of cases while paying respects at Turkish memorials, my guide pointed out errors of factual accuracy or factual accounts where some poetic licence on the inscriptions had been taken in the name of building patriotism. It is interesting to note that the Turkish people very early noted the lack of a Turkish commemoratory presence on the battlefield. One Turkish visitor in 1925 commented:

> *The sea was cheerful as if she did not remember anything; the earth was covered by deep green scrub from one end to the other as if it did not embrace the bodies of thousands of men… only foreign cemeteries were like white flower gardens on the sides of the hills close to the sea. The only visible traces are not of those who won, but those who were defeated.*[296]

Similarly, as my guide Celik pointed out, the Turks are not the only ones to embellish the truth or emphasise a factual inaccuracy, Australia also has a fine tradition of developing a yarn. There were three interesting examples of this that Celik brought to my attention. In each of the accounts I was initially defensive and somewhat dismissive of the different perspective brought by Celik's details of the campaign and history that I have found to be quite accurate and impartial.

The first was in regard to the landing boat that is on display in the main entrance to the Australian War Memorial in Canberra. Like many during my visits to the Memorial, I have stood and marvelled at the sight of the boat, looked inside and pictured the boat packed with eager Australian soldiers rowing for shore among a hail of rifle and machine-gun fire, seeing the bullet-ridden sides and wondering did any of these bullets reach a victim. While

I have not yet had a chance to confirm or deny, it is believed that the boat is actually a Turkish craft recovered from Palestine with markings that were not of Australian or British origin and did not match any of the ships used during the campaign. Instead, it was repainted and promoted as an Anzac landing craft used on the 25th April, 1915. Moreover, the technician who was fixing and restoring the boat for display found spent Lee Enfield bullets, fired from rifles used by the Australian soldiers, at the bottom of the boat rather than Turkish bullets. No reason could be provided to Celik following a line of questioning, apart from the fact that in the heat of battle firing can become confused. When I am next at the Australian War Memorial, I will make some enquiries on this and try to confirm these facts.

The second was that there were no Turkish machine-guns close to the beaches, or in fact firing down on the beaches when the first few landings of Australian troops took place on the morning of the 25th April, 1915. Nor was there wholesale slaughter of the first wave of Australian troops on the beaches at Anzac Cove. Again many accounts outline that there was a hail of bullets, machine-gun fire and artillery fire that rained down on the men as they left the landing craft at Anzac Cove and dashed up the steep hills and ridges. This is almost a standard part of the history handed down. Paintings and pictures have been drawn that illustrate the murderous fire unleashed and the deadly run from the boats to the first of the hills just in from the beach taught to Australians over many decades. My Turkish guide, Celik indicated that on the morning of the 25th April, 1915, there were only four machine-guns in the entire Anzac area, and they were preciously guarded and only brought into action later in the day when it had been confirmed that indeed the area around Anzac Cove was the site for the landing of a large enemy force. Each Turkish regiment had a machine-gun company, which had approximately four guns. The Turkish historical documentation and records indicate that the equipment available for the initial defence of the Anzac Cove and nearby surrounds were only rifles used by the Turkish defenders. The machine-gun company was only brought forward from the reserve position beyond the Third Ridge well after the 3rd Brigade had landed and moved inland. This account is documented by the Turkish platoon commander[297] and is the widely held view of most, if not all, Turkish historians and military commentators.

What makes this discussion all the more interesting is that most Australian historians and writers express the opposite view. It has become a much argued point and one that strikes at the heart of national pride in both countries. My view is that there were machine-guns present on the morning of the landing, although not as many and in so many places as one might think. Refer to appendix 17.

Of greater significance is that for the Turkish Army of approximately 700,000 men prior to the outbreak of hostilities there were only about 200 machine-guns, and many of the soldiers were still using old slow-firing guns just prior to the landing, whereby they were issued the model 1893 Mausers, bolt-action rifle. The Anzac Cove area on the morning of the 25th April, 1915 was only thinly defended by Turkish soldiers. At Ari Burnu, where the initial wave of Anzacs landed, there were only two companies of Turkish soldiers (160 men), and at Hell Spit, where the next wave of men from the 9th Battalion landed, there were no more than about 85 Turks, all operating mainly as coastal sentries and part of the 27th Regiment located in and around Anzac Cove. Most of these Turks would be killed within the first two hours of the start of the landings. One notable exception was three Turkish soldiers, one being an officer who had been wounded and two of his men who managed to carry him to safety. It is estimated that roughly 30 Australian soldiers were killed on the beaches at Anzac Cove during the first few waves of attacks. By far the majority of the casualties suffered by the 3rd Brigade were when they strove inland, victims of artillery fire, and more frequently, by sniper fire as discussed earlier. For the 9th Battalion men in the covering force landing at Anzac Cove, the key reason they did not suffer many more casualties landing first on the beach was due to a number of reasons. The first was due to the fact that it was still dark when they landed. Moreover, to the benefit of the 9th Battalion men that were in the first group of boats coming ashore, the order was given to the Turkish soldiers that they were not to start firing until the enemy were about to get out of the boats. This enabled the first of the Australians landing to only come under fire when they were running across the beach. Last, when the Turks did start firing, the machine-guns at the front of one of the 9th Battalion steamboats suppressed some of the Turkish fire being directed at the landing troops.

This observation is supported in the writings of Lieutenant Colonel Aker who after the war states:

> *Although it is certain that the platoon at Ari Burnu was not taken by surprise, it is clear that the platoon did not open fire until the landing craft were about to put the troops ashore.... This was a mistake. If this platoon at Ari Burnu had engaged these landing craft with fire at a distance of 100*

> *metres there is no doubt that getting the Australians ashore would have been a very costly operation. But the firing that was opened up ... on the twelve landing craft that first approached came from not more than 60 rifles ... and it is most unlikely that this firepower, dispersed among the twelve landing craft in the darkness, could have been effective in preventing all these boats from approaching land. It is clear that the causes of the Australian forces getting ashore with so few losses were withholding fire until the craft got near to land, the fact that the motor boats towing the craft fired back with machine-guns and the dispersal of firepower weakly among the twelve craft.*[298]

The written accounts indicate that the Turks in most cases did not stay long in defending the beaches and were soon overwhelmed by the sheer weight of numbers of Australians landing. Many of the Turkish sentries, if not killed by the initial wave of Anzacs, retreated quickly back to regroup with reserve units moving forward, or took up sniping positions at key vantage points until they were silenced.

However, for those men of the 3rd Brigade landing soon after the first few boats hit the shore at Anzac Cove, effectively after the alarm had been raised, the casualty rate was much higher and there was a mad rush to reach the shore and get to cover. Also for the covering force, and for that matter those in the second wave that landed to the north and south of Anzac Cove, casualties in the boats on approach and on the beaches were much greater as these landing areas were more exposed and better covered by enemy fire. Once the Anzac Cove area had been secured and the coastal sentries pushed back by the covering force and the second wave of the 3rd Brigade, it was a reasonably sheltered landing zone and became the preferred point of disembarkation for those landing later in the day.

The third point was in regard to the charge at the Nek by the 8th and 10th Australian Light Horse Regiments (LHR). Clearly the bravery of the men who charged that day is unquestioned, and their devotion to their mates and country incredible. It has, however, been mentioned in some accounts that by the time the third row of the 10th LHR was standing readying themselves to go over the top, the Australian soldiers were questioning the recklessness and folly of the orders. In some cases, the Australians had to be prodded and forced to attack, as witnessed by Turkish officers that day. While I have not researched this claim in any detail, I personally believe that while there is likely to be some truth to this, I would expect that the same Australians who did not take kindly to drill and orders in Egypt and were renowned for speaking their mind if they felt unfairly treated, would have created some noise about the scenario that was being presented to them. They were not like the British. Moreover, there would have been a great deal of patriotic fervour from the Turkish officers at the time, keen to ensure their men were kept zealous. The fact of the matter, however, is that the third and fourth line went and met a fate similar to the 8th LHR troopers of the first and second lines.

It is impossible to travel around the peninsula without noticing the high admiration and affection afforded to Mustafa Kemal (or Ataturk, Father of the Turks) by the Turkish people. The myriad of inscriptions outlining his bravery and leadership, the statues and the portraits of the leader seem to be located at every turn. Certainly his influence and presence during the campaign ensured that, to a large degree, the Turkish forces retained the upper hand for most of the fighting, particularly in the Anzac theatre. While Ataturk was not the commander-in-chief during the campaign (it was a German officer, General Liman Von Sanders) he was through his influence on three occasions, at the Anzac landing, the Suvla Bay landing and on the slopes of Chunuk Bair, able to contribute significantly to the outcome of the campaign. Carlyon indicates in a lecture he gave during the 85th year anniversary of the Gallipoli campaign that a good definition of a great commander is a man who knows instinctively what he has to do, and does it – quickly and ruthlessly. This was a quality that distinguished Ataturk from several British commanders at Gallipoli, whom Carlyon describes as spending much time doing imitations of the Spanish knight Don Quixote, forever winning fantastic battles in their minds while skating around the responsibilities of the real world. At 34, Ataturk was only a Colonel, but clearly a man of destiny.[299]

Bean refers to Mustafa Kemal as, "the greatest leader of the Eastern Front". Kemal clearly understood the need for the presence of a commander at the critical moment of battle to lead the way, unlike many of his British counterparts that were content to direct troop movements well behind the battlefront, or even from ships anchored offshore, or at Headquarters located miles away from where their men were engaged. This was best demonstrated when he personally led his men in the attack at Chunuk Bair that forced the British out of the strategically important mountain position.

It is therefore more poignant when trying to communicate the true spirit of respect shown by both Australian and Turkish people alike to the fallen men of the Gallipoli campaign to reflect on the words acknowledged by Mustafa Kemal:

> *Those heroes who shed blood and lost their lives; You are now living in the soil of a friendly country, therefore rest in peace. There is no difference between the Johnnies and the Mehmets to us where they lie side by side, here in this country of ours. You, the mothers, who sent their sons from faraway countries, wipe away your tears; your sons are now lying in our bosom and are in peace. After having lost their lives on this land, they have become our sons as well.*

While the old Anzac battlefield now is quiet and nature has since reclaimed her rightful place and concealed most of the battle scars, there is hardly anything left from the war years to suggest that men fought and died here over 90 years ago. Away from the memorials, when sitting off by oneself though, there is a strong presence of those men from a time long ago and an Australia long ago that abounds. The stories of ordinary men from the bush and city alike who performed extraordinary service, endured, suffered and sacrificed so much on this foreign shore for their country have helped us define our national identity and the uniqueness of the Australian character. The confident, wide-eyed, all conquering faces of the men of the 11th Battalion on the Great Pyramid of Cheops and the larrikin smile of Brisbane's Bert White (25th Battalion – KIA on 10th June, 1918) just prior to embarking for the war, is the way I like to think of these ordinary men.

I will, we will, continue to remember them.

Anzac Cove Beach, looking south towards Hell Spit or Little Ari Burnu.

Looking up to the heights of Plugge's Plateau with MacLagan's Ridge on the right. This is the ascent that the first wave of the 9th Battalion, landing on the morning of the 25th April, 1915, were confronted with, climbing to the top under fire.

Looking south towards Plugge's Plateau on the left and then to the right down to Ari Burnu headland, north end of Anzac Cove.

View from Plugge's Plateau, looking south over Shrapnel Valley, the end of Razorback Ridge, then across to McCay's Hill and then to Bolton's Ridge running down to the sea.

9th Battalion – C Company landed at the mouth of this valley (Shrapnel), running south over the First Ridge in view (Razorback) and then on to the Second Ridge (McCay's Hill) where they met up with "D" Company coming up the other side. Both companies then followed this ridge up to the left and on to 400 Plateau.

This view from the top of Plugge's Plateau shows the path taken by the 9th Battalion men from A and B Companies. The trees up on the horizon line mark 400 Plateau and Lone Pine.

View down the "highway" from Quinn's Post. Monash Valley, then into Shrapnel Valley through to the beach just south of Anzac Cove.

Shell Green Cemetery. To the left is Artillery Road and Bolton's Ridge. The 9th Battalion had its first roll call here a few days after the landing.

The Nek Cemetery, this is a view of the area where the Australian Light Horse charged. Left of the photo were the Australian trenches, and to the right, where the monument is, marks the line of Turkish trenches.

Sunset on Chunuk Bair, looking out towards Imbros Island.

A quiet afternoon overlooking Beach Cemetery at Little Ari Burnu headland.

Appendices

During the writing of this book there were many times when an interesting topic arose but was more preferable to deal with separately outside of the chapters. Some of these topics are therefore covered below.

Appendix 1 – Two Fathers and Two Sons

In Chapter two, I mentioned that the 9th Battalion at its inception had two sets of father and son within the unit. This is believed to be an unparalleled occurrence in an AIF battalion in active service.[300] Both families were from the Maryborough area of Queensland and all four were commissioned officers in the 4th Wide Bay Regiment prior to joining up into the newly formed 9th Battalion. Both fathers, who were approaching their 50s at the time, were highly trained and had served with their regiments from before the Boer War. There was no indecision when war broke out and it was clear what was required. Within 24 hours all four were on their way to Brisbane to volunteer for overseas service.

The four officers were:

- Lieutenant Colonel H.W. Lee (First Commanding Officer of the 9th Battalion)
- Captain H.W. Lee Jnr.
- Major W.C. Harvey
- 2nd Lieutenant H.C. Harvey

What happened to them?

Lieutenant Colonel Lee was part of the landing on the 25th April where on the first day he was wounded in the hand. On Tuesday, 28th April while returning to the beach with some of his men from the front-line for a rest and climbing the steep slopes, he slipped over and sprained his ankle, which effectively meant that his initial time at Anzac Cove was very short. Command of the Battalion had to be handed on. He was taken back to Alexandria, although he had tried to stay on the ship off the coast hoping that the swelling in the ankle would subside. It did not. After spending a few months in hospital he eventually returned to the peninsula on 19th July, 1915, only to be evacuated again due to sickness on the 21st July, 1915, where he was then transferred on to hospital in England. However, given his ankle was still highly suspect, he was then returned to Australia. It was a very unfortunate end to his military career. He returned and took up work as a school headmaster at Chermside, the family living in Alderley. The family later moved to Toowoomba, where he died in November 1932 at the age of 64.

Captain H.W. Lee Junior had been the original Transport Officer of the 9th Battalion and seems to have survived with the Battalion throughout the Gallipoli campaign and after the evacuation, he attended a Senior Staff College at Aldershot prior to transferring to the 25th Battalion as their second in-charge. He was unfortunately killed on 2nd March, 1917 in France.

There is very little mentioned of Major W.C. Harvey's time on Gallipoli. From my research I believe he was in the role of Quartermaster and hence had responsibility for the supplies and material, including clothing for the troops and equipment, which included ammunition and firearms. He also had high-level responsibility for the transport of the troops. Therefore, he would not have been involved in the fighting directly and may not have landed with the Battalion on the first day. I did note that he was seconded from Gallipoli in October 1915 and made Commandant of a Turkish POW camp in Egypt. He was then invalided home to Australia in August 1916. He died in April 1947.

Lieutenant H.C. Harvey was wounded on the 25th April following the landing and evacuated, but seems to have rejoined the Battalion in July 1915. The next reference I could find was that he was invalided to Australia in April 1916, whether this was from being wounded again or suffering from sickness I could not determine. He died in 1929 at the age of 30, possibly from complications from wounds sustained on active service.

Appendix 2 – The Lifeboat found at Anzac Cove

The Australian War Memorial in Canberra has on display a lifeboat found on the beach at Anzac Cove, with the only marking on the boat being a white-painted number 6. It was a lifeboat from the British transport ship HMT *Ascot* (A33) and was used to bring the 13th Battalion AIF into the beaches during the landings at Anzac Cove on 25th April, 1915. The 13th Battalion landed after 9.30pm on the night of the 25th April, 1915. The lifeboat became stranded on the beach at Anzac Cove and it was found by Charles Bean when he returned to Gallipoli in 1919, immediately after the war. It, however, remained on the beach until 14th September, 1921, when an Imperial War Graves Unit recovered it from the beach, having to cut it in half to get it around the sharp curves in the roads they had built along the hills. There are many bullet holes in the boat, several especially in both sides of the bow. Refer also to the comments made in chapter 9 concerning this boat and its questioned origins.

Appendix 3 – The Battle of Lone Pine (August 1915 – Gallipoli)

Lone Pine is a heart-shaped clearing on the Second Ridge above Anzac Cove and a part of the 400 Plateau (furthest section inland secured by the Anzacs) and took its name from a solitary pine tree. The position itself was taken on the 25th April, 1915 as noted in chapter 5, but not held by the Australians, who moved back to entrench across the main area of the 400 Plateau and an area just forward of Lone Pine called the Pimple. The next day the 4th Battalion crossed the Plateau towards Lone Pine, only to be greeted by a hail of rifle, machine-gun and artillery fire.

The depleted Battalion withdrew that night and the Turks moved in. Between May and August 1915, the Turks developed a formidable trench system. The Turkish trenches were about three metres deep and the main trench, which essentially ran north to the south, was roofed with timber and covered with earth. A pilot flying overhead would have seen the intricate network of both the Anzac and Turkish trenches facing one another, with no more than 150 metres separating them at the furthest point. In front of the main Turkish trenches was barbed wire and beyond the trenches and further inland lay a gully called the Cup, which was where the Turks had established their administration and Battalion headquarters. In this position there were no trenches, only dugouts and terraces. If the Australians were successful in forcing a path through the system of Turkish trenches through to the Cup, they would have achieved the desired breakout from the positions they had been holding for several months and into open country through towards the Turkish headquarters based at Scrubby Knoll.

The frontal assault required to be made by the Australian troops on Lone Pine on the 6th August was intended as part of the August offensive to break out of the stalemate that had taken hold. The main breakout was from the north of Anzac to capture the dominating heights of Conk Bayiri and Hill 971. Ekins[301] contends that this was the primary offensive action. The British landing more troops further to the north at Suvla Bay and further large-scale attacks taking place at the Cape Helles front were secondary and supplementary actions. He writes that in no sense were the Anzac operations intended as mere diversions to allow the British to land unopposed at Suvla Bay.

Lone Pine itself was not tactically significant or key terrain for the Allied Command. Diversionary attacks were used often during the campaign to ensure that other areas of the peninsula, where a fresh offensive were about to be launched, meant the Turks would be so tied up defending other sectors that they would not be able to spare moving troops and would be spread thinly across several fronts.

The Australians faced an enormous task. Essentially they had to make a frontal attack across between 55 and 130 metres of some of the flattest terrain on the entire peninsula. They had to assault well-defended trenches over ground that would be well covered by both Turkish gun and artillery fire. Both Harold Walker, the officer commanding the 1st Brigade, and Charles White, the senior Australian staff officer, could see the risks involved with the plans and argued against the attack with their superiors but were not successful. Nevertheless, they set out to meticulously plan the assault as best they possibly could in the hope of limiting the loss of life and improve the overall chances of success of the attack.

Walker and White ordered tunnels to be dug out from the Australian trenches towards the Turkish trenches. In some of these tunnels, large landmines were placed in them, to be detonated before the attack began. The intention was to break up the flat ground and provide some cover for the attacking troops.

For three days before the attack the Turkish position was bombed by artillery fire, which was able to destroy most of the barbed wire. When the bombardment lifted, the Australian soldiers of the 1st Brigade were in position with the sun setting behind them. At 5.30 pm, an hour after the bombardment had finished, the Australians attacked on a 220-metre front. On their arms they wore white bands and on their backs they had sewn calico squares for recognition. They moved out in two lines. The Turks had not expected an attack would be made on one of their strongest posts, in fact some Turks thought that the bombardment was a payback for some placards that they had put up reporting the capture of Warsaw by the Germans.

The Turks were slow to respond and the first line of troops reached the main trench with surprisingly few casualties. Then for the staff officers watching the battle unfold, they looked with amazement at the Australian troops stopping at the Turkish parapet and beginning to bunch up. What they were witnessing was the men of the first line of the advance suddenly coming across the elaborate trench system that had not been noted by aerial reconnaissance, given its camouflage and concealment, and for a while the men stood around thinking of ways to enter the trenches. Some jumped over the roofed trenches and into the open communication trenches, some fired through the logs into the trenches below, and others prised up the logs with their bayonets and jumped down into the musty galleries below. One group of Australians even managed to reach the Turkish Battalion Headquarters at the Cup, only to be cut–off and killed.

"The Taking of Lone Pine", by Fred Leist, accurately depicts how the men of the Australian 1st Brigade had to lift heavy logs that covered the Turkish trenches to penetrate their front-line.

Bean indicated that perhaps half the Turkish defenders had been killed or wounded during what turned out to be a reasonably effective Allied bombardment.

During the next half-hour, there was fierce hand-to-hand and close-quarter fighting underground, with a lot of confusion among the combatants. The attackers and defenders were very mixed. Men fought frantically with bayonets and bombs, they kicked and punched; shouts and curses could be heard coming out of the trenches all along the front. Interestingly, most bombs because of their longer fuses did not explode on the first landing, but were often thrown back and forth until at last the fuse was complete. Many men consequently had hands and arms blown off. In some cases it was even noted that men having lost one hand took to throwing other bombs back with the other one. Three other waves of Australians followed into the Turkish trenches, running over the bodies of their own dead, which in places were piled three and four high in order to get them out of the way so men could pass through the trenches.

Private John Gammage of the 1st Battalion, writing about the incidents of the day in which he entered as part of the second wave, states:

> *The wounded bodies of both Turk and Australian were piled up three and four deep, the bombs simply poured in but as fast as our men went down, another would take his place. Besides our own wounded the Turks wounded lying in our recently taken trenches were cut to pieces with their own bombs. We have not time to think of our wounded... their pleas for mercy were not heeded... some poor fellows lay for 30 hours waiting for help and many died still waiting.*[302]

By 6pm, Lone Pine was in Australian hands. The Turks over the next four days unleashed many fierce counterattacks, but could not get their original positions back. There was never a moment to think and the men fought until they dropped from exhaustion, unable to rise up from their knees. Australians from the 2nd Brigade (elements of the 5th Battalion and the 7th Battalion) and 3rd Brigade (12th Battalion) were called up as reinforcements. Other Australian troops that were being held in reserve begged to get into the fight; some offered bribes of £5 to be allowed through.[303]

Lieutenant Jack Merivale of the 4th Battalion was killed on the first day of fighting at Lone Pine. Among his papers was a letter written by an unknown officer, who had watched the first line of the assault and had written:

> *"My batman and I were fearfully excited, and I'm not ashamed to own we both wept with excitement at not being in it, but our turn was to come." Of the next day, he wrote, "the sights in the Lone Pine works were too terrible for words, so I won't describe that at all, but the way those chaps took the trenches, and the way they held on, was equal of any feat of arms ever accomplished. One must remember that these men had been constantly*

fighting for four months, and are thin and worn. The Turks are magnificent fighters, and are very brave men".[304]

When the fighting had ended the Australians had lost 80 officers and 2197 men. The Turkish casualties were about 5000 men. Attesting to the fighting and the bravery of the men engaged, seven Victoria Crosses (VC) were won during the battle, two of them posthumously. Carlyon writes that all the medals were won in the three days after the opening charge. Most were related to bomb throwing and the subterranean "anarchy" of the second part of the battle. All were about furious little scraps around trench corners and over piles of sandbags. A VC requires the action to be witnessed by an officer. Had the officers' casualties from the assault not been so high, it is expected that more VCs would have been awarded.[305]

The battle for Lone Pine was one of the few decisive Australian victories during the campaign, although achieved at significant cost, as was the prevailing case during the Gallipoli campaign.

Turkish and Australian dead on the parapet of a Lone Pine trench. In the foreground is Captain Leslie Morshead, 2nd Battalion. (AWM A02025)

Appendix 4 – Captain Alfred Shout – 1st Battalion

Lieutenant Alfred Shout was born in Wellington, New Zealand and emigrated to Australia in 1907. He was a carpenter and applied his trade in Sydney before joining the army. Shout arrived at about 10am with the 1st Battalion on the shore at Anzac Cove and was destined to become the most decorated Australian soldier to serve on the Gallipoli Peninsula.

Shout was the casual hero with a cheery manner; he made things look easy and had the ability to make the men around him feel better. Carlyon believes that he deserves to be seen as one of the larger figures of the Gallipoli campaign.[306]

As a Lieutenant at the landing he fought all day with the Battalion on the northern heights of the battlefield around Baby 700 and Walker's Ridge. After two days of solid fighting he had carried more than a dozen wounded men out of the firing line. Although repeatedly wounded himself and with his arm almost useless, he refused to leave the battlefield, and leading by example he told his men, "I am with you boys to the finish". He received the Military Cross for his actions over the first few days following the landing and was mentioned in dispatches.

Back at the front-line again in May after having recuperated, he was wounded again in action and promoted to the rank of Captain. At Lone Pine on 9th August during the attack on the Turkish trenches, Shout charged the Turks with bombs, and was heard to be cracking jokes and cheering his men on. However, it seems he became too ambitious and tried to light three bombs at once. While managing to throw one, either the second or the third bomb exploded as it left his hand. Both his hands were severely impacted by the blast and he lost his right hand entirely. His left eye was blown out, his cheek gashed and his chest and one leg were badly burnt. Through all of this he still managed to talk optimistically to those around him and drank tea after they carted him off, announcing that he would soon recover and return to be with his men.[307] This was not to be and Shout died at the age of 33 a few days later on a hospital ship and was buried at sea. For his final actions at the battle of Lone Pine, he was awarded the Victoria Cross posthumously.

Captain C.K. Millar of the 2nd Battalion later remarked in a very honest manner of the situation he had found himself in when he first came across Shout:

Here was a man – a born leader, with wonderful control. I first saw him when we lay behind a ridge with bullets cutting the leaves and twigs of bushes just above our heads. Hell! I was scared; almost every second man was dead, and hope was lost! I prayed as I had been taught as a kid. If somebody had said run for the beach I would have been an easy winner. Along the ridge came an officer, just strolling, carrying a stick and a revolver – it was Shout! A brave leader who sensed the position, he rushed over the skyline into a better possie; gave fire orders, and passed on, unhurt. This was my first experience of individual courage – the stuff we call "guts" – and I've never forgotten Shout.[08]

The ever-cheerful Captain Alfred Shout, VC, MC. (AWM G01028)

Appendix 5 – The Life of Private James Martin

Private James Martin of the 21st Battalion is listed on the embarkation records as an 18 year old who worked as a farmhand in Victoria prior to enlisting. He left Melbourne for training in Egypt on the 28th June, 1915 on the ship HMT *Berrima*. Private Martin had a rough start to his war experience, however, and spent some time in the water after his troop ship the *Southland* was torpedoed en route to the fighting. Having survived the sinking, he managed to reach Anzac Cove on 5th September, 1915. After a month on the peninsula, he wrote to his parents, who lived in the Melbourne suburb of Hawthorn, in boyish scrawl:

> *Just a line hoping all is well as it leaves me at present. Things are just the same here the only difference is that we are expecting a bit of rain which will not be welcomed by us… There was one Turk who tried to give himself up the other night and got shot by the sentry. We dragged him into our trenches to bury him in the morning and you ought to have seen the state he was in (He comments about the Turk's clothes. He had probably become used to the sight of dead bodies during his stay on the peninsula). …We are not doing too bad for food, we got a little present from Lady Ferguson [wife of the Australian Governor-General] that was two fancy biscuits, half a stick of chocolate and two sardines each. I think I have told you all the news so I must draw to a close with fondest love to all.*[309]

Private Martin craved a letter, no doubt feeling somewhat homesick. Across the top of his letter he scrawled: "Write soon. I have received no letters since I left Victoria and I have been writing often".

A little over a fortnight later, on the 25th October, 1915 (just under two months since arriving at Gallipoli), he was evacuated and brought on board the hospital ship *Glenart Castle* suffering from typhoid fever, but he died that evening from heart failure and was buried at sea.[310]

Although as noted above, Private Martin claimed he had reached the minimum age to be able to enlist of 18. Like many others he had actually given a false age to ensure that he would be able to join the others and go off to fight. The saddest thing, however, is that at the time of his death he was only 14 years and nine months old and is considered to be one of the youngest Australian soldiers to have died in the World War I.[311]

Among his effects that were returned to his family, along with his letter, was a scrap of red and white streamer that he had picked up and stowed away in his pack as his troopship left Melbourn.[312]

Private James Martin, aged 14, posing with his sister, Millie, before sailing off to fight at Gallipoli. (King)

Appendix 6 – The Charge of the Light Horse at the Nek (August 1915 – Gallipoli)

The battle for the Nek was another diversionary attack that formed part of the Allies' August Offensive and occurred the day after the Australians attacked the Turkish Lone Pine defences. This attack, however, was a great failure and resulted in a wasteful loss of life that occurred over a very short period of time. It is a sobering story about the incompetence of many of the officers involved at Gallipoli and the supreme disregard that many had for men's lives. It is also the story of supreme courage and bravery by men that knew clearly what dire circumstances awaited them, and that any charge would almost certainly result in death or wounding. Indeed many men would have also have concluded that their efforts would ultimately have only a limited chance of success. Knowing all this, they were still willing to lay down their lives for their country, mates and uphold honour. They were carrying out the orders given to them no matter how difficult it was to comply with and how futile the exercise would be. As Bean stated, there was no greater example of reckless obedience than the charge by the Australians at the Nek. The attack also demonstrated the sheer bloodymindedness of senior officers who should have known better.

North of the 400 Plateau and higher up the Second Ridge was a small area of land called the Nek. It is a narrow ridge about 300m long, tapering to 60m at the waist. At the Anzac line it was about 50m wide and at the Turkish line it was about 30m wide. There was only about 40m that separated the trenches, roughly two tennis courts joined together in area. The Turks had at least five machine-guns positioned to cover the ground between the two trenches, sited to provide interlocking arcs of fire. The ridge that the attack would need to be made across was so narrow that the Australians would have to move forward in four waves of 150 men. Behind the Turkish trenches of the Nek, rising up a hill called Baby 700, lay another seven lines of Turkish trenches. Breaking through the Turkish trenches at the Nek represented a way out of the stalemate for the Allies, a way to get to the heights of Chunuk Bair and on to Hill 971, the highest point in the Sari Bair Range. Both armies were well aware of the advantage the high ground provided to the occupying army, and countless attempts had been made by each to take the possession of the heights away from the other.

The Turks in their failed May offensive tried to cross this ground and were cut to pieces by Australian fire, now it was the Turks' turn to repay the debt.

Before dawn on the 7th August, 1915, the men of the 8th Light Horse Regiment (LHR) from Victoria and the 10th LHR from Western Australia, their chests warmed by a double ration of rum, stood in the dog–legged trenches of Russell's Top. Bean indicated that the spirits of the men at that stage were high and they were keen for action, having noted with interest the assault of the 1st Battalion on the trenches of Lone Pine, albeit at a distance, the previous day. They would have heard the sounds of battle ranging on the plateau below. They too expected to be successful in what would be their first offensive action since arriving at Gallipoli.

The men of the Light Horse Regiments, like those in the infantry battalions, had all volunteered because they thought the war was going to be a fine romance. They would get to ride horses with their mates, wear leather leggings and a slouch hat with emu plumes. But the romance soon started to fade. They had left their horses back in Egypt and were now fighting on foot, wearing pith helmets, shorts and puttees. The reality of the circumstances would have by this stage been clearly understood and confirmed by the lice that was rampant throughout their clothing, the growing number of their mates that were now listed as killed or wounded and the bouts of dysentery that most of the soldiers would have had to endure while trying to fight at some stage since landing at Gallipoli. In their 11 weeks on the peninsula, they had carted water and dug trenches in which many times their picks had thudded into bodies of Turks and Australian soldiers who had died earlier.[313] Their situation was now so far removed from what they had first expected.

The basic plan of attack was simple enough. The first two waves of men would take the first line of trenches at the Nek, moving forward immediately after an intense naval artillery barrage had been directed at the Turkish trenches. Given that the Turkish machine-guns were located some 200 metres beyond the Turkish front-line trenches, the initial waves were not expected to silence these guns. The first wave would also take with them two scaling ladders that they would use to clamber out of the deep Turkish trenches, along with red and yellow marker flags that would be used to indicate that the trenches had been taken. The third and fourth waves would move through the first two waves and move forward to attack the trenches further on up the hill. Surprisingly, another hurdle would be given to the Australians, just to make it harder still to succeed, in the form of an order that required that the rifles carried by the Light Horsemen would have bayonets fixed, but were not to be loaded until they reached the Turkish trenches. The plan went on to outline that it was hoped that the New Zealanders would take and secure their objective of Chunuk Bair, which lay further up the ridge behind Baby 700, and put pressure on the Turks from the other side of the Nek. Simultaneous attacks on the Turkish trenches in front of Pope's Hill and Quinn's Post would also be undertaken by Australian soldiers.

Like many plans at Gallipoli, this sounded reasonable on paper, but the strength of the Turkish defences had again been underestimated and the plan fell apart soon after it started. The artillery barrage was limited, and one officer remarked that it was a joke. In addition, the order to move forward and attack was not given until seven minutes after the barrage had stopped and the advantage of attacking while the Turks were in disarray had been lost. Instead the men then waited in the trenches for the eventual order to go. Lieutenant Colonel John Antill, who was left in charge of the planning and providing the orders for the attack, had failed to synchronise the timing of the gunners with that of the assault troops. It was never expected that the front row of Turkish trenches would be significantly impacted by the barrage given their close proximity to the Australian trenches. Bean notes that the barrage had, however, been highly effective in wrecking havoc among the Turks in the trenches that lay on the slopes behind the first rows of trenches. It is interesting to note that an order had been given by the Turkish command that the trenches at the Nek should be covered with logs, in much the same way that the Turkish trenches at Lone Pine were constructed in order to provide protection for the soldiers against the Allied naval bombardments, which had proven to be very successful to date against open-trench systems that were capable of being shelled. However, this order was declined by the Turkish commanders at the Nek, who stated that it was too restrictive on their capacity to suppress attacks with machine-gun and rifle fire. Had the order been carried out though, the outcome of the charge at the Nek may have been different. The Turks have long held a belief that it was the enclosed trenches at Lone Pine that aided the attackers and the success the Australians were able to achieve in capturing the Turkish trench systems following their advance.

In another unfortunate turn of events, the New Zealand troops had not been able to take Chunuk Bair as had been planned. In fact, it would not be until the following day that the objective would be taken, and then it would only be held in Allied hands for a short time. Effectively, this meant that the charge at the Nek was no longer part of a pincer movement as had been originally planned without success at Chunuk Bair. Rather it now took the form of a feint to take the pressure off the New Zealand forces that were struggling further up the ridge.

In the meantime, starting from 4.23am when the guns stopped, the Turks, now aware that an attack was imminent, had time to regroup and set themselves up, some sitting up on the parapet. The Australians waiting in the trench would have heard the Turkish machine-guns off to the flanks of the killing grounds and further up the hill fire warming rounds. They knew the firestorm that lay ahead for them!

The 8th LHR was commanded by Lieutenant Colonel Alexander White, a well-known Melbourne businessmen before the war, who was well respected by his men. No doubt aware of the impossibility of the task he had been given, he decided to lead by example and place himself in the first line of the assault troops. As he left Antill, he put out his hand and said simply "goodbye". He would lead his troops and be with them until the end, as was his character. White ordered "Go" at 4.30am and climbed out of the Australian trench to be followed by the first 150 of his men. White managed only 10 paces and then fell dead. Most of his men in the first wave did not get as far, dying within six metres of their starting point above the parapet or falling back into the trench on to the second wave of men waiting below. In the half light, the Turkish machine-guns and rifles belched flames. Bean indicated that he had heard the fusillade in which he described as "a continuous roaring tempest" and he shivered. The Australians were shot to pieces. An observer on Pope's Hill said it was "as though men's limbs had become like string". Three men reached the Turkish trenches on the right, but did not last much longer, and on the left, 23 year old Lieutenant E.G.Wilson a grazier from Warrnambool, reached the Turkish parapet and was then killed by a bomb. The first wave of the 8th LHR had been wiped out within half a minute.

The sensible thing would have been to call off the attack, given it was clear that any further attempts would be futile. However, two minutes later the second wave of the 8th LHR charged out of the trench to meet a similar fate. In two and a half minutes, almost the entire regiment had been wiped out without any Turkish casualties.

Lieutenant Colonel Noel Brazier, commanding the 10th LHR, who was next to go into the firestorm, had been watching through a periscope. No doubt concerned about what he had seen, he went to Antill having hoped to speak to his superior, Brigadier General Fredric Hughes, who was not there, and told the Brigade Major that any further attack was futile. Antill told Brazier that an Australian marker flag had been seen in the Turkish trenches (it hadn't) and then shouted at him, "Push on!". Brazier went back to his men saying, "I'm sorry lads, but the order is to go." The West Australians of the third and fourth lines knew they were doomed. They had heard the terrible sound of the deadly fusillade and no doubt noted the wounded survivors of the 8th LHR being rushed past them in the crowded trench. They shook hands and said goodbye, each man considering no doubt how death would occur. Trooper Harold Rush, in his now famous final words that have been engraved on his headstone in the cemetery at Walkers Ridge, turned to his mate and said, "Goodbye, cobber. God bless you". At about 4.45am, in Bean's words, "the 10th went forward to meet death instantly… with that regiment went the flower of the youth of Western Australia". Two brothers died in the third wave, Gresely Harper, a barrister, and Wilfred, a farmer. Wilfred was either 25 or 26 years of age and was last seen running like a schoolboy in a foot race. He was the inspiration for the Archie Hamilton character in Peter Weir's film *Gallipoli.*[314] When I think about the character of the men that were in the third and fourth lines and what drove them to get out of the trench, having heard the sounds of death from among the earlier waves, knowing what would no doubt happen to them, their courage was astounding. They were very much were men from another time and another era. With a true sense of duty as a soldier, they intended to carry out the order given to them no matter what the cost.

About this time, a message from a wounded Major Todd reached Brazier. Todd was seeking instructions on what to do given the fourth wave of men were preparing to attack. Brazier took the note to Antill and pleaded with him to reconsider the order. Antill refused to listen to him. "Push on!" was the repeated order.

It is said that before the fourth line charged, a Turkish officer appeared at the parapet at the end of one of the lines of Australian trenches and implored then to "Stop, Stop" the slaughter was so terrible. The last line of the 10th LHR went ahead anyway.

At 5.15am, the fourth line attacked, to meet the same fate as its predecessors. Of the 300 in the 8th LHR, 156 were dead and 80 wounded. In the 10th LHR, 80 were dead and 58 wounded. Bean noted:

At first here and there a man raised an arm to the sky, or tried to drink from his water bottle. But as the sun of that burning day climbed higher, such movement ceased. Over the whole summit the figures lay still in the quivering heat.[315]

In fact the bodies of the men would not be recovered and buried until after the end of the war. When Bean and his entourage returned in 1919, they could see a white patch, like snow, on the ground just below the Nek. It was the bleached bones of the two Light Horse regiments.

The cemetery that is now located at the Nek is built on the former no-man's-land. On this small rectangular piece of land, the dead would lay for almost four years unburied, as it was far too dangerous to venture out during the campaign. Hence, there are very few headstones, as most of the 316 men killed at this place could not be identified and lie in unmarked graves in six rows beneath the thick, green grass. The Turks also had lost a large number of men at this place a few weeks earlier in their own disastrous offensive. They named this same piece of ground "Cesaret Tepe" or in English, Hill of Valour.

Bean notes that the 10th Light Horse Regiment was one to which the sons of almost every well-known pastoralist and farmer in Western Australia came bringing their own horses and their own saddles. Just a year later half of the regiment was wiped out in a few seconds in one of the bravest charges ever made.

Boys who never came home. Officers of the 8th Australian Light Horse Regiment in Melbourne before the outbreak of war. They are (standing) Major Thomas Redford, Lieutenant Edward Henty, Lieutenant Eliot Wilson and (seated) Lieutenant Keith Borthwick and Lieutenant Robert Baker. Only Baker survived the charge at the Nek to return to Australia. (AWM P00265.001)

"The Charge at the Nek", painting by George Lambert.

Appendix 7 – Lieutenant Hugo Throssell – 10th Light Horse Regiment

This was an interesting story about a war hero that survived some of the worst battles of the Gallipoli campaign and was recognised for his valour and courage under extreme conditions, only to become a casualty of life after coming back home. Carlyson recounts his story and I have taken a summary of this below.

Lieutenant Hugo Throssell of the 10th Light Horse Regiment had taken part in the ill-fated charge at the Nek on 7th August, 1915. Throssell, like most other officers at the time, knew that the charge was hopeless and would amount to wholesale slaughter of his men well before the actual order to move out of the trenches was given. He had seen the devastation that befell the first and second lines of the 8th LHR when they had charged earlier and heard the roar of the Turkish guns. His story was that during the charge, once confirmation that the attack would likely end in disaster, he called out to the remaining men of his line to lie down and they huddled with him in a hollow blasted out by the preparatory bombardment on dead ground. This may have been one of the reasons why in comparison to the 8th LHR that charged earlier, their casualties were much less severe. He and a number of other men, including his brother, Ric, who was wounded, managed to crawl back to the trench.

Then on August 29th, Throssell again found himself fighting for his life in a trench at Hill 60, in a fierce bomb fight with the Turks that was as fierce as the fighting that had taken place at Lone Pine. Throssell and his men were on one side of a barricade in a trench and the Turks on the other side in their trench, with only 12 metres separating them at times. Both sides pelted each other with bombs and the Australians fired until their rifles became too hot to handle and they had to exchange them for guns from the wounded or dead. Throssell had been shot in the shoulder and neck, but he stayed in the trench, rallying the men around him and held it against Turkish insurgencies. When he came out of the trench at the end of the fight he could not raise his hand to his mouth to smoke a cigarette, his cloths were shredded from bomb fragments and one of his Australian badges had been driven into his shoulder.

Throssell, the 31 year old farmer from Western Australia, was awarded the Victoria Cross for his bravery in this action. After his wounds had healed he rejoined the Light Horse Regiment in Palestine in 1917 and was again wounded in the thigh and foot during the battle of Gaza. His brother Ric, was killed in the same battle. Throssell spent the night following the battle searching in vain for his brother's body. His men noted that after this event, the Lieutenant was never the same. The happy-go-lucky leader who had led them by example had lost his spark.

Once repatriated to Australia, he married a writer by the name of Katharine Prichard and they settled on a farm near Perth. Things did not work out for him and his wife and they started to go broke as the Great Depression took hold of the country. Unfortunately his war service pension did not provide the financial security he wanted for his family and in 1933, aged 49, the hero of the World War I sat out on his veranda and shot himself in the head. His war was finally over.

Appendix 8 – The Queenslanders' Charge at Quinn's Post

At about the same time that the first line of the 8th LHR charged at the Nek i.e. 4.30am, at Quinn's Post the Queenslanders of the 2nd LHR, who had been based at Enoggera camp with the 9th Battalion, carried out a similar diversionary charge. They planned for four lines of 50 men to charge equally well-defended enemy trenches.

The first line charged into a hail of Turkish bullets and 49 of the first wave of 50 men, were either killed or wounded. The difference, however, this time, was that Major G.H. Bourne told the second line to stand fast and stopped the attack. Charles Chauvel, the Brigade commander, also fortunately agreed with him.

Appendix 9 – The British Landings at Cape Helles on 25th April, 1915

Like the plan for the Anzac landings, the British also had big plans for landing large numbers of men from the sea at Cape Helles on the 25th April. In fact for General Hamilton, this was the main Allied strike force for the Gallipoli campaign. Also like the plan prepared for Anzacs, the British would land a covering force and then following, a second wave would be landed. Similarly, at the same time the French 1st Division (which included units from the French Foreign Legion and Colonial Senegalese) would carry out feints at Kum Kale and at Besika Bay, which are on the Asiatic side of the Dardanelles, on the 25th April.

Just prior to landing, the ships carrying the British and French soldiers headed for the island of Tenedos to assemble in invasion order. The 29th Division was the selected British Division for the landings and 6000 men from this Division would land at five designated beaches at Cape Helles as the initial covering force. The main landing, however, would be at "W" and "V" beaches, which unfortunately were landing sites that favoured the defenders more than those attacking. Following the landings of the covering force, 12,000 more men would land across each of the five beaches, linking up and advancing up the peninsula with the aim of taking Achi Baba, which was the high ground commanding the Cape Helles area.

The beach designated as "V", is a strip of sand about 10 metres wide and about 300 metres long. It is an ampitheatre, made for defence, and is flanked by the ruined Seddulbahir castle and the village of the same name on the right and a newer fort located on the left. There is a bank four to five feet high where the sand ends and from here the land rises to a height of 100 to 150 feet. The plan was for the 4000 tonne ship the *River Clyde,* which was painted a yellow-brown colour, to be beached here.

Both W and V beaches could be considered death traps unless the naval guns could silence the Turkish defenders, particularly those located in and around Seddulbahir Fort. Both beaches were identified as possible landing places by the German High Command on Gallipoli and now the beaches were covered in a matrix of barbed wire, complex trench systems had been created and artillery strategically placed inland. These formidable defences had been confirmed by none other than General Hamilton and General Braithwaite in their reconnaissance from ships off the coast well before the landings took place.

The thinking behind the use of the *River Clyde* was that as V Beach at Cape Helles was so small, it would be hard to get troops ashore quickly there. Commander Edward Unwin came up with the Trojan Horse idea, being that they would run the old ship aground and land 2000 troops from eight sallyports cut in the ship's sides. The men would run along wooden gangplanks into grounded lighters and then jump on to shore. [316]

At 5am, the guns on the HMS *Albion* opened fire on the Turkish held Seddulbahir Fort and other ships then started to join in across the whole of the Cape. The purpose of the bombardment was to destroy the entrenched positions around the beaches and force the enemy to flee the beachheads. Again the British had underestimated their enemy, and while the Turks did leave the area, they returned soon after the bombardment had finished to take up their original trench positions.

The Allied landings at Y, X and S beaches had been successful and there was minimal Turkish opposition encountered. However, the Lancashires that landed at W Beach were decimated. The naval guns did little damage to the wire entanglements that stretched from the beach into the water. While there was only a company of Turkish soldiers defending at W Beach, the progress of the 1st Battalion of Lancashire Fusiliers was slowed by wire barriers both in the water on approach that caught boats and also thickly placed on the beach. Before the Turks could be driven out of their defensive positions, they took a terrible toll on the British soldiers. The Battalion that left Egypt for Gallipoli numbered 1029 men, but after the end of the first day the number of fighting men available was down to 410. A Captain commanding D company was noted as saying that the front of the barbed wire facing to the sea was now a thick mass of men that had been shot trying to get through and over. Most would not make it alive off the wire.

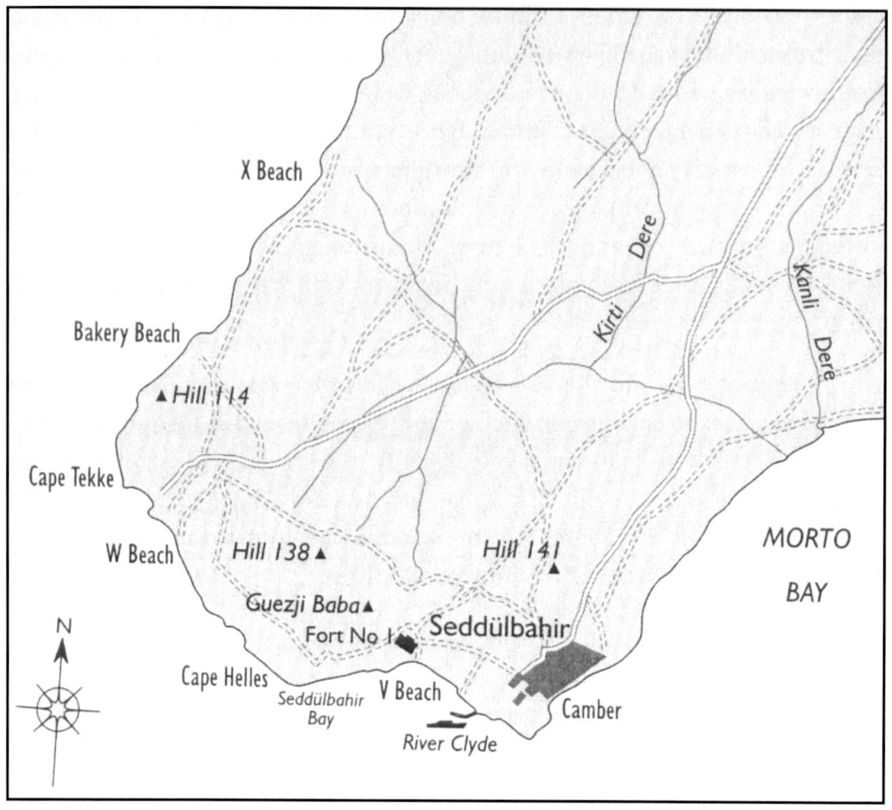

The landing beaches, Cape Helles. (Carlyon)

At V Beach the landings started at about 6.22am. In conjunction with troops heading to the shore in boats, the *River Clyde* was also run ashore. Concealed in its hull were the 2000 men of the Munster Fusiliers and the Hampshire Regiment, and they waited for the lighters to be put in place. The lighters, however, started to drift away and two men from the *River Clyde's* crew had to jump into the water in a bid to secure them. When the troops appeared running down the gangplanks to the lighters, they were literally mowed down by the Turkish machine-guns that were lying in wait. Unfortunately, there was only one real connection with the beach and the men moved across in single fire making easy targets. Not more than one in 10 of the British soldiers made the journey, as the machine-gun fire from the Turks was disciplined and accurate.

Very little damage had been done to the fort or the defences from the naval bombardment and in general, the bombardment was highly inaccurate. Only a handful of the first 1000 men made the beach and therefore some relative safety behind a sand bank. The lighters that linked the ship to the shore again drifted loose and the disembarkation was called off, and the men were then ordered to run back to the ship under fire. The drifting lighters were left full of dead and wounded men. Turkish Major Mahmut recorded that "the shore became full of enemy corpses, like a shoal of fish. At Seddulbahir, five boatloads of men were completely sunk."

A British airman, Commander Charles Samson, flying above the scene later stated that he had looked down on a sea "absolutely red with blood". The stain, he said, spread for 50 yards from the shore.[317]

The remaining men in the hull of the *River Clyde* would not leave again until night time and then they had the problem of how to get off the beach to contend with.

The fatal shore. This photo was taken from the bridge of the *River Clyde* a few hours after it was beached. The bodies of the dead Hampshires and Munsters can be seen sprawled in the lighters, as well as groups of men sheltering behind a low bank on the beach. Beyond the ruins of Seddulbahir's fort, above V Beach, are well entrenched Turkish units. (AWM A03076)

View from the headland today, where the Turkish trenches were located looking down on to V Beach at Cape Helles. Top left of the picture is the ruins of Seddulbahir Fort. The top end of V Beach is where the *River Clyde* was beached.

Appendix 10 – Y Beach, An Opportunity Lost – Cape Helles

In regard to the strategy for the landings at Cape Helles, the key objective for the first day was the peak of the 700 feet Achi Baba hill, which lies about two kilometres in from Y Beach and is the highest point of the Kilitbahir Plateau. Much like the Anzac battlefield, capture and securing of the high ground was vital. In the case of Achi Baba, it was believed that capturing this hill would stop the Turks from bringing further reinforcements down the Peninsula towards Cape Helles and allow the attackers to dominate the defensive positions in the Dardanelles along the coastline.

While the first consideration was true, the capacity to dominate the defensive positions at the Dardanelles, however, in particular Kilitbahir Fort, was not correct. In fact the hill of Achi Baba was far more valuable to the defenders than the attackers, given the vantage point it provided over the entire bottom section of the peninsula. Specifically it provided a view of all of the landing points at Cape Helles and a clear view of the plateau that the Allied attacking forces would need to move along. When I stood on Achi Baba in October 2008, the view of the plateau that the Allied forces would need to cross was clear, along with a view of the exit points from each of the beach landing zones. Conversely, the northern view from Achi Baba did not provide a vantage point for any of the forts that the Allies would have liked to target on the Dardanelles coastline. This was also noted by Commodore Roger Keyes in charge of the March 1915 naval battle, who following the war climbed up Achi Baba and was "unpleasantly shocked" at this revelation.

View from the top of Achi Baba, looking towards the eastern side of Cape Helles. On the right of the photo is S Beach.

A British artillery officer who served on Gallipoli during the campaign wrote on revisiting the battlefield in the 1920s that the Helles battlefield could be compared to a hollow like the dish of a spoon, while the rim of the spoon prevented observation from the Allied ships at sea. He wrote:

> *The possession of Alcitepe (Achi Baba) ... Gave the Turks the most wonderful and complete observation into the whole of this area except for the strips of beaches under the cliffs. It was the fact that made the development of a subsequent offensive from Helles on a large scale practically impossible. He concluded that, the true value of the hill is obvious; to defense its retention was invaluable because of the observation it gave. But its capture by the Allies could not have produced the decisive results expected.*[318]

In between Achi Baba and Y Beach is the town of Krithia (present-day Alcitepe), which at the time of the landings by the British at Y Beach (the northernmost landing point by the British at Cape Helles that morning) was clearly visible across the wheatfields. There were no Turkish soldiers present in the town on the morning of 25th April, 1915. In my discussions with Kenan Celik, my Turkish Gallipoli guide, he indicated that the actions of the British on the first day at Cape Helles displayed a lack of initiative that would cost them dearly over the next few months.

Looking to the west from the top of Achi Baba, towards the old town of Krithia, Gully Ravine and then over to the Y Beach landing area.

The best example of this were the actions of the British under the command of Lieutenant Colonel Godfrey Matthews, who landed at Y Beach on the morning of the 25th April. Matthews landed with 2000 men (Plymouth Battalion of the RND and a company of South Wales Borderers). They were unopposed and scaled to the top of the cliffs off the beaches without a casualty. Matthews' orders were to capture a Turkish gun emplacement thought to be inland from Y Beach, divert Turkish forces away from the more heavily defended beaches further to the south and then to met up with the men having landed at X Beach further to the south of the Peninsula. Then later that afternoon, to take part in the advance on Achi Baba.

Matthews and his men landed at 5.45am and without any opposition, and no Turkish gun to be found, strolled to within 500 metres of the town of Krithia and then made their way back to the beach. His men made tea and lugged water up from the beaches and waited for the men from X Beach, deciding to dig in at 3pm that afternoon rather than take the initiative offered to them by capturing and securing the town of Krithia at the very least, even if they did not move directly on to Achi Baba. On the 25th April, the Turkish forces in the whole area south of Achi Baba, covering all of the five landing areas, were limited and there were no more than two Battalions of the 26th Regiment, or roughly 2000 men. This number was the equivalent of the British soldiers landing at Y Beach alone. Moreover, there were very few defenders in and around Achi Baba itself, and it is conceivable that Matthews and his men, possibly having made contact with the other British forces that had landed with little resistance at both X and W beaches, could have taken the objective that morning. This would have changed the course of the campaign, certainly in the Cape Helles area. They would have had what little high ground advantage was available and cut off the Turkish reinforcements from the 25th Regiment that were moving en masse towards the Cape.

The other option that they could have taken was to take the pressure off their comrades who were being massacred down at V and W beaches by marching down to support them and enable them to advance inland towards the objective much sooner with far less casualties. This unfortunately was not what happened, mainly due to poor communications, failure of commanders to take any initiative and to seize the opportunity that was presented. Orders were there to be followed, so the most expensive cup of tea was had that afternoon on the 25th April at Y Beach.

By 5.30pm, the three Battalions of the Turkish 25th Regiment had reached Y Beach and a Battalion attacked Matthews and his casualties mounted quickly. The British had not dug themselves in nearly as much as they should have and fell back, eventually evacuating Y Beach by mid morning on the 26th April, 1915. The town of Krithia and the Y Beach area was now in Turkish hands.

By day three after the landings, the British forces had just managed to clear the Turkish coastal defensive areas and secure beachheads (one Turkish Battalion had hung on doggedly for two days and stopped an earlier breakout), however, by this time it was too late. Turkish reinforcements had arrived and by day four, 28th April, 1915, a stalemate similar to the Anzac area had developed. The Turks were dug in between Achi Baba and the British forces moving up from Cape Helles, and the town of Krithia had been garrisoned by the Turks.

During this first battle of Krithia, some 14,000 British soldiers were engaged and they suffered almost 3000 casualties, after having made attack after attack in broad daylight across open country on the plateau with limited protection. The main advances were cut down by heavy fire from entrenched Turkish positions. The battle lasted three days and cost a total of 6000 Allied casualties, nearly a third of the troops involved, and resulted in a net gain of ground of roughly 600 metres.

The view of a French liaison officer on the Gallipoli Peninsula of the British High Command was that:

The British only get some idea about enemy strength by crashing into them, and by that time it is often too late.

After their losses during the landings on the 25th April, the 29th Division again suffered severely from 26th April to 10th May, 1915, with over 10,000 casualties being evacuated. From a very similar period of time, the French had suffered 12,600 casualties from a total strength of 22,450 men.

The trench systems quickly resembled those on the Western Front and the Allied front-line stretched for five kilometres in length, cutting across the toe of the peninsula and would not move substantially for the rest of the campaign. Interestingly, the town of Krithia was still almost two kilometres inland beyond the Allied trenches.

After many months of fighting and a significant loss of men, all aimed at taking possession of the town and the hill of Achi Baba, which had been the key objectives for the very first day of the landings, but neither were ever taken by the Allies over the course of the campaign.

Appendix 11 – The Tragedy at Gully Ravine

There is a long gorge that runs out to the Aegean Sea on the southern end of the Gallipoli Peninsula named Gully Ravine. It is on the western side of the peninsula and lies just south of the town of Krithia and west of the hill named Achi Baba, which were the key strategic objectives for the Allied Army landing at Cape Helles.

As had occurred early at the Anzac battlegrounds, the Cape Helles landings by the British and French had now ground to a halt, and a stalemate of Allied trenches facing off against Turkish trenches stretched across the southern end of the peninsula. Both the town of Krithia and Achi Baba were firmly in the hands of the Turks and both objectives were now over a mile and half behind Turkish front-lines.

In another ill-conceived effort to advance up the peninsula and take Achi Baba, following the failed attempt during the Third Battle of Krithia, the British (29th Division) made their first assault during the Battle of Gully Ravine along Gully Spur at 10.45am in the hot sun on the 28th June, 1915. The battle that took place over the next few days would be one of the bloodiest of all battles that took place throughout the Gallipoli campaign, especially for the Turkish soldiers.

During my tour to the Gallipoli Peninsula, Kenan Celik took me around the Cape Helles and Krithia battlefields. One of the more sombre times during the tour was standing with Kenan as he pointed to the key features of the area where the battle for Gully Ravine had taken place and recounted the horrors that occurred in this area. On that day of my visit it was a serene picture of a rolling countryside, very dry with golden grass shimmering in the sun's rays and a light, soft sea breeze blowing in from the beautiful blue Aegean Sea. It is mostly cleared farming land now, with the odd tree or green clump of trees still standing. We could clearly make out the gorge that formed Gully Spur and then ran into Gully Ravine, as it was marked by a thick tree line. Behind us is the Turkish "Nuri Yamut" memorial, which is shrouded with trees. It was difficult to picture the scene of devastation that took place here over 90 years ago, but in his mild, mannered, matter of fact way, Kenan outlined what had taken place and the significance of the Turkish memorial that has now been erected. Slowly the hairs on the back of my neck began to rise and a sickly feeling of the suffering that occurred over these fields began to sink in.

The advance by the British on the left-hand side during the opening exchanges of the battle had progressed reasonably well, as they had the support of the heavy guns from the naval warships that were blasting away at the Turkish defenders. However, the right- hand side of the advance suffered badly, mainly due to the fact that this area had limited support from the naval guns, and subsequently the British casualties began to mount. Over the three days to 30 June, 1915, the British casualties numbered about 3800 men.

Worried about the British advance on the left, the Turkish commanders ordered a series of wild counterattacks back down Gully Spur on the night of 1st July, and it was then the Turkish Army's turn to die in their thousands. The guns of the British warships were particularly devastating. The Turks, while plentiful in manpower, advanced with limited artillery or machine-gun support. They made incessant attacks over the next few days, each being repulsed, culminating in the strongest attack up to that point at dawn on the 5th July. It also failed everywhere, and the Turkish losses that day alone, were worse than the losses suffered in the Anzac sector during the Turkish May offensive. The Turkish casualties between 28th June and 5th July were estimated to be between 14,000 and 16,000 men, four times the British losses, and most of them around Gully Ravine.

It was a scene of horrendous brutality, death and carnage all along the ravine. Carlyon notes that even 85 years later, one still sees many bones there, and why even on a smiling spring day, the place seems haunted in a way that is hard to explain, as if corrupted.[319]

The Allies witnessed great fires over the next few nights, which were the Turks burning their dead.

The Turks had requested of the Allied Command that a truce be observed to bury the dead that were strewn all over the battlefield. However, the request was turned down by General Ian Hamilton in what the Turks believed was an act that questioned the standards of the British. Even though Hamilton was overheard to state, "Although on the grounds of humanity as well as health, I should like the poor chaps to be decently buried", he believed that the Turks had made the request because they could not get their men to charge across the corpses of their comrades. Dead Turks were therefore better than barbed wire.[320]

The bodies of the Turks that fell over the days of the battle stayed on the field until 1943. The Greeks that had lived in the area had long gone and nobody occupied this land until Turks came back to settle around 1938. In 1943, a former Turkish officer arranged for a Turkish memorial to be built in honour of the men that had died there during the war, the Nuri Yamut memorial. The locals went around the battlefield and collected thousands of bones in carts and placed them in the tomb that lies at the centre of the memorial. Kenan added that there were now hardly any objects remaining on the battlefield, as farming had resumed across the area, particularly following the end of World War II and farmers sold items found, especially scrap metal, to supplement their earnings from their crops.

Appendix 12 – The New Zealanders (Wellington Infantry Battalion) and the battle for Chunuk Bair

August 7th,1915 had become a crucial day for the Allies. The charges at the Nek, Pope's Post and Quinn's Post had gone disastrously. However, while the New Zealanders were late, they had done well to get within reach of Chunuk Bair, which was a key part of their objectives during the offensive. Brigadier–General Francis Johnson commanded the New Zealand Infantry Brigade, which was made up of the Canterbury, Otago, Wellington and Auckland Battalions, a Mountain Battery and a company of Engineers. The Brigade, with a theoretical strength of 4000 men, was down to about 2800 men. The New Zealand troops had been in the May struggle for Baby 700 and the second battle of Krithia; they had also garrisoned Quinn's Post and other areas at the head of Monash Gully. Each of these actions had taken a toll on the strength of the New Zealand forces.

At 5.30am (4.30am the attack at the Nek had occurred), Colonel William Malone and his Wellington Battalion had advanced to a point called the Apex, which was only 500 yards from the summit of Chunuk Bair. They were joined by the Otago and Auckland Battalions, but the Canterburys were still missing (in fact they had become lost and most ended up back at the starting point). At this time they were more than six hours behind schedule.

By mid-morning, three companies of the Auckland Battalion were ordered to attack and move towards the summit. Within 10 yards of the starting point at the Apex, they started to fall. The leading Auckland platoons were "simply devastated; the sight sickening" recalled one New Zealand officer. About 100 men reached the unoccupied Turkish trench at the Pinnacle and hastily began to deepen it. Behind the trench, there were about 300 dead and wounded men laying in the sun. Johnson then promptly urged the Wellingtons under Malone to follow after the Aucklanders. Malone, however, refused the order outright and his men heard him do so. Malone shouted to his men to "Stop where you are! No we're are not taking orders from you people. Wellington is not going up there. My men are not going to commit suicide." Malone said that he would take full responsibility for his actions and any follow–on punishment. The Wellingtons would take Chunuk Bair at night, not in daylight, he said. Colonel Malone looked after his men and his men loved him in return. It is interesting to note that even after 60 years since the battle, men that had served under him still held "Molly Malone" in high reverence.[321] It is little wonder considering the amazing achievements the Battalion, under the leadership of Malone, would display over the next few days of hard fighting.

The Wellington Battalion march down Cuba Street, Wellington, NZ, in October 1914, to their embarkation. Lieutenant-Colonel William Malone (mounted with drawn sword) is in the centre of the photo. The officer at the head of the column is Colonel Francis Johnston, Commander of the New Zealand Infantry Brigade. (Alexander Turnbull Library, Wellington New Zealand G-17072-/4)

The Canterbury Battalion had suffered heavy casualties from artillery and gunfire on their way up to the Apex and the Otago Battalion had also suffered and were low in numbers. Only the Wellingtons Battalion was still left relatively unscathed at this point.

At 4.30am the next morning, the 8th August, the Wellingtons moved out towards the summit, which was being heavily shelled by naval and Anzac batteries. The men advanced 16 abreast along the ridge towards the Pinnacle, over the fallen men from the Auckland Battalion, past their shallow trench and down the dip, then up towards the summit itself, spreading out as the hill opened up in front of them. Not a shot was fired as the Wellingtons climbed, and when the barrage ended they charged the summit. It was a bit of an anti climax as there was only a single Turkish gun crew below the summit, given that most of the Turkish defenders had fled the artillery barrage because their trenches were too shallow to protect them.

Lieutenant–Colonel William Malone, just prior to the assault on to the crest of Chunuk Bair. (Kippenberger Military Archive, National Army Museum, New Zealand - 2006575-8)

Some prisoners were taken and Malone and his men saw the silvery waters of the Narrows of the Dardanelles. However, all was not secure, and the men realised that this place was going to be hard to defend. The ground was very rocky and hard and worst of all, the summit was open to artillery fire from the north (Hill Q) and from the south (Battleship Hill). Having only been on the high ground for a short period of time, the Battalion and those following in reserve came under heavy fire from the artillery, and also from Turkish riflemen that could now see their targets after the haze lifted.

Malone and his men hastily began to dig. Two companies were placed forward of the crest in the existing Turkish trench, the other two would dig a new trench behind the crest and then drive saps forward to join the two lines. The Turks were now starting to pick off the Wellingtons at will, and the reinforcements behind the Battalion were cut–off. The Turks were also able to creep within 20 yards of the Wellingtons positions without being seen. The front trench, which was too shallow anyway, became clogged with dead and wounded, and by 6.30am Malone was running a tremendous battle. The rifles of the New Zealanders became too hot to handle and many used three or four rifles, which were being loaded by wounded men. Private Nicholson of the Battalion later recalled that the bayonet fighting seemed to last for weeks, "although I suppose it was only a few minutes" he stated.

Malone moved around among the men throughout the day keeping up morale and using encouraging words, indicating that it would ease off shortly and that "the Turks will get tired of this". The Wellingtons at times made short bayonet charges at the advancing Turks and then returned quickly to the trenches, which were filling with casualties from the fighting.

At about 5pm, Malone was hit by a shrapnel burst, possibly fired from an Anzac battery or a warship and was killed. Carlyon indicates in his book that by the standards set at Lone Pine, he should have received a Victoria Cross, instead he received no posthumous decoration for his day on Chunuk Bair.[322] Possibly on account of his subordination earlier in turning down a direct order. It is highly conceivable that Malone would have been court martialled had he survived the battle. I am certain he also had considered this a possible outcome.

The Turks were bringing up reinforcements all day and knew the importance of getting the summit back. There were many panicky messages from the Turks throughout the day back to their commander, Mustafa Kemal, and there was a lot of confusion, even though they had taken back most of their side of the crest of the summit. For the Turks, this was becoming a crisis, and Kemal, indicating that he could change the situation if given the mandate during discussions with his German commanders, was given command of all the troops within the Suvla Bay area and also those on Sari Bair. Carlyon indicates that Kemal was made for crisis. He was very thin and his face looked haunted. He had not slept for three nights and was suffering from malaria, yet despite all of this his spirit was soaring, it was his battle now. [323]

At Chunuk Bair, the Turkish fire eased off as darkness came. The Otago and Wellington mounted units moved up without a casualty to take over the trench line. Of the 760 Wellingtons who had arrived on the crest that morning only two officers and 47 men remained unwounded. Their uniforms were torn and splattered with blood, they had hardly slept for two days and they had lost their leader. According to Bean they talked in whispers, trembled and cried.

Hundreds of wounded New Zealand soldiers lay across the battlefield at this time. Some bled to death and others went mad with thirst. Some asked when the stretcher bearers were coming and were told they weren't. The problem wasn't that there were so many wounded and so few stretcher bearers, but also how to carry them to the beaches. Some of the wounded would take three days to travel down to the beaches. Six men were often needed to carry men over the rougher parts and often it was completed under fire. When they did reach the beach, the lighters they had been loaded on to had to "shop" around to overcrowded ships to find someone to take them. Many had to lose limbs following the onset of gangrene. The suffering of the wounded Anzacs at Gallipoli in August 1915 was horrific, no worse than the New Zealanders wounded during the battle for Chunuk Bair. When the stretcher bearers reached the beaches they dipped their stretchers in the sea to wash off the blood and then headed back into the hills for others.[324]

On the night of August 9th, what was left of the New Zealanders were pulled out of the line and replaced by British Battalions, the Loyal North Lancashires and the Wiltshires. As this was happening, Turkish reinforcements were massing behind Chunuk Bair and the Turks under their leader Kemal were moving from defensive action to the offensive. The British generals, however, thought that the summit was secure. The following day, however, the massed Turkish forces came swarming over the crest in complete surprise, without any bombardment to signal their intentions like the British would have expected. They swept away the British soldiers and then rolled down the hill and annihilated the forces that were holding the Allied slopes. The Allied forces had lost the high ground of the summit and would not gain it back again.

The Wellingtons wait, under fire at the Apex, making their final preparations for their last push on to the summit of Chunuk Bair (Kippenberger Military Archive, National Army Museum, New Zealand – 2004 – 236)

Their faces say it all. The exhausted men of the Wellington Mounted Rifles stop their advance on Table Top to rest during the night of the 6th August, 1915(Alexander Turnbull Library, Wellington, New Zealand – F58131-1/4)

Appendix 13 – Queensland Point – Gallipoli Peninsula

Queensland Point was the name given to a point just above the beach just south of Hell Spit and Anzac Cove where D Company of the 9th Battalion (second wave) were fired upon by the Turks when landing. The naming of this point illustrates the persistence of State loyalties in a newly formed Federated Australia among the AIF.

Later, the name of the cemetery, which has many 9th Battalion graves, was changed to Beach Cemetery.

Appendix 14 – Research on Officers of the 11th Battalion in the photo on the Pyramid of Khufu (Cheops)

The picture referred to in both the introduction and then in chapter 3 shows the men of the 11th Battalion AIF, who were recruited from Western Australia, spread over the Pyramid of Khufu (Cheops). Of interest, it has 30 officers sitting or kneeling at the very front rows of the photo. Fortunately, I was able to locate a guide prepared by an historian of the 11th Battalion that indicates each of the officers' names (although some were incorrect), which then enabled me to verify/correct against other photos and documents held by the Australian War Memorial. Out of interest, I have taken some time to research what happened to each of these officers, mainly to find out who survived the fighting at Gallipoli and then who made it home after the war. I have not tried to ascertain who was wounded, as there is a high proportion of men who enlisted in 1914 and survived the war who were wounded at least once during their service. It would, however, be the exception to the rule that if they had survived the war, that these men would have managed to make it through unscathed.

The names of the officers who are standing and sitting in the first two rows of men, quite separate from the men on the pyramid, from left to right in the photo are as outlined below. For each officer listed, a brief account is provided that outlines whether they returned home or were killed in action (KIA), and if so, the date of death.

2nd Lieutenant F.P. Strickland – survived the war

2nd Lieutenant J. Newman – survived the war

Major S.R. Roberts – survived the war

Lieutenant A.R. Selby – returned to Australia October 1915 due to wounds (Gallipoli)

Captain J.S. Denton – survived the war

Captain A.E.J. Croly – returned to Australia September 1917 due to wounds (Western Front)

Captain C.A. Barnes – KIA 28th April, 1915 (Gallipoli)

Lieutenant K. McLennan – survived the war

Padre Fahey

Lieutenant C.A. Lanauze – KIA 28th June, 1915 (Gallipoli)

Lieutenant A.P.H. Corley – KIA 17th September, 1915 (Gallipoli)

Lieutenant J. Peat – KIA 27th June, 1917

Captain J.H. Peck – survived the war

Captain W.R. Annear – KIA 25th April, 1915 (Gallipoli)

Lieutenant R.R. Reilly – returned to Australia March 1918, likely due to wounds (Western Front) ended his war in the 51st Battalion

2nd Lieutenant M.L. Reid – KIA 25th April, 1915 (Gallipoli)

Lieutenant D.H. MacDonald – KIA 28th June, 1915 (Gallipoli)

Lieutenant Colonel J. Lyon Johnston – survived the war

Captain R.W. Everett – no information available – transferred into 44th Battalion following Gallipoli, no indication that he was killed in records

Major E.A.D. Brockman – survived the war, promoted to Brigadier General 4th Brigade

Captain E.T. Brennan – survived the war (medical unit) – many times mentioned in dispatches for bravery, particularly at Gallipoli

Captain R.L. Leane – survived the war

2nd Lieutenant A.H. Darnell – died of wounds 24th September, 1918

2nd Lieutenant A.H. Priestly – returned to Australia July 1915 due to wounds (Gallipoli)

Lieutenant W.H. Rockliff – survived the war, promoted to Major

2nd Lieutenant J.H. Cooke – KIA 10 April, 1916 (Western Front)

2nd Lieutenant H. James – survived the war, promoted to Major

2nd Lieutenant C.F. Buttle – survived the war

Lieutenant J. Morgan – survived the war

Lieutenant J. Williams – died of wounds 29th July, 1916 (Western Front)

Of the 29 officers of the 11th Battalion that were researched (excludes the Padre) from this photo, 10 men were killed in action (35% of the total). Of those killed, five were killed within the first two months of the Gallipoli campaign.

Appendix 15 – Private John Leak (VC)

It was interesting to note that for Private John Leak, the most highly decorated soldier of the 9th Battalion, having been awarded the only Victoria Cross (VC) earnt by a 9th Battalion soldier during the World War I there was surprisingly little information about him in either of the two Battalion histories. I was, however, able to find a lot of detail on a website called the "AIF Project", which provides details of Australian soldiers serving in the World War I. It revealed why this brave soldier has had such low profile and why he, interestingly, remained only a private in rank throughout the war. This alone seemed strange given he served from June 1915 at Gallipoli right through until the end of the war on the Western Front, with a VC decoration.

Private Leak was born in Portsmouth, England in 1892 and later immigrated to Australia. There is no detail whether he came alone or with his family and there was only the GPO address shown on his enlistment forms. He was listed as single and his occupation was shown as a teamster, enlisting at the age of 23 in Rockhampton, Queensland, on 28th January, 1915.

He embarked from Brisbane for the war on 16th April, 1915, nine days before the original men of the 9th Battalion landed at Anzac Cove.

Private Leak joined up with the 9th Battalion as part of one of the early reinforcements (at least after the second reinforcement of the 9th Battalion) at Gallipoli on 22nd June, 1915. He is noted to have been hospitalised in September 1915 suffering from illness while at Gallipoli and was transferred back to the Battalion in April 1916, when they were then located at the Western Front. As outlined in chapter 8, his brave actions at Pozieres in July 1916 are recognised and he was awarded the VC. However, within one month of this date, he received a gunshot wound to his back and was hospitalised again and later discharged from hospital in October 1916. From this point on, Private Leak's record is hardly that of a model soldier and his list of misdemeanors grows ever longer. Possibly the injury he had suffered and the stress of the war may have had something to do with this breakdown of discipline.

From January 1917, when he was found guilty of entering the Staff Sergeants Mess and demanding a drink and then not obeying orders to leave, right up to October 1917, he was found guilty of no less than three other charges. Most of them associated with being absent without leave. In March 1917, for some reason he was transferred to the 69th Battalion before being transferred back into the 9th in October 1917, to join up again with his unit in Belgium.

However, by 25th November, 1917, he was again in trouble, this time for a far greater crime and found guilty and court martialled in the field for absenting himself from the line. He served a few weeks in jail, suspended sentence (possibly because the Army needed all the soldiers they could for the fighting) rather than the firing squad. He then rejoined the Battalion after serving some time in prison in December 1917, until he was gassed while in action in March 1918. Having been discharged from hospital at the end of March 1918, he was again charged for ill discipline in both May and June 1918, before returning to the Battalion at the end of June 1918.

Private Leak then contracted bronchitis in August 1918, and after recovering he subsequently fractured his arm in September 1918, and again after being away from the Battalion for a few weeks, he returned for service with the Battalion in October of that year. By this time the war was almost over and following the armistice he married a 21 year old spinster in Cardiff. He returned to Australia in May 1919, arriving in Brisbane on 31 May, and there is no mention of his new wife.

His highly eventful period of service during the war, which in no doubt labelled him as a troublemaker, meant that he went from pin-up boy and hero to army misfit and criminal in the short space of a few months. It is an amazing story and one that the army and historians have not obviously been keen to dwell on. I would like to think that this hero was badly affected by the war following his wounding and living through the horrors of the battle of Pozieres and this caused him to go "off the rails". It is probably best just to remember him as the hero of Pozieres who won a VC for bravery, and not dwell on the other details of his history in the AIF.

John Leak died in October 1972 in South Australia at the age of 80.

Appendix 16 - Infantry Structures and Commissioned Officers (AIF)

Body of Soldiers AIF	***Commanded By:***
Supreme Commander	5 Star – Field Marshal
Army Made up of 3 Corps Approx. = 180,000 men	4 Star – General
Corps Made up of 3 Divisions Approx. = 60,000 men	3 Star – Lieutenant General
Division Made up of 4 Brigades Approx. = 16,000 – 20,000 men	2 Star – Major General
Brigade Made up of 4 Battalions. Approx. = 4000 men plus	1 Star – Brigadier General (Note Colonel is an interim rank).
Battalion Made up of Rifle Companies and support company, Approx. = 800 – 1000 men	Lieutenant Colonel
Company Made up of 4 platoon Approx. = 120 men	Major commands and a Captain is second in charge. A Lieutenant is an assistant to the Captain.
Platoon Made up of 3 sections each of 10 men	Second Lieutenant
Section of 10 men	Non Commissioned officers – Corporal/ Lance Corporal

Appendix 17 – Turkish Machine-guns – Were they used on the morning of the landing?

As mentioned earlier, this topic has been the cause of ongoing debate and argument among historians and those interested in the Gallipoli campaign. It is difficult to conclusively argue either way, however, most of my conclusions are based on the accounts of soldiers and eyewitnesses that morning. Turkish documentation, specifically the detailed account of Turkish defences provided by Lieutenant Colonel Sefik Aker of the battles that took place on the 25th April, 1915, do not indicate the presence of any Turkish machine-guns in the Anzac sector, specifically at Anzac Cove that morning during the Anzac landings.

There seem to be four main locations around the Anzac battlefield where Australian soldiers and historians (principally Australian) indicate that Turkish machine-guns were operating on the morning of the 25th April, 1915. The first was at Gaba Tepe, the second was located on Plugge's Plateau (behind Ari Burnu headland), the third being in the lower and upper ridges above North Beach – Walker's Ridge or Russell's Top, and the fourth location was at Fisherman's Hut on North Beach.

Starting with the Gaba Tepe location, I think this is probably one of the easier to conclude on given that Major Halis Bey, commander of the 3rd Battalion, 27th Regiment, confirmed this site did have a machine-gun. He indicated that it was their intention to have coverage of the beach between Ari Burnu (effectively this would have been the northernmost point visible to Gaba Tepe, being Hell Spit) and Kaba Tepe (Gaba Tepe), given that this was identified as a potential suitable landing site for the British. Indeed, even prior to landing men from C Company of the 9th Battalion under Captain Milne, the destroyer HMS *Beagle* which was located the furthest south of the landings off Gaba Tepe, came under both artillery and machine-gun fire.

The second location, being on Ari Burnu headland, is less likely. Although there were up to three separate accounts made of Australians coming under machine-gun fire, including Lieutenant Colonel Stanley Weir, Commander of the 10th Battalion, and Medical Officer of the 11th Battalion, Captain Brennan, it is the stated recollection of 21 year old Corporal Tom Louch of the 11th Battalion that offers the most vivid account:

There were two Turks in the machine-gun nest, and our boat almost to their direct front… When they saw us and the other boats approaching, I watched them for a few seconds while they got their gun into action. They fired one or two short bursts, but fortunately not at us, and then the picket boat came in and silenced them. The two men were knocked over backwards, taking their gun with them.

The issue with this is that it was still very dark when Corporal Louch came into shore and it would have been very difficult to see such detail. In addition, there were many Turkish rifles aimed down at the men in the boats landing after the first few boats of the 9th Battalion hit the shore which, when firing all at once, would have provided a heavy fusillade.

The Turkish coastal sentries located at Ari Burnu were decimated by the first wave of Australians and very few of the Turks managed to survive. Among the accounts of the Anzac soldiers that swarmed through this area, I would have expected that if machine-guns were in use in this location then some account of them being uncovered or captured would have been recorded. Moreover, if one machine-gun had been located at Ari Burnu, then it would not have been at the level of the landing craft i.e. beach level. The Turks believed that the beach south of Ari Burnu (later named Brighton Beach) was the likely landing site and would have had the gun higher up to cover this landing zone. Given the limited supply of machine-guns within the Turkish Army, I find it difficult to believe that they would have sited such a valuable piece of equipment in such a place where there was a strong possibility that it could be lost so early in the fighting. What the Australian soldiers who landed at Ari Burnu may have heard instead that morning was the firing of the machine-gun located on the front of one of the towing Anzac steamboats.

There is a possibility that there were machine-guns on the upper or lower slopes above North Beach, however, there is no confirmation by Turkish sources, and only general accounts provided of machine-guns in this area by Australians. In addition, given the proximity to Fisherman's Hut, there may have been some confusion given that I believe a Turkish machine-gun was certainly in operation at Fisherman's Hut.

There are many detailed accounts provided by Australians landing around and attempting to take the Turkish positions at Fisherman's Hut that indicate the presence of a Turkish machine-gun. Men of the 11th Battalion speak about the water around their landing boat being churned into foam by a machine-gun in the Turkish trenches at Fisherman's Hut. So heavy was the fusillade that they diverted their boats south towards Ari Burnu instead. In addition, the 7th Battalion War Diary entry on the 25th April, 1915 at 5.00am indicated the dramatic effect that machine-gun fire had on the 120 men of B company who had drifted some way from their intended landing to a place just offshore from Fisherman's Hut. Such was the impact of the Turkish machine-gun fire on the Australian troops that orders were given by Lieutenant Colonel Clarke to two parties of men respectively by Lieutenant Rafferty and Lieutenant Strickland to specifically silence the machine-guns at Fisherman's Hut. I am inclined to believe that a Turkish machine-gun had been here on the morning of 25th April.

Appendix 18 – Charles Bean – Official World War I AIF Correspondent

Charles Bean was a 35 year old trained lawyer and journalist writing for *The Sydney Morning Herald*. When the World War I broke out, he won an Australian Journalists Association ballot and became the official correspondent to the AIF. Bean accompanied the first Division AIF from Australia, spent time with them during their training in Egypt and went on to land with them at Gallipoli, where he stayed for most of the campaign, only leaving a few days before the last of the soldiers were evacuated. He then went on to the Western Front with the Australian forces, documenting the successes and tragedies that befell the AIF. Bean was a very thorough man and believed he needed to be where the action was to understand what was taking place. He had a great ability to mix with both privates and generals alike, and liked to be where the action was, which often meant he would be up with those fighting. This style endeared him to the men, who would take him into their confidence, and he gained a significant level of respect across the AIF. The Australian public more importantly relied on him to provide cables that would provide details regarding the whereabouts and actions involving the AIF, describing in some detail the deeds of Australian soldiers on the distant battlefield. His cables were used principally by the newspapers and the government to communicate war news and events, in some cases specifically to provide the enthusiasm at home to keep the recruitment lines ticking over.

Bean became a prolific writer of Australian military history, particularly during the World War I in a diary that recorded what he saw and events that took place each day, and subsequently used his diaries as a base for the six volumes written after the war. This historical account of the war was completed over a two-decade period of time. His writing now stands as the cornerstone for any study or research concerning the Australian Imperial Force (AIF) during the World War I and he had a significant hand in the establishment of the Australian War Memorial in Canberra. Bean stated that due to the lack of official records available concerning the war, in order for him to complete his work recording the actions of the AIF he really had to rely on his own diaries that he kept in his notebooks. His notebooks numbered some 226 over the course of the war and contained information taken while talking to soldiers and officers about events that had taken place. Even after the war, Bean spent a lot of time with returned soldiers filling in gaps in his knowledge or providing further details to events.

Alec Hill outlines in the preface to Bean's second volume – *The Story of Anzac*, that Bean compiled his notes close to the events he described. At Krithia, for example, some of his notes were written under fire in a shallow pit he shared with Colonel James M'Cay (Commander of the 2nd Brigade –AIF) and his signallers. Sometimes, he would write in his dugout throughout the night, sleeping during the morning hours. He drew rough sketches of the ground and incidents ... and made a particular point of questioning as many leaders as possible immediately after a battle. Such careful compilation of after-action accounts by an observer who not only knew the plan, but also had followed the operation on the ground, went far towards creating the realism and freshness that distinguished Bean's work.[325]

Such was his drive to provide a complete coverage he returned to the Gallipoli Peninsula in 1919 to survey the battlefield and answer the questions that had hounded him throughout the campaign. During what he describes as his Gallipoli Mission, Bean wanders the battlefield recounting certain events, seeing what was on the enemy's side of the battlefield, observing different vantage points and trying to piece together events that had occurred during the campaign. He also met with Major Zeki Bey, a Turkish commander of the 1st Battalion, 57th Regiment, and had him spend a week with his small team as they wandered over the battlefields and helped them answer questions about the battle in broken French, gaining an understanding from him of the Turkish experience. He therefore has chapters in his book titled – "Gallipoli Mission" such as; "the Turkish side at Lone Pine", "the Turks and the Evacuation" and "What the Turks could see". Zeki Bey was wounded on the 25th April, 1915, but returned to the front and was commanding his men during the battle of Lone Pine.

For Bean it was a walk down memory lane without the constant risk of being fired upon, being able to go across no-man's-land and into the once Turkish trenches, remembering where men were killed and trying to identify the site where he had slept in his dugout. Most importantly he tried to get a better understanding of the Turkish perspective of the fighting and the reasoning behind decisions made in the heat of battle.

Alec Hill states that Bean's writing was complete and described the detail of battles and terrain with a focus on the individual soldier. The degree of Bean's success is directly related to his presence at nearly every battle he describes; for example, he was in the old front-line for Lone Pine and he was trudging forward in the darkness of the wake of the 4th Brigade on 6th August when he was hit by a stray bullet. At Krithia on 8th May, he moved with M'Cay's Brigade Headquarters in that desperate attack, and at one stage dashed out under fire to bring in a wounded man. He spent the night on the battlefield under machine-gun fire, carrying water and helping the wounded. As the Military Cross for which he was recommended could not be awarded to a civilian, he was mentioned in dispatches, but his true reward was the high regard of the AIF that he quickly won on the peninsula.[326]

Bean received a number of honourary degrees and even declined a knighthood. He died in 1968 after a long illness in Concord Repatriation Hospital in Sydney.

Me, my mate and my "Bully Beef". 20 year old Lance-Corporal George Henry Barker, 12th Battalion, and 21 year old Private George Hill (10th Battalion) pose for a photo in their Gallipoli home at about 3pm on 25th April, 1915. George Barker was shot in the left leg on 2nd May, 1915 and was invalided back to Australia in November 1915. George Hill, although receiving a gunshot wound to the right foot in July 1915, fought on the Western Front until mortally wounded from a shell blast in November 1916. He later died in hospital. (King)

Endnotes

Introduction

1 Carlyon, *Gallipoli.*

2 Conway, *Courier-Mail.*

3 Carthew, *Voices from the Trenches.*

Chapter 1: Prelude to War

4 Kyle, *An Anzac's Story.*

5 Broadbent, *Gallipoli.*

6 Ibid.

7 Pedersen, *The Anzacs.*

8 Kyle, *An Anzac's Story.*

9 Wrench, *Campaigning with the fighting 9th.*

10 Carthew, *Voices from the Trenches.*

11 Ibid.

12 *Times History of War,* Ch. 1, in Wrench *Campaigning with the fighting 9th.*

13 Hamilton, *Gallipoli Sniper.*

14 Ibid.

15 Bean, *Official History,* Vol. 1, Ch. 1, paraphrased in Wrench, *Campaigning with the fighting 9th.*

16 Ibid.

17 Ibid.

18 Wrench, *Campaigning with the fighting 9th.*

19 Kyle, *An Anzac's Story.*

20 Bean, *Official History,* Vol. 1, Ch. 1.

21 Ibid.

22 Bean, *Official History,* Vol. 1, Ch. 1.

23 Hamilton *Gallipoli Sniper.*

24 Ibid.

25 Ibid.

26 Kyle, *An Anzac's Story.*

27 Ibid.

28 Fewster, *Gallipoli.*

29 Carlyon, *Gallipoli.*

30 Kyle, *An Anzac's Story.*

Chapter 2: The Queenslanders Depart for Adventure

31 Wrench, *Campaigning with the fighting 9th.*

32 Carlyon, *Gallipoli.*

33 *Ibid.*

34 Broadbent, *Gallipoli.*

35 Kyle, *An Anzac's Story.*

36 Carlyon, *Gallipoli.*

37 Pedersen, *The Anzacs.*

38 Harvey, *From Anzac to the Hindenburg Line.*

39 Wrench, *Campaigning with the fighting 9th*.

40 Scrivener Family, AWM.

41 Harvey, *From Anzac to the Hindenburg Line.*

42 Ibid.

43 Ibid.

44 *Western Star* (regional), quoted in Hamilton, *Gallipoli Sniper.*

45 Diary of Lance Corporal Neal, AWM.

46 Harvey, *From Anzac to the Hindenburg Line.*

47 Diary of Lance Corporal Neal, AWM.

48 Harvey, *From Anzac to the Hindenburg Line.*

49 Wrench, *Campaigning with the fighting 9th*.

50 Bean, *Official History*, Vol. 1, Ch. 6.

Chapter 3: Welcome to Egypt

51 Wrench, *Campaigning with the fighting 9th*.

52 Harvey, *From Anzac to the Hindenburg Line*, notes that reference to camp is really an understatement in that there were no tents or anything resembling a camp, only a lot of sand.

53 Ibid.

54 Wrench, *Campaigning with the fighting 9th*.

55 Diary of Lance Corporal Neal, AWM.

56 Bean, *Official History*, Vol. 1.

57 Pedersen, *The Anzacs.*

58 Loch, *To Hell and Back.*

59 Wrench, *Campaigning with the fighting 9th*.

60 Diary of Lieutant Ross, quoted in Wrench, *Campaigning with the fighting 9th*.

61 Bean, *Official History*, Vol. 1, Ch. 7.

62 Pedersen, *The Anzacs.*

63 Wrench, *Campaigning with the fighting 9th*.

64 Diary of Lance Corporal Neal, AWM.

65 Ibid.

Chapter 4: The 3rd Brigade AIF is Going to War

66 Carlyon, *Gallipoli.*

67 Ibid., which references a comment made by Winston Churchill in his writings in 1930.

68 Cameron, *25th April 1915.*

69 Diary of Lieutant Ross, quoted in Wrench, *Campaigning with the fighting 9th*.

70 Harvey, *From Anzac to the Hindenburg Line.*

71 Diary of Lance Corporal Neal, AWM.

72 Diary of Lieutant Ross, quoted in Wrench, *Campaigning with the fighting 9th*.

73 Pedersen, *The Anzacs.*

74 Chambers, *Anzac.*

75 Aker, "The Dardenelles", in Rayfield Papers, Imperial War Museum.

76 Carlyon, *Gallipoli.*

77 Ibid.

78 Ibid.

79 Afflerbach, "Impact of the Ottoman Empire", in Gallipoli Conference Papers.

80 Carlyon, *Gallipoli.*

81 Pedersen, *The Anzacs.*

82 Carlyon, *Gallipoli.*

83 Speech by Colonel MacLagan, 3rd Brigade CO, quoted in Cameron, *25th April 1915.*

84 Pedersen, *The Anzacs.*

85 Discussions between General Bridges and Colonel MacLagan, quoted in Bean, *Official History*, Vol. 1, Ch. 9.

86 Diary of Lieutant Ross, quoted in Wrench, *Campaigning with the fighting 9th*.

87 Pedersen, *The Anzacs.*

88 Ibid.

89 Bean, *Official History*, Vol. 1, Ch. 12.

90 Pedersen, *The Anzacs.*

Chapter 5: The Landing at Anzac Cove

91 Carlyon, *Gallipoli.*

92 Personal account of Private Percival Young, 9th Battalion, in the *School Paper,* Queensland Department of Public Instruction, Anzac Day 1916, Vol. 7, quoted in Wrench, *Campaigning with the fighting 9th*.

93 Carlyon, *Gallipoli.*

94 Cameron, *25th April 1915.*

95 Carlyon, *Gallipoli.*

96 Ibid.

97 Pedersen, *The Anzacs.*

98 General Birdwood, quoted in Bean, *Official History.*

99 Cameron, *25th April 1915.*

100 Ibid.

101 Harvey, *From Anzac to the Hindenburg Line.*

102 Cameron, *25th April 1915.*

103 Personal account of Private Percival Young, quoted in Wrench, *Campaigning with the fighting 9th.*

104 Cameron, *25th April 1915.*

105 Aker, "The Dardenelles", in Rayfield Papers, IWM.

106 Hampson, *The Brothers Keid.*

107 Pedersen, *The Anzacs.*

108 Harvey, *From Anzac to the Hindenburg Line.*

109 Personal account of Private Percival Young, quoted in Wrench, *Campaigning with the fighting 9th.*

110 Broadbent, *Gallipoli.*

111 Carlyon, *Gallipoli.*

112 Ibid.

113 Major McNicoll, quoted in Carlyon, *Gallipoli.*

114 Pedersen, *The Anzacs.*

115 Personal account of Private Percival Young, quoted in Wrench, *Campaigning with the fighting 9th.*

116 Records for Sergeant Herbert Fowles, NAA website.

117 Bean, *Official History*, Vol. 1, Ch. 12.

118 Harvey, *From Anzac to the Hindenburg Line.*

119 Fewster, *Gallipoli.*

120 Carlyon, *Gallipoli.*

121 Ibid.

122 Ibid.

123 Ibid.

124 Diary of Lieutenant Colonel Malone, quoted in Chambers, *Anzac.*

125 The *Courier-Mail*, "Anzac 90th Anniversary", 2005, provided extracts from letters home in an article titled "Letters to Loved Ones". In Winter 1916 it devoted several columns to these letters including one from Lance Corporal Rydon, which the article quotes.

126 Bean, *Official History.*

127 Chambers, *Anzac.*

128 Harvey, *From Anzac to the Hindenburg Line.*

129 Broadbent, *Gallipoli.*

130 Chambers, *Anzac.*

131 Cameron, *25th April 1915.*

132 See Bean, *Official History*, Vol. 1, Ch. 16 regarding the 3rd Brigade on 400 Plateau.

133 Diary of Corporal Mitchell, quoted in Cameron, *25th April 1915.*

134 Pedersen, *The Anzacs.*

135 Diary of Corporal Loud, quoted in Cameron, *25th April 1915.*

136 *The Military Adventures of John Rutherford Gordon 1895-1983, quoted* in Cameron, *25th April 1915.*

137 Diary of Corporal Loud, quoted in Cameron, *25th April 1915.*

138 Service records of Corporal Harrison, NAA website.

139 Cameron, *25th April 1915.*

140 Bean, *Official History,* Vol. 1.

141 Harvey, *From Anzac to the Hindenburg Line.*

142 Letter by Private Robert Hamilton to his family, quoted in King, *Gallipoli Diaries.*

143 Service records of Private Hamilton, NAA website.

144 Craven & Blackledge, *Peninsula of Death,* in Chambers, *Anzac.*

145 Wrench, *Campaigning with the fighting 9th.*

146 Ibid.

147 Chambers, *Anzac.*

148 Private Fred Symonds, quoted in Ibid.

149 Service records of Sergeant Fred Scrivener, NAA website.

150 Hamilton, *Gallipoli Sniper.*

151 Ibid.

152 Diary of Trooper Jack Idriess, in Hamilton, *Gallipoli Sniper.*

153 Pedersen, *The Anzacs.*

154 Diary of Lance Corporal Neal, AWM.

155 Wrench, *Campaigning with the fighting 9th.*

156 Ibid.

157 Diary of Lieutant Ross, quoted in Wrench *Campaigning with the fighting 9th.*

158 Ibid.

159 Bean, *Official History,* Vol. 1, Ch. 17.

160 Trooper S.G. Millar, in *Brisbane Grammar School Magazine,* Vol. 17, No. 50, Aug 1915, p.16, on Anzacs.org website.

161 Service records of Sergeant Steele, NAA website.

162 Sergeant Steele, quoted in Wrench, *Campaigning with the fighting 9th.*

163 Personal account of Private Percival Young, quoted in Wrench, *Campaigning with the fighting 9th.*

164 Pedersen, *The Anzacs.*

165 Diary of Lance Corporal Neal, AWM.

166 Broadbent, *Gallipoli.*

167 Aker, "The Dardenelles", in Rayfield Papers, Imperial War Museum.

168 Pedersen, *The Anzacs.*

169 Ibid.

170 Bill Gammage, *The Broken Years,* in the *Age* 8th May 1915, quoted in Pedersen, *The Anzacs.*

Chapter 6: Hardship and Suffering at Gallipoli

171 Hampson, *The Brothers Keid.*
172 Pedersen, *The Anzacs.*
173 Loch, *To Hell and Back.*
174 Ibid.
175 Harvey, *From Anzac to the Hindenburg Line.*
176 Scrivener Family, AWM.
177 Pedersen, *The Anzacs.*
178 Ibid.
179 Carlyon, *Gallipoli.*
180 Harvey, *From Anzac to the Hindenburg Line.*
181 Pedersen, *The Anzacs.*
182 Harvey, *From Anzac to the Hindenburg Line.*
183 Ibid.
184 Pedersen, *The Anzacs.*
185 Gammage, *The Broken Years*, quoted in Fewster, *Gallipoli.*
186 Carthew, *Voices from the Trenches.*
187 Loch, *To Hell and Back.*
188 Broadbent, *Gallipoli.*
189 Diary of Lieutant Ross, quoted in Wrench *Campaigning with the fighting 9th.*
190 Service records, NAA website.
191 Harvey, *From Anzac to the Hindenburg Line.*
192 Ibid.
193 ABC, "Andrew Denton's Gallipoli", in which Alf Gardiner was one of the featured soldiers.
194 Service records, NAA website.
195 Diary of Lieutant Ross, quoted in Wrench, *Campaigning with the fighting 9th.*
196 Kyle, *An Anzac's Story.*
197 Hamilton, *Gallipoli Sniper.*
198 Carlyon, *Gallipoli.*
199 Wrench, *Campaigning with the fighting 9th.*
200 Carlyon, *Gallipoli.*
201 Kyle, *An Anzac's Story.*
202 Hamilton, *Gallipoli Sniper.*
203 Wrench, *Campaigning with the fighting 9th.*
204 Harvey, *From Anzac to the Hindenburg Line.*
205 Ibid.
206 Ibid.
207 Carlyon, *Gallipoli.*
208 Ibid,

209 Ekins, "A Ridge Too Far", Gallipoli Conference Paper.

210 Carthew, *Voices from the Trenches.*

211 Reid, *Gallipoli 1915.*

Chapter 7: Now on to the Western Front

212 Wrench, *Campaigning with the fighting 9th.*

213 Embarkation details in service records, NAA website.

214 Diary of Private Desmond Pitty, AWM.

215 Bean, *Official History,* Vol. 1.

216 Kyle, *An Anzac's Story.*

217 Wrench, *Campaigning with the fighting 9th.*

218 Ibid.

219 Copy of diary not obtainable from AWM.

220 Wrench, *Campaigning with the fighting 9th.*

221 Harvey, *From Anzac to the Hindenburg Line.*

222 Bean, *Official History,* Vol. 3, Ch. 15.

223 Wrench, *Campaigning with the fighting 9th.*

224 Bean, *Official History,* Vol. 3, Ch. 17, quoted in Wrench, *Campaigning with the fighting 9th.*

225 Diary of Archie Barwick, ML, and Service records, NAA website.

226 Corporal Arthur Thomas, quoted in Carlyon, *The Great War.*

227 Carlyon, *The Great War.*

228 Bean, *Official History,* Vol. 3.

229 Carthew, *Voices from the Trenches.*

230 Ibid.

231 Carlyon, *The Great War.*

232 Harvey, *From Anzac to the Hindenburg Line.*

233 Ibid.

234 Diary of Lieutant Ross, quoted in Wrench *Campaigning with the fighting 9th.*

235 National Service records of Private Fred Williams, NAA website.

237 Harvey, *From Anzac to the Hindenburg Line.*

238 Bean, *Official History,* Vol. 4, Ch. 19.

239 Conway, "Remembering Passchendaele".

240 Ibid.

241 German General, quoted in Ibid.

242 Pedersen, *The Anzacs.*

243 Lieutenant Russell Harris, quoted in Pedersen, *The Anzacs.*

244 Service records, NAA website.

245 Kyle, *An Anzac's Story.*

246 Ibid.

247 Service records, NAA website.
248 Wrench, *Campaigning with the fighting 9th*.
249 Ibid.
250 Harvey, *From Anzac to the Hindenburg Line.*
251 Scrivener Family, AWM.
252 Harvey, *From Anzac to the Hindenburg Line.*
253 Carthew, *Voices from the Trenches.*
254 Carlyon, *Gallipoli.*
255 Carlyon, *The Great War.*
256 Ibid.
257 Ibid.
258 Carthew, Voices from the Trenches.
259 Service records, NAA website.

Chapter 8: The War is Over

260 Carthew, *Voices from the Trenches.*
261 Carlyon, *The Great War.*
262 Section on the Victoria Cross award, AWM website.
263 Diary of Archie Barwick, ML.
264 Wrench, *Campaigning with the fighting 9th*.
265 Pedersen, *The Anzacs.*
266 Scrivener Family, AWM.
267 Carthew, *Voices from the Trenches.*
268 Harvey, *From Anzac to the Hindenburg Line.*
269 Ibid.
270 Hampson, *The Brothers Keid.*
271 Carlyon, *Gallipoli.*
272 Hampson, *The Brothers Keid.*
273 Hamilton, *Gallipoli Sniper.*
274 Carthew, *Voices from the Trenches.*
275 Ibid.
276 Kyle, *An Anzac's Story.*

Chapter 9: Final Thoughts

277 Carlyon, *The Great War.*
278 L. Carlyon, quoted in interview by Bantick, "The Western front of Death".
279 Carthew, *Voices from the Trenches.*
280 Ibid.
281 Ibid.
282 Bean, *Gallipoli Mission.*

283 Geoffrey Blainey, *A Shorter History of Australia*, quoted in Carlyon, "Where Great Deeds Were Done".

284 Ibid.

285 Ibid.

286 Ibid.

287 Carlyon, *Gallipoli.*

288 Kyle, *An Anzac's Story.*

289 Carlyon, *Gallipoli.*

290 Ibid.

291 Fewster *Gallipoli.*

292 Ibid.

293 Scates, "Return to Gallipoli".

294 Carlyon, *Gallipoli.*

295 Chambers, *Anzac.*

296 Fewster, *Gallipoli.*

297 The battle account by Lieutenant Colonel Sefik Aker during the morning of the first day of the landings does not indicate there were any Turkish machine-guns present and being used by coastal sentries. Aker, "The Dardenelles", in Rayfield Papers, Imperial War Museum.

298 Ibid.

299 Carlyon, *Gallipoli.*

Appendices

300 Wrench, *Campaigning with the fighting 9th*.

301 Ekins, "A Ridge Too Far", Gallipoli Conference Paper.

302 Carlyon, *Gallipoli.*

303 Ibid.

304 Ibid.

305 Ibid.

306 Ibid.

307 Ibid.

308 Captain K. Millar. "Control Over Fear: The Secret Of Leadership". *Reveille* Vol. 9, No. 8, 1 Apr 1936 p.12, on Anzacs.org website.

309 Carlyon, *Gallipoli.*

310 Woodcock, "The Youngest Anzac".

311 Ibid.

312 Carlyon, *Gallipoli.*

313 Carlyon, "Where Great Deeds Were Done".

314 Ibid.

315 Bean, *Official History*, Vol. 2, Ch. 21.

316 Carlyon, *Gallipoli.*

317 Reid, *Gallipoli 1915*.

318 Ekins, "A Ridge Too Far", Gallipoli Conference Paper.

319 Carlyon, *Gallipoli*.

320 Ibid.

321 Ibid.

322 Ibid.

323 Ibid.

324 Ibid.

325 Alec Hill, Preface to Bean's, *Official History*, Vol. 2.

326 Ibid.

Bibliography

Records, Australian War Memorial

9th Infantry Battalion, AIF, Nominal Roll.

9th Infantry Battalion, AIF, *Unit War Diary,* War Diaries, 1914-18 War.

25th Infantry Battalion, AIF, *Unit War Diary,* War Diaries, 1914-18 War.

Neal, Lance Corporal Frederick W., Diary, 9th Battalion, Private record No. PR88/074.

Pitty, Private Desmond, Diary, 9th Battalion, Private Record No. PR84/128.

Scrivener Family, *Case Study, Memorial Box 01.*

Records, Mitchell Library, State Library of NSW

Barwick, Private Archibald, Diary, 1st Battalion AIF, on website.

Books

Bean, Charles E.W., *Anzac to Amiens,* Australian War Memorial, Canberra, 1948.

Bean, Charles E.W., *Gallipoli Mission,* Australian War Memorial, Canberra,1948.

Bean, Charles E.W., *The Official History of Australia in the War of 1914-1918. Volume 1: The Story of Anzac from the Outbreak of War to the End of the First Phase of the Gallipoli Campaign,* 11th edition, University of Queensland Press, St Lucia, 1941.

Bean, Charles E.W., *The Official History of Australia in the War of 1914-1918. Volume 2: The Story of Anzac from 4th May 1915, to the Evacuation,* 11th edition, University of Queensland Press, St Lucia, 1941.

Broadbent, Harvey, *Gallipoli: The Fatal Shore,* Penguin Group, Camberwell VIC, 2005.

Cameron, David W., *25th April 1915: The Day the Anzac Legend was Born,* Allen & Unwin, Crows Nest NSW, 2007.

Carlyon, Les, *Gallipoli,* Pan Macmillan, Sydney, 2001.

Carlyon, Les, *The Great War,* Pan Macmillan, Sydney, 2007.

Carthew, Noel, *Voices from the Trenches: Letters to Home,* New Holland Publishers, Sydney, 2002.

Chambers, Stephen, *Anzac: the Landing,* Pen and Sword, Barnsley UK, 2008.

Charlton, Peter, *The Warriors: State of War,* Queensland Newspapers, Brisbane.

Cochrane, Peter, *Australians at War,* ABC Books, Sydney, 2001.

Cross, Robin, *World at War: World War I and World War II in Photographs,* Mustard, Bath UK,1999.

Ekins, Ashley, *Gallipoli Guide: Guide to the battlefields, cemeteries and memorials of the Gallipoli Peninsula,* AWM, Canberra, 2000.

Fewster, Kevin and others, *Gallipoli: The Turkish Story,* Allen & Unwin, Crows Nest NSW, 2003.

Hamilton, John, *Gallipoli Sniper: The Life of Billy Sing,* Pan Macmillan, Sydney, 2008.

Hampson, Cedric, *The Brothers Keid,* CopyRight Publishing, Brisbane, 2005.

Harvey, Norman K., *From Anzac to the Hindenburg Line: The History of the 9th Battalion AIF,* William Brooks, Brisbane, 1941.

Hill, A.J., Introduction, in *Bean, Official History, Vol.2, 1941.*

King, J., *Gallipoli Diaries: The Anzacs' Own Story Day by Day,* Kangaroo Press, East Roseville NSW, 2003.

King, Jonathan. & Michael Bowers, *Gallipoli: Untold Stories from War Correspondent Charles Bean and Front Line Anzacs,* Random House Australia, 2008.

Kyle, Roy, *An Anzac's Story,* ed. Bryce Courtenay, Penguin Books, Camberwell VIC, 2003.

Loch (De Loghe), Sydney, *To Hell and Back: The banned account of Gallipoli,* Harper Collins Publishers, Pymble NSW, 2007, *incl. biography by Susanna and Jake De Vries.*

MacDougall, Anthony K., *Australians at War: A Pictorial History,* Five Mile Press, Noble Park VIC, 2002.

Pedersen, Peter A, *The Anzacs: Gallipoli to the Western Front,* Penguin Group, Camberwell VIC, 2007.

Prior, Robin, *Gallipoli: The End of the Myth,* University of NSW Press, Sydney, 2009.

Rayner, Michael, *Battlefields: Exploring the Arenas of War, 1805-1945,* New Holland Publishers, London, 2006.

Reid, R., *Gallipoli 1915,* ABC Books, Sydney, 2002.

Uluaslan, Huseyin, *Gallipoli Campaign: Gentlemen's War,* 2008.

Wrench, C.M., *Campaigning with the Fighting 9th: In and out of the line with the Ninth Battalion AIF,* Boolarong Publications for the 9th Battalion Association, Salisbury QLD, 1985.

Articles, Journals

Aker, Sefik (Lieutenant Colonel), "The Dardanelles. The Ari Burnu Battles and the 27th Regiment: The Battles of the 25th April, 1915 Ankara, 1935", *Military Journal, Turkish General Staff,* trans. in Rayfield Papers, Imperial War Museum, London, ref. 69/61/9.

Burness, Peter, "Men of Pozieres" *Wartime (AWM Magazine),* Issue 34, 2006.

Cameron, David W., "Gallipoli: A Turkish View", *Wartime,* Issue 42, 2008.

Duncan, Susan, "Return to Gallipoli", *Australian Women's Weekly,* April 2007.

Ekins, Ashley, "The Battle of Fromelles", *Wartime,* Issue 44, 2008.

Faulkner, Andrew, "Blackburn's Place", *Wartime,* Issue 42, 2008.

Gray, Andrew. "Courage at Lone Pine", *Wartime,* Issue 34, 2006.

Londey, Peter, "Bulair: The Attack that Didn't Happen", *Wartime,* Issue 34, 2006.

Losik, Sharon, "Baptism of Fire", *Wartime,* Issue 28, 2004.

McMullin, Ross, "The Butcher of Fromelles", *Wartime, Issue 27, 2004.*

Molkentin, Michael, "Like cats in the night", *Wartime,* Issue 43, 2008.

Pedersen, Peter, "Reflections on a Battlefield" (Fromelles), *Wartime,* Issue 44, 2008.

Robertson, Emily, "Who was the Man with the Donkey?" *Wartime,* Issue 41, 2008.

Scates, Bruce, "Return to Gallipoli", *Wartime,* Issue 34, 2006.

Williams, Peter D., "Ottoman Artillery Bombardment", *Wartime,* Issue 34, 2006.

Woodcock, John, "The Youngest Anzac?", *Wartime,* Issue 34, 2006.

Articles, Newspapers

Bantick, Christopher, "The Western Front of Death", *Courier-Mail,* 11th -12th November 2006.

Bean, Charles, "Gallipoli. How the Australians Fought. Imperishable Fame", *Sydney Morning Herald,* 15th May 1915.

Bean, Charles, "Battle Country. Around Gaba Tepe", *Argus, 26th July1915.*

Bean, Charles, "Fighting at Gallipoli. A Six Days' Battle. Glorious Feat Described. Australians Charge and Capture Trenches", *Age, 25 August 1915.*

Bean, Charles, "Quinn's Post. How it is Defended. The Enemy at Arm's Length. A Near View of the Turkish Trenches", *Age, 4th September 1915.*

Carlyon, Les, "Where Great Deeds Were Done", *Sydney Morning Herald,* 25th April 1998.

Conway, Doug, "Remembering Passchendaele", *Courier-Mail,* 14th July 2007.

Courier-M ail, Saturday 24th April 1915 (full issue).

Courier-M ail, Monday 26th April 1915 (full issue),

Courier-M ail, "Anzac 90th Anniversary", 23rd -24th April 2005, by Peter Charlton, Peter Stanley, Vecihi (John) Basarin and others.

Lennon, Troy, "Bravery above and beyond imagination", *Daily Telegraph* 10th November 2006.

Noonan, Kathleen, "A Day to Remember", *Courier-Mail,* 11th-12th November, 2006.

Sunday Mail, "My Dad took a Wallaby to War", 22nd April 2007, Anzac Day article.

Films

"Andrew Denton's Gallipoli: Brothers in Arms", ABC TV documentary, 2007

"Gallipoli: The Fatal Shore", ABC Video documentary, 1988

"Gallipoli", R&R Films, Australia, 1981, directed by Peter Weir.

"Monash: The Forgotten Anzac", ABC TV documentary, 1988.

"Not Forgotten: 90 years after the Fighting Stopped", SBS TV documentary, 2009, narrated by Mark Lee.

Websites

anzacs.org, Lost Leaders of Anzacs, by Bryn Dolan & John Myers, 2000-2008.

anzacsite.gov.au, Gallipoli and the Anzacs/Australians at War/World War 1, Australian Department of Veterans Affairs, 2011.

awm.gov.au, biographical on-line database records and collections, 2011.

naa.gov.au, personal service records, World War I, National Archives of Australia, 2011.

Other

Bean, Charles, Report, *Commonwealth of Australia Gazette,* No. 39, 17th May 1915.

Cownie, Stewart, *Gallipoli Battlefield Guide Map.*

Gallipoli Campaign: International Perspectives 85 Years On Conference papers, Canakkale, Turkey, Ataturk and Gallipoli Campaign Research Center, Canakkale Onsekiz Mart, 2000: Ashley Ekins, AWM, "A ridge too far: Military objectives and the dominance of terrain in the Gallipoli Campaign"; Holger Afflerbach, "Dusseldorf: The impact of the Ottoman Empire in the German strategy of 1915"; Peter Doyle, University of Greenwich, "Terrain and the Gallipoli Campaign 1915"; Yulug Tekin Kurat, METU, "Perspectives on the Gallipoli Campaign"; Les Carlyon, Australia, "The Influence of the Gallipoli Campaign on Australia and Turkey"; Bruce Skates, Britain, "Gallipoli's Shadow: Australian Pilgrimages to Great War Cemeteries".

Holt, Major Tonie and Valmai, Battle Map of Gallipoli, Slouch Hat Publications, 2000.

Regimental Books Newsletter, "History of the 9th Battalion: Formation and Gallipoli", No. 4, June 2009.

Regimental Books Newsletter, "History of the 9th Battalion: The Western Front (France to Belgium)", No. 5, July 2009.